By the Same Authors

The Penguin Book of

Poetry from Britain and Ireland since 1945

EDITED BY SIMON ARMITAGE
AND ROBERT CRAWFORD

VIKING

VIKING

Published by the Penguin Group
Penguin Books Ltd, 27 Wrights Lane, London w8 5tz, England
Penguin Putnam Inc., 375 Hudson Street, New York, New York 10014, USA
Penguin Books Australia Ltd, Ringwood, Victoria, Australia
Penguin Books Canada Ltd, 10 Alcorn Avenue, Toronto, Ontario, Canada m4v 3b2
Penguin Books (NZ) Ltd, Private Bag 102902, NSMC, Auckland, New Zealand

Penguin Books Ltd, Registered Offices: Harmondsworth, Middlesex, England

First published in Great Britain in Hardback and Trade Paperback by Viking 1998
1 3 5 7 9 10 8 6 4 2

Set in 11.5/14.5 pt PostScript Monotype Bembo
Typeset by Rowland Phototypesetting Ltd,
Bury St Edmunds, Suffolk
Printed in England by Clays Ltd, St Ives plc

A CIP catalogue record for this book is available from the British Library

Hardback ISBN 0-670-86829-9
Trade Paperback ISBN 0-670-88325-5

CONTENTS

INTRODUCTION:
THE DEMOCRATIC VOICE

This books offers many kinds of enjoyment. It is the first anthology to survey the poetry from Britain and Ireland which was published in the half-century after the Second World War. It seeks to present work of consistent quality and surprise. Poetic vitality was our essential criterion. In an age of electronic communications and information overload, the niftiness, attentiveness and numinous vibrancy of poetry have become more, not less, important. Poetry is language which delivers its own promise, and which may often trip reader and writer beyond the expected, into an otherworld potent with spiritual experience. It is poetry's power which makes it for some people embarrassing and unconfinable. Yet almost everyone has written a poem at some time, and has known poetry as intimately important – a source of delight, nurture and illumination that need not always be po-faced. In assembling good poems this volume aims to deliver some of that nourishment. At the same time, the titles both of this book and of its Introduction announce a philosophy and argument. The anthology gathers work from a cluster of islands off the mainland of western Europe which encompasses several nations and two states that share a common language (though they also contain other minority languages with a long literary history). Arguments about what is 'British', what is 'English', or 'Irish', or 'Welsh', or 'Scottish' run through the period and sometimes energize its poetry, but the existence of the two geographical entities, Britain and Ireland, and their mutual awareness remains throughout unarguable.

In looking at the work of poets of these islands in the period since the Second World War, we are alert to a shift in poetry and in the perception of poetry, as well as to an alteration in politics and history. World War II marks a fissure in history and poetry in Britain as well as Ireland. Before it, Irish verse is dominated by Yeats, his aristocratic stance producing a voice which often makes him sound as if (as he put it in 'All Things Can Tempt Me') 'he had a sword upstairs'. In Britain, the brilliant, highly educated poetry of Eliot and Auden held sway. Greek epigraphs guarded the portals of Eliot, while readers marvelled at what Dylan Thomas called 'young Auden's coded chatter'. Whether it was written by William Empson or Edith Sitwell, the most admired poetry was a bit like an exam and often carried a mandarin tone – one heard movingly, harrowingly in the music of Eliot's *Four Quartets*. Yeats died in 1939 and Eliot slipped away towards the theatre, where he attempted to catch a popular audience. The publication of *Four Quartets* in 1942 is the high-water mark of modernist poetry in Britain. After it came the delayed publication of the biblioholically demanding late poetry of the Scottish poet Hugh MacDiarmid (mostly written in the 1930s), the ambitious and Eliot-supported myth-manoeuvrings of Welshman David Jones, and the Pound-sponsored northern English modernist poetry of Basil Bunting; but each of these seems something of an isolated, if exciting, outcrop in the post-war geography. Some of the established poets, such as Edwin Muir and Dylan Thomas, continued on courses mapped out in the pre-war years, though they registered (as would the generations that followed in Britain) the shock of the war. Yet strikingly, after spending the Second World War in the United States, Auden grew less telegraphically compressed, less 'coded', more relaxed. The short-lived, strained and clotted New Apocalyptic movement of the early 1940s was sloughed off like a skin. The democratic voice was arriving.

This voice's emergence was heralded and later schooled by the Butler Education Act of 1944, which extended the educational franchise, bringing about a movement in the constituency of readers and writers. Where Auden in the early thirties wrote from, and most immediately addressed, a public-school-educated Oxbridge coterie audience, post-war poets as diverse as Philip Larkin, Ted Hughes and Stevie Smith wrote subtle, accessible and surprising poetry, communicating more directly with a wider public:

> Piggy to Joey,
> Piggy to Joe,
> Yes, that's what I was –
> Piggy to Joe.
>
> (Stevie Smith, 'Piggy to Joey')

In the generation that followed, Douglas Dunn, Seamus Heaney and Tony Harrison (none educated at public school or at Oxbridge) wrote consciously as 'barbarians' from outside the traditional cultural centre. Where T. S. Eliot, nicknamed 'the Pope of Russell Square', had pronounced *ex cathedra* in *Four Quartets* on the poet's mission 'to purify the dialect of the tribe', more and more post-war poets delighted in the impure 'mud flowers of dialect', as Heaney called them. Poetry *was* possible after Auschwitz, but it was subtly different from before. Largely rejecting pontifical tones, poets in Britain and Ireland wrote as part of a shift towards post-imperial, pluralist societies and communities. The notion of a hieratic voice of authority (whether that of received pronunciation, the BBC, the Irish Catholic priest, the Oxford don, or the patriarchal male) was rejected, though poets' voices were increasingly part of the public sphere.

Especially since the 1960s, poetry readings throughout Britain and Ireland have become a popular phenomenon, while a wide variety of spoken verse has been broadcast through (particularly BBC) radio and, more occasionally, television. Though poetry remains a medium of risk and exploration, it need not be at odds with popular culture. If, at times, the mass media may have lacked the courage to trust poetry, then there are also instances where poets as different as Tony Harrison and Sorley MacLean have had their work published in broadsheet newspapers, filmed, and broadcast through radio, tapes and more modern electronic media. It may have become easier in this period to publish books of verse. Certainly, and often with support from public bodies such as Arts Councils, important poetry publishers have established themselves in such diverse locations as Newcastle, Manchester, County Meath, Edinburgh, Belfast and Mid Glamorgan. Though some of the most significant poetry presses and magazines remain London-based, the strength and range of publishing established elsewhere encouraged new readers and writers, disseminating a proliferation of poetries. Some of the voices that emerged were blokish, some consciously female, some clearly un-English. All appear aware of existing among a plurality of speakers and writers. The notion of 'the democratic voice' is not intended to suggest that all post-war poets sound alike or speak with one intonation – quite the opposite. Continually, these poets display an awareness of inhabiting one voice that is among others, part of a vernacular community surrounded by further vernacular communities. The democratic voice may speak Gaelic or English. It may be gendered as male or female. It is unhieratic, belonging to a culture of pluralism, where its authority is both challenging and challenged. It is an allied self-awareness and bite that allows Peter Reading to combine traditional poetic techniques, such as couplets, rhythm and rhyme, with mixed colloquial and formal English, reported speech, everyday expletives and a gravestone epitaph, all within the one piece:

> Inside a shed with the Council's coat-of-arms blazoned on it
> there is a Flymo and spades. Here comes a gent with a pick:
>
> 'Wouldn't it make you want to dip your bread in the piss-pot
> – some of the bilge they write there? Fuckin daft sods' (he opines).
>
> Sweet peas are cunningly wrought in a huge pink crucifix resting
> fresh on damp just-replaced turf. Wet clay outlines a new slot.
>
> Biro-smeared sympathy cards blow about and one is signed
>   'Viv, The
> Deepest Regrett Always Felt' (it shows a wren on a wreath).
>
> On a diminutive gravy-hued sandstone wafer is chiselled
> that which, despite mawkishness, prompts a sharp intake of breath.
>
> *Aged 10.*
> *Little Boy,*
> *We Would Not*
> *Wake You To*
> *Suffer Again.*
>
> (Peter Reading, 'Ukulele Music')

The contemporary culture of pluralism evolved in Britain to a large degree through the gradual development of modern democracy and the winding-down of British imperial power. In Britain, all women over the age of twenty-one received the right to vote in 1928, while as late as the mid-1940s a small minority of men had two votes rather than one. What we now consider democracy was long and slow in evolving, and continues to evolve. Having only recently established its independence from Britain, the Republic of Ireland remained neutral during the Second World War. In 1945, however, the United Kingdom, triumphantly exhausted after playing a crucial role in the then concluding war against fascism, was still in control of the world's largest empire, covering over one quarter of the globe. The decades that followed brought a vast relinquishing of imperial territories, from India and Pakistan (which became independent in 1947), through Nigeria, Kenya, Rhodesia (now Zimbabwe) and South Africa, to Hong Kong (Britain's last major colony, which reverted to Chinese control in 1997). While this might be presented in terms of a narrative of imperial decline, it also represents a pragmatic and principled recognition that the ideology of empire was no longer desirable, and that democratic institutions across the former empire, whether in Australasia, India, Africa, or Canada, had largely replaced British rule. The rise of the economic, military and cultural power of the United States accompanied Britain's cession of empire and her sometimes awkward relationship with the developing European Community. These political and historical developments had a crucial impact on language.

From being the widely acknowledged fount and centre of English-language culture in the early 1900s, England, as the century developed, became more and more an anglophone culture within an English-speaking world. Having spread throughout the atlas English, as the language of global science, became the world's most desired language, but it was one more and more vestigially, if discernibly, linked to its country of origin. England became in some senses one of many provinces within the English-speaking world. London remained a capital of publishing, but was not so clearly a capital of cultural or poetic authority. Though political devolution within the United Kingdom (giving Scotland its own Parliament and Wales its own Assembly) was not democratically chosen until 1997, a process of literary devolution has been taking place over a long period, and is linked to changes within the operation of British democracy. Some of these shifts have been awkward and remain unresolved. The status of Northern Ireland within the island of Ireland, and within the United Kingdom of Great Britain and Northern Ireland, has been a persistent source of (often violent) friction that has

left its mark on the work of poets as different as Michael Longley, Seamus
Heaney and Paul Muldoon. In a 1976 lecture, 'Englands of the Mind',
Heaney pointed out that poets of what he still called 'the mother culture
[i.e., England] are now possessed of that defensive love of their territory
which was once shared only by those poets whom we might call colonial
– Yeats, MacDiarmid, Carlos Williams'. For Heaney, 'The loss of imperial
power, the failure of economic nerve, the diminished influence of Britain
inside Europe, all this has led to a new sense of the shires, a new valuing
of the native English experience.' This sense of English poetry being
bound up at times with an awareness of English nationalism or regionalism
can be detected in work by Philip Larkin, Tony Harrison, Ted Hughes,
Geoffrey Hill and Glyn Maxwell, all of whom compose very different
kinds of poetry. It connects what some English poets are doing with the
attunement to (and interrogation of) national cultures in Scotland, Ireland
and Wales. In Scotland, for instance, poets from Norman MacCaig and
Edwin Morgan, to Tom Leonard, Douglas Dunn and Kathleen Jamie,
continually latch on to situations, terrains and kinds of language that are
at once peculiarly Scottish yet can also resonate more widely within
Britain, Ireland and beyond:

> The museums of Scotland are wrang.
> They urnae arraheids
> but a show o grannies' tongues,
> the hard tongues o grannies
> aa deid an gaun
> back to thur peat and burns,
> but fur thur sherp
> chert tongues, that lee
> fur generations in the land . . .
>
> (Kathleen Jamie, 'Arraheids')

A sense of local accents, dialects, languages attaining their own authority, at the same time as ideas of absolute central authority dissolve,
characterizes the poetry of the period and plays a strong part in the
evolution of the democratic voice. In this climate it is right that as
anthologists who are aiming at an English–language audience we also

acknowledge the outstanding work in Scottish Gaelic, Irish and Welsh which forms part of the manifold body of modern poetry from Britain and Ireland. We have chosen to represent these languages through a small, but highly significant, selection of parallel texts. So, among our democratic voices is the following:

> Cuirim mo dhóchas ar snámh
> i mbáidín teangan
> faoi mar a leagfá naíonán
> i gcliabhán
> a bheadh fite fuaite
> de dhuilleoga feileastraim
> is bitiúman agus pic
> bheith cuimilte lena thóin
>
> I place my hope on the water
> in this little boat
> of the language, the way a body might put
> an infant
>
> in a basket of intertwined
> iris leaves,
> its underside proofed
> with bitumen and pitch . . .
>
> (Nuala Ní Dhomhnaill, 'Ceist na Teangan'/
> 'The Language Issue', trans. Paul Muldoon)

It was important to us to present the work in its original language, if only to stress the poetry's distance from English-language culture, to give it its independent head. At the same time, as English speakers aiming at an English-speaking audience, we have had to select only poems that seemed to work convincingly in modern English translation, rather than in translations which seemed weak or unfulfilled. To some, this may seem an awkward half-way house, but we are confident that a policy of total exclusion, or undiscriminating inclusion, would have betrayed our desire to represent in the strongest way the pluralism of modern poetry from these islands. An anthology which omitted Sorley MacLean's work would be as unthinkable to us as one which omitted Sylvia Plath's. That said, and perhaps because in much of Ireland and Scotland there is a friendlier relationship between English and Gaelic than exists in Wales between English and the Welsh language, we have had difficulty in finding English versions of some Welsh poets which convinced us that they demanded inclusion.

It would be possible to elaborate on the themes of nationalism and regionalism within modern poetry from Ireland and Britain, but it would be wrong to see this as the sole defining feature of the map. If older narratives of post-1945 poetry in these islands dwelt on the rejection of modernist aesthetics by the poets of The Movement (a group which crucially included Philip Larkin), then that now seems a dated and misleading oversimplification. Modernist interests in the run-down city, jazz and mixing unusual with demotic language, resurface in Larkin's work, for instance, while the experimentalism of Larkin's near-contemporaries W. S. Graham, Edwin Morgan and Ian Hamilton Finlay shows an openness to language and international poetic currents (whether of concrete poetry or concerns about the materiality of language), which challenges ideas of post-1945 verse as Movement-dominated. If sometimes heated debates over free verse had erupted in the earlier part of the century, then increasingly in the post-1945 period attitudes towards form became more relaxed. The outcome was not an across-the-board triumph for *vers libre*, but rather an acceptance of a wide variety of forms and styles, with poets choosing, or being chosen by, the most appropriate. If recent American poetry has produced a proselytizing New Formalist movement, then nothing so regimented has appeared in Britain or Ireland. The poetry of the period, like its politics, contains strong voices which may seem irreconcilable, but that is the character of strong poetic voices, and in picking what seem to us to be the best of these we are seeking to dispel the notion that there is one straightforward, quasi-monarchical line of succession in this period of the democratic voice.

Indeed, one of the striking things about the poetry of this era is how apparent genealogies become disrupted, not least through poetic emigration and immigration. At a time when global travel and communications are taken for granted, and the international circulation of poetry through magazines and volumes developed further, it would be absurd to insist on notions of 'pure' Irish or English or other poetries. We have not insisted on too precise a notion of subjecthood or citizenship to define what constitutes a poet from Britain or Ireland. Many of the writers here were born in the Anglo–Celtic archipelago, but some were born in Australasia, the United States, the Caribbean or other parts of the world, and have become part of the literary communities in Britain and Ireland through extended residence. We have also included poets born in these islands who spent much of the post-war period living abroad, as Robert Graves or Denise Levertov did, for example. We wanted to make a lively and valid anthology, rather than staff a literary passport control point. The poet of

> Inglan is a bitch
> dere's no escapin' it
> Inglan is a bitch
> y'u haffi know how fi survive in it
>
> (Linton Kwesi Johnson, 'Inglan Is a Bitch')

is as much a part of this anthology as

> Crocus in the Fellows' Garden, winter jasmine up the wall
>   Gleam gold.
>
> Shadows of Victorian chimneys on the sunny grassplot fall
>   Long, cold.
>
> (John Betjeman, 'I. M. Walter Ramsden')

Most older notions of poetic succession assumed that the male line was what mattered. Again, this has been rightly, and often, challenged in the years since 1945. Whether in Ireland or in Britain, changing attitudes to gender have been accompanied by a growth in the assurance with which women poets write, and in the confident way their work is received. The poetry suggests that these changes may not have occurred at a uniform rate across the islands. The quite different, yet equally strong, voices of Eavan Boland and Liz Lochhead in Ireland and Scotland postdate those of Anne Stevenson, Sylvia Plath and Fleur Adcock in England – it is also worth pointing out that these latter two poets are incomers,

Plath arriving from the United States (where Anne Stevenson was also educated), Adcock from New Zealand. Just as there may be pressures (not least from academia) to manufacture teachable lines of succession in post-war poetry in general, so there may be pressures to identify a clear genealogy of female poets. While readers of this book can attempt this, the editors are at least as aware of the differences between the voices of the women poets of this era, and we have attempted to complicate rather than simplify the picture by including, for instance, work by the English-American Denise Levertov. Stevie Smith, Kathleen Raine, Elizabeth Jennings are among the senior female poets of this anthology, and each can show an awareness of writing from a female perspective, yet to suggest that their voices were identical, or even similar, would be reductive. They too are part of the community of democratic voices in which the articulation of identity may take many forms. At the same time, it may be undeniable that the growing number of women poets in the later pages of the anthology reflects an increasingly confident generation of women writers, several of whom (including Selima Hill, Medbh McGuckian, and Carol Ann Duffy) incorporate into their work a strategic and imaginative awareness of issues of gender.

If one's sex or gender, race or religion, nationality or language, automatically commits one to a set of opinions or forms, then a limitation is being placed on imaginative freedom. Since poetry thrives on, and encourages, imaginative freedom, it is essential to state that while this book's title may indicate something of its contents, and while its introduction may set out a trajectory in terms of cultural and political currents in Britain and Ireland, the editors were determined to include only writing of high poetic worth in the wide variety of work they chose. Poetry can take many different forms, and quite often what succeeds most is the poetry that doesn't fit any tidy attempts at categorization. Indeed, as with any imaginative activity, one of poetry's fundamental urges is always to push at its own boundaries. This anthology includes work which hovers between verse and the visual arts, and work where the poem seems like a libretto or performance script. On the whole, though, we have preferred poems which seemed to work both on the page *and* acoustically.

While casting the net widely, we were conscious that all anthologists must face up to questions of poetic value. As a rule of thumb, four or five poems were selected from each of the poets who seemed to us particularly important in the period, with the hope that these selections would provide a spine for the anthology. Considerations of space did have an impact on our thinking, and sometimes we chose a smaller number of longer poems (even, in the case of Paul Muldoon, one long poem) to represent a significant talent. We had our rules, and we broke them. Like a poem, an anthology involves sheer idealism and actual solutions – a kind of pragmatic dreaming. All the poems we have included are valuable to us, and we hope readers will enjoy them rather than simply look at 'major figures'.

We wished to represent the work of poets best known for their pre-1945 writing who had gone on to produce strong verse after that date, and we wanted to try to do justice to the work of writers now less fashionable, yet in whose poems we believe. We also gave a generous amount of space to the poets of our own generation, since it seemed both right and inescapable that this book should carry something of the accent of its time and its editors' experience. In the earlier period, time had done some sifting for us; in the later, we tried to be as discriminatingly inclusive as we could. A number of recent anthologies have surveyed the ground, but only partially. This book hopes to demonstrate a certain catholicity of taste which will disrupt over-exclusive readings of modern poetry, at the same time as presenting only poems that, however varied, are of a high calibre. It is the kind of anthology in which the editors might have liked their work to appear; as editors, however, we thought it inappropriate to parade our own wares.

In all the material we read we have looked for the unpredictability of poetic life. Sometimes, as in Karen Gershon's 'I Was Not There' or Blake Morrison's 'The Ballad of the Yorkshire Ripper', the poems came markedly charged with the pressure of historical occurrences. But we were not searching simply for work which would be about events that have shaped modern Ireland and Britain. So, while one can find in this volume poems that clearly speak of the Troubles in Northern Ireland, or of issues of race in contemporary England, the poems that treat such matter have won their place in the book because they seemed to the editors to have a characterful poetic life, rather than because they were of sociological note. As one might expect, experiences such as the Second

World War and its aftermath have left a powerful impression on many poets in the period, yet as editors we had to judge the quality of the imaginative response rather than the subject matter. In listening to the democratic voice, while we have not inclined towards the street-cred populism of the Liverpool Poets (impressive performers who have had their rewards elsewhere), we would argue that Irish and British poetry may seem more grounded in the details of historical and sociological experience than French poetry of the same period, for instance; but it is still the case that many of the poems in this book are powered as much by the mysterious and intuitive as by the historiographical impulse. It is not the function of poetry to work only at a rational level, or to legislate for a state. Poetry can be highly documentary, but must also make the imagination manifest itself as fully as possible in language. It loves language. It carries its own authority. Subtler and more sly than politics, it weaves, dips and submerges at least as often as it stands up to be counted. The stuff of strong dreams and sideways glances rather than of five-year plans, it calls on the rhythms of the body as well as on the brain:

> When he was turning on the riverbank,
> The horse had rusted and reared up and pitched
> Cart and sprayer and everything off balance
> So the whole rig went over into a deep
> Whirlpool, hoofs, chains, shafts, cartwheels, barrel
> And tackle, all tumbling off the world,
> And the hat already merrily swept along
> The quieter reaches.
>
> (Seamus Heaney, 'Seeing Things')

Poetry's authority depends on an absolute aptness of verbal shape. The right words need to be in the right order. The line-breaks, and whatever other technical devices, need to be spot-on too, disrupting and conducting the flow of rightness exactly. If poetry is too nudge-nudgily jokey or flatly programmatic, too grandiose, too handwringing – it fails.

On the whole, neither British nor Irish poetry of the last half-century has imploded into universities, though increasingly the teaching of creative writing there is bringing poets on to campus. While a good number of the writers in this book have, or have had, some university affiliation, many have none. For some readers and poets there may be a conflict between the culture of poet as bard or even shaman, reading to an audience either face-to-face or through the mass media, and poet as seminar-room habitué. Yet tensions between the wildly bardic and the bookishly academic have energized poetry in these islands since at least the time of Ossian, and may help define the figure of 'the modern poet'. What is good, surely, is that there remains and continues to develop a range of voices – some tenured, some not – yet all alert to the importance of the imagination's independence. Certainly, the situation in Ireland and Britain still contrasts with that in the United States where so many writers of verse are connected to an academic institution, with the term 'poet' almost denoting a salary point.

We would like to think that, from the work of Stevie Smith and John Betjeman, to that of Paul Durcan and John Agard, this book contains a lot that may make the reader laugh or smile. Since it is as human to laugh as to cry, this seems to be appropriate. Poetry is not just a way of telling jokes, but it can include that; indeed, many of the poems mix humour with other emotions. But poetry is no more a form of stand-up comedy than it is the new rock and roll or the new religion; it has its own being and its own demands. As a kind of nimbleness, humour can meet these often as well as can the nuanced lacerations of a lamenting imagination.

Whether ululating or whispering, the poems in this book show the many ways in which language lives in the various parts of Ireland and of Britain. If poems are linguistic distillations then this anthology will remind readers of how complex and rich remains the mixture of tongues and linguistic possibilities present in these north-west European islands. On the one hand, with access to a world language, there is the possibility to attempt, modify and develop kinds of American-driven post-modernism; on the other hand, articulations of Englishness, or voicings of dialect and non-English languages, may be used as tools of cultural resistance, ways of relating to long and rich traditions, or simply as the most available way in which to speak. Language, for many of the poets in this book, is something to be negotiated with and through, rather than something simply transparent. An alertness to the often tricksy grain of words may be the product of a late twentieth-century sensibility educated in a kind of after-world (post-modern, post-Christian, post-war, post-Hiroshima, post-structuralist), but it may owe as much to a sense of choice between languages, whether for Tony Harrison or Paul Muldoon or Iain Crichton Smith. As we move towards the beginning of a new millennium a sense of belatedness grows, mixed with a sense of anticipation. Just as it is unlikely that either war or religion will be left behind, so it may be that many of the poems in this book will come to be seen, not so much in terms of what they followed, as in terms of what they preceded. We hope that we have selected here a good number of the poems from post-1945 Britain and Ireland which will continue to have a lasting life.

EDWIN MUIR (1887–1959)

Edwin Muir was born in 1887 on Deerness, Orkney, and grew up on the island of Wyre and then in Glasgow. He worked in a variety of settings before moving to London, then in 1921 to Europe, where he began to write poetry at the age of thirty-five. After spells in Prague and Rome and a lectureship at Harvard, he eventually returned to Britain, settling finally in Cambridgeshire. His Autobiography *was published in 1954, and a revised edition of the* Collected Poems *in 1984. He died in 1959.*

The Interrogation

We could have crossed the road but hesitated,
And then came the patrol;
The leader conscientious and intent,
The men surly, indifferent.
While we stood by and waited
The interrogation began. He says the whole
Must come out now, who, what we are,
Where we have come from, with what purpose, whose
Country or camp we plot for or betray.
Question on question.
We have stood and answered through the standing day
And watched across the road beyond the hedge
The careless lovers in pairs go by,
Hand linked in hand, wandering another star,
So near we could shout to them. We cannot choose
Answer or action here,
Though still the careless lovers saunter by
And the thoughtless field is near.

We are on the very edge,
Endurance almost done,
And still the interrogation is going on.

The Annunciation

The angel and the girl are met.
Earth was the only meeting place.
For the embodied never yet
Travelled beyond the shore of space.
The eternal spirits in freedom go.

See, they have come together, see,
While the destroying minutes flow,
Each reflects the other's face
Till heaven in hers and earth in his
Shine steady there. He's come to her
From far beyond the farthest star,
Feathered through time. Immediacy
Of strangest strangeness is the bliss
That from their limbs all movement takes.
Yet the increasing rapture brings
So great a wonder that it makes
Each feather tremble on his wings.

Outside the window footsteps fall
Into the ordinary day
And with the sun along the wall
Pursue their unreturning way.
Sound's perpetual roundabout
Rolls its numbered octaves out
And hoarsely grinds its battered tune.

But through the endless afternoon
These neither speak nor movement make,
But stare into their deepening trance
As if their gaze would never break.

The Horses

Barely a twelvemonth after
The seven days war that put the world to sleep,
Late in the evening the strange horses came.
By then we had made our covenant with silence,
But in the first few days it was so still
We listened to our breathing and were afraid.
On the second day
The radios failed; we turned the knobs; no answer.
On the third day a warship passed us, heading north,
Dead bodies piled on the deck. On the sixth day
A plane plunged over us into the sea. Thereafter
Nothing. The radios dumb;
And still they stand in corners of our kitchens,
And stand, perhaps, turned on, in a million rooms
All over the world. But now if they should speak,
If on a sudden they should speak again,
If on the stroke of noon a voice should speak,
We would not listen, we would not let it bring
That old bad world that swallowed its children quick
At one great gulp. We would not have it again.
Sometimes we think of the nations lying asleep,
Curled blindly in impenetrable sorrow,
And then the thought confounds us with its strangeness.

The tractors lie about our fields; at evening
They look like dank sea-monsters couched and waiting.
We leave them where they are and let them rust:
'They'll moulder away and be like other loam'.
We make our oxen drag our rusty ploughs,
Long laid aside. We have gone back
Far past our fathers' land.
                              And then, that evening
Late in the summer the strange horses came.
We heard a distant tapping on the road,

A deepening drumming; it stopped, went on again
And at the corner changed to hollow thunder.
We saw the heads
Like a wild wave charging and were afraid.
We had sold our horses in our fathers' time
To buy new tractors. Now they were strange to us
As fabulous steeds set on an ancient shield
Or illustrations in a book of knights.
We did not dare go near them. Yet they waited,
Stubborn and shy, as if they had been sent
By an old command to find our whereabouts
And that long-lost archaic companionship.
In the first moment we had never a thought
That they were creatures to be owned and used.
Among them were some half-a-dozen colts
Dropped in some wilderness of the broken world,
Yet new as if they had come from their own Eden.
Since then they have pulled our ploughs and borne our loads,
But that free servitude still can pierce our hearts.
Our life is changed; their coming our beginning.

HUGH MACDIARMID (1892–1978)

Hugh MacDiarmid was born Christopher Murray Grieve in 1892 in Langholm in the Scottish Borders. In his early years he taught, worked as a journalist and served in the armed forces during the First World War. In the 1920s he adopted his pseudonym and wrote in Scots such work as A Drunk Man Looks at the Thistle *(1926). He went on to become the major Scottish literary figure of the twentieth century, and one of the most controversial. A member of the National Party of Scotland and later the Communist Party of Great Britain, he settled in Brownsbank near Biggar in later life and lived there until his death in 1978. His two-volume* Collected Poems *was published in 1978 and reissued in 1985 with additional poems.*

Crystals Like Blood

I remember how, long ago, I found
Crystals like blood in a broken stone.

I picked up a broken chunk of bed-rock
And turned it this way and that,
It was heavier than one would have expected
From its size. One face was caked
With brown limestone. But the rest
Was a hard greenish-grey quartz-like stone
Faintly dappled with darker shadows,
And in this quartz ran veins and beads
Of bright magenta.

And I remember how later on I saw
How mercury is extracted from cinnebar
– The double ring of iron piledrivers
Like the multiple legs of a fantastically symmetrical spider
Rising and falling with monotonous precision,
Marching round in an endless circle
And pounding up and down with a tireless, thunderous force,
While, beyond, another conveyor drew the crumbled ore
From the bottom and raised it to an opening high
In the side of a gigantic grey-white kiln.

So I remember how mercury is got
When I contrast my living memory of you
And your dear body rotting here in the clay
– And feel once again released in me
The bright torrents of felicity, naturalness, and faith
My treadmill memory draws from you yet.

To a Friend and Fellow-Poet★

It is with the poet as with a guinea worm
Who, to accommodate her teeming progeny
Sacrifices nearly every organ of her body, and becomes
(Her vagina obliterated in her all-else-consuming
Process of uterine expansion, and she still faced
With a grave obstetrical dilemma calling for
Most marvellous contrivance to deposit her prodigious swarm
Where they may find the food they need and have a chance in life)
Almost wholly given over to her motherly task,
Little more than one long tube close-packed with young;
Until from the ruptured bulla, the little circular sore,
You see her dauntless head protrude, and presently, slowly,
A beautiful, delicate, and pellucid tube
Is projected from her mouth, tenses and suddenly spills
Her countless brood in response to a stimulus applied
Not directly to the worm herself, but the skin of her host
With whom she has no organized connection (and that stimulus
O Poets! but cold water!) . . . The worm's whole musculocutaneous
   coat
Thus finally functions as a uterus, forcing the uterine tube
With its contents through her mouth. And when the prolapsed uterus
   ruptures
The protruded and now collapsed portion shrivels to a thread
(Alexander Blok's utter emptiness after creating a poem!)
The rapid drying of which effectually and firmly
Closes the wound for the time being . . . till, later, the stimulus being
   reapplied,
A fresh portion of the uterine tube protrudes, ruptures, and collapses,
Once more ejaculating another seething mass of embryos,
And so the process continues until inch by inch
The entire uterus is expelled and parturition concluded.

★ Ruth Pitter.

Is it not precisely thus we poets deliver our store,
Our whole being the instrument of our suicidal art,
And by the skin of our teeth flype ourselves into fame?

DAVID JONES (1895–1974)

David Jones was born in Brockley, Kent, in 1895, and served with the Royal Welsh Fusiliers during the First World War, an experience which formed the basis of his best-known work, In Parenthesis, *published in 1937. Calligrapher, artist, engraver, he also wrote many essays on art and related subjects. His other works include* The Anathemata *(1952) and* The Sleeping Lord and Other Fragments *(1974). He suffered mental health problems throughout his life becoming virtually a recluse in his later years and died in Devon in 1974.*

from The Sleeping Lord

And is his bed wide
                           is his bed deep on the folded strata
is his bed long
                           where is his bed and
                           where has he lain him
from north of Llanfair-ym-Muallt
                           (a name of double *gladius*-piercings)★
south to the carboniferous vaultings of Gŵyr†
                           (where in the sea-slope chamber
they shovelled aside the shards & breccia

★ *Llanfair-ym-Muallt*: 'Mary's church in Buellt'. The town now called Builth Wells. It was between Llanfair and Llanganten that the Lord Llywelyn, Prince of Wales was killed in 1282. Hence my reference to a *double* piercing in that any place-name with Marian associations necessarily recalls the passage in the gospel of the *gladius* that would pierce the heart of the God-bearer. Pronounce: llan-veir-um-mee-allt.
† *Gŵyr*: The Gower Peninsula; pronounce approximately goo-eer. It was in Gŵyr that human remains, ritually buried, were discovered of a young man of the Palaeolithic period, so many, many millenniums prior to Britain becoming an island.

the domestic litter and man-squalor
of gnawed marrowbones and hearth-ash
with utile shovels fashioned of clavicle-bones
of warm-felled great fauna.
Donated the life-signa:
the crocked viatic meal
the flint-worked ivory agalma
the sacral sea-shell trinkets
posited with care the vivific amulets
of gleam-white rodded ivory
and, with oxide of iron
ochred life-red the cerements
of the strong limbs
of the young *nobilis*
the first of the sleepers of
Pritenia, *pars dextralis*, O! aeons & aeons
before we were insular'd.)
Is the tump by Honddu★
his lifted bolster?
does a gritstone outcrop
incommode him?
does a deep syncline
sag beneath him?
or does his dinted thorax rest
where the contorted heights
themselves rest
on a lateral pressured anticline?
Does his russet-hued mattress
does his rug of shaly grey
ease at all for his royal dorsals
the faulted under-bedding.
Augite-hard and very chill
do scattered *cerrig*†

★ *Honddu*: pronounce hón-thee.
† *cerrig*: stones; pronounce ker-rig 'er' as in errand.

jutt to discomfort him?
>Millenniums on millennia since
this cold scoria dyked up molten
when the sedimented, slowly layered strata
(so great the slow heaped labour of their conditor
the patient creature of water) said each to each other:
'There's no resisting here:
>the Word if made Fire.'

ROBERT GRAVES (1895–1985)

Robert Graves was born in Wimbledon in 1895 and went from school to the First World War, where he became a captain in the Royal Welsh Fusiliers. For much of his life he lived on the Spanish island of Majorca. Apart from a year's teaching in Egypt he made his living entirely from writing, and is as well-known for his prose books, which include the novel I, Claudius, *the autobiographical work* Goodbye to All That *and the visionary poetic manifesto* The White Goddess, *published in 1948. Graves also published criticism and books on mythology, but poetry was his main passion, and he wrote continuously from an early age up until his death in 1985. His complete works, poetry and prose, were re-edited and reissued in 1997 and 1998.*

The White Goddess

All saints revile her, and all sober men
Ruled by the God Apollo's golden mean –
In scorn of which we sailed to find her
In distant regions likeliest to hold her
Whom we desired above all things to know,
Sister of the mirage and echo.

It was a virtue not to stay,
To go our headstrong and heroic way
Seeking her out at the volcano's head,
Among pack ice, or where the track had faded

Beyond the cavern of the seven sleepers:
Whose broad high brow was white as any leper's,
Whose eyes were blue, with rowan-berry lips,
With hair curled honey-coloured to white hips.

Green sap of Spring in the young wood a-stir
Will celebrate the Mountain Mother,
And every song-bird shout awhile for her;
But we are gifted, even in November
Rawest of seasons, with so huge a sense
Of her nakedly worn magnificence
We forget cruelty and past betrayal,
Heedless of where the next bright bolt may fall.

Apple Island

Though cruel seas like mountains fill the bay,
Wrecking the quayside huts,
Salting our vineyards with tall showers of spray;

And though the moon shines dangerously clear,
Fixed in another cycle
Than the sun's progress round the felloe'd year;

And though I may not hope to dwell apart
With you on Apple Island
Unless my breast be docile to the dart –

Why should I fear your element, the sea,
Or the full moon, your mirror,
Or the halved apple from your holy tree?

Surgical Ward: Men

Something occurred after the operation
To scare the surgeons (though no fault of theirs),
Whose reassurance did not fool me long.
Beyond the shy, concerned faces of nurses
A single white-hot eye, focusing on me,
Forced sweat in rivers down from scalp to belly.
I whistled, gasped or sang, with blanching knuckles
Clutched at my bed-grip almost till it cracked:
Too proud, still, to let loose Bedlamite screeches
And bring the charge-nurse scuttling down the aisle
With morphia-needle levelled . . .
                                        Lady Morphia –
Her scorpion kiss and dark gyrating dreams –
She in mistrust of whom I dared out-dare,
Two minutes longer than seemed possible,
Pain, that unpurposed, matchless elemental
Stronger than fear or grief, stranger than love.

AUSTIN CLARKE (1896–1974)

Austin Clarke was born in Dublin in 1896 and apart from a period in London lived there throughout his life. His published works include many verse plays, essays and journalism, prose fiction and autobiography. His Collected Poems *was published in 1974 – the same year as his death – and a* Selected Poems *appeared in 1991.*

from Eighteenth Century Harp Songs

1: Mabel Kelly

> Lucky the husband
> Who puts his hand beneath her head.
> They kiss without scandal
> Happiest two near feather-bed.
> He sees the tumble of brown hair
> Unplait, the breasts, pointed and bare
> When nightdress shows
> From dimple to toe-nail,
> All Mabel glowing in it, here, there, everywhere.

> Music might listen
> To her least whisper,
> Learn every note, for all are true.
> While she is speaking,
> Her voice goes sweetly
> To charm the herons in their musing.
> Her eyes are modest, blue, their darkness
> Small rooms of thought, but when they sparkle
> Upon a feast-day,
> Glasses are meeting,
> Each raised to Mabel Kelly, our toast and darling.

> Gone now are many Irish ladies
> Who kissed and fondled, their very pet-names
> Forgotten, their tibia degraded.
> She takes their sky. Her smile is famed.
> Her praise is scored by quill and pencil.
> Harp and spinet
> Are in her debt
> And when she plays or sings, melody is content.

No man who sees her
    Will feel uneasy.
He goes his way, head high, however tired.
    Lamp loses light
    When placed beside her.
She is the pearl and being of all Ireland
Foot, hand, eye, mouth, breast, thigh and instep, all that we desire.
Tresses that pass small curls as if to touch the ground:
    So many prizes
    Are not divided
Her beauty is her own and she is not proud.

RUTH PITTER (1897–1992)

Ruth Pitter was born in Ilford, Essex, in 1897, and published her first poems while still at school. In 1955 she became the first woman to receive the Queen's Gold Medal for Poetry. Collected Poems, published in 1990, contains poems written between 1908 and 1976. She died in 1992.

Old Nelly's Birthday

She knows where to get cracked eggs, does Nelly.
Knows where to get them cheap:
Ninepence a dozen from that Mrs Kelly.
Of course they will not keep,
But Nelly will make them into a jam sandwich
Of most portentous size.
Now this jam sandwich is her secret language,
And sacred in her eyes;
And to go with this sandwich, her love, her treasure,
She'll make a pot of tea,
Her urn, her cauldron of almost unholy pleasure,
For in that tea will be

Never a drop of shivering starving water,
But milk with all its cream;
A boiling foaming snow, by pleasure's daughter,
Obedient to the dream,
Brewed and kept hot and poured out and delected,
This once of all the year,
Most cordial to the hearts of those selected,
Those delicate, those dear,
Mystical inmost friends of fervent Nelly,
Who will consume with glee
And blessings on the decent Mrs Kelly,
That sandwich and that tea.

But this year it was really extra special;
For when old Nelly went
Down to the dairy, she beheld a vessel
Of marvellous extent,
Full of fine milk soured by the spring thunder,
With cream on top galore:
And Mrs Kelly, who really is the world's wonder,
Skimmed her a quart and more;
And Nelly with light heart and little trouble
Beat it and made it turn
Into lovely butter that made the pleasure double:
Her sandwich and her urn,
Flanked by the light new loaf and heavenly butter,
Home-made from magic cream,
Ravished the creature till words could not utter
The glory of the dream.

BASIL BUNTING (1900–1985)

Basil Bunting was born in Northumberland in 1900, and was to return there in later years after something of a nomadic life. In the First World War he spent time in prison as a conscientious objector, then lived in London, Germany, Italy, the United States, the Canary Islands and Paris, where he met and was greatly influenced by Ezra Pound. He published his first book in Milan in 1930, and Poems 1950 *was published in Texas. He eventually returned to England after joining the RAF in the Second World War and serving a posting in what was then Persia. He began to publish in Britain for the first time in the sixties and* Briggflatts, *the long poem which established his reputation, appeared in 1966. A* Collected Poems *was published in 1978 and an* Uncollected Poems *in 1991. He died in 1985.*

from Briggflatts

I

Brag, sweet tenor bull,
descant on Rawthey's madrigal,
each pebble its part
for the fells' late spring.
Dance tiptoe, bull,
black against may.
Ridiculous and lovely
chase hurdling shadows
morning into noon.
May on the bull's hide
and through the dale
furrows fill with may,
paving the slowworm's way.

A mason times his mallet
to a lark's twitter,
listening while the marble rests,
lays his rule
at a letter's edge,

fingertips checking,
till the stone spells a name
naming none,
a man abolished.
Painful lark, labouring to rise!
The solemn mallet says:
In the grave's slot
he lies. We rot.

Decay thrusts the blade,
wheat stands in excrement
trembling. Rawthey trembles.
Tongue stumbles, ears err
for fear of spring.
Rub the stone with sand,
wet sandstone rending
roughness away. Fingers
ache on the rubbing stone.
The mason says: Rocks
happen by chance.
No one here bolts the door,
love is so sore.

Stone smooth as skin,
cold as the dead they load
on a low lorry by night.
The moon sits on the fell
but it will rain.
Under sacks on the stone
two children lie,
hear the horse stale,
the mason whistle,
harness mutter to shaft,
felloe to axle squeak,
rut thud the rim,
crushed grit.

Stocking to stocking, jersey to jersey,
head to a hard arm,
they kiss under the rain,
bruised by their marble bed.
In Garsdale, dawn;
at Hawes, tea from the can.
Rain stops, sacks
steam in the sun, they sit up.
Copper-wire moustache,
sea-reflecting eyes
and Baltic plainsong speech
declare: By such rocks
men killed Bloodaxe.

Fierce blood throbs in his tongue,
lean words.
Skulls cropped for steel caps
huddle round Stainmore.
Their becks ring on limestone,
whisper to peat.
The clogged cart pushes the horse downhill.
In such soft air
they trudge and sing,
laying the tune frankly on the air.
All sounds fall still,
fellside bleat,
hide-and-seek peewit.

Her pulse their pace,
palm countering palm,
till a trench is filled,
stone white as cheese
jeers at the dale.
Knotty wood, hard to rive,
smoulders to ash;
smell of October apples.
The road again,

at a trot.
Wetter, warmed, they watch
the mason meditate
on name and date.

Rain rinses the road,
the bull streams and laments.
Sour rye porridge from the hob
with cream and black tea,
meat, crust and crumb.
Her parents in bed
the children dry their clothes.
He has untied the tape
of her striped flannel drawers
before the range. Naked
on the pricked rag mat
his fingers comb
thatch of his manhood's home.

Gentle generous voices weave
over bare night
words to confirm and delight
till bird dawn.
Rainwater from the butt
she fetches and flannel
to wash him inch by inch,
kissing the pebbles.
Shining slowworm part of the marvel.
The mason stirs:
Words!
Pens are too light.
Take a chisel to write.

Every birth a crime,
every sentence life.
Wiped of mould and mites
would the ball run true?

No hope of going back.
Hounds falter and stray,
shame deflects the pen.
Love murdered neither bleeds nor stifles
but jogs the draftsman's elbow.
What can he, changed, tell
her, changed, perhaps dead?
Delight dwindles. Blame
stays the same.

Brief words are hard to find,
shapes to carve and discard:
Bloodaxe, king of York,
king of Dublin, king of Orkney.
Take no notice of tears;
letter the stone to stand
over love laid aside lest
insufferable happiness impede
flight to Stainmore,
to trace
lark, mallet,
becks, flocks
and axe knocks.

Dung will not soil the slowworm's
mosaic. Breathless lark
drops to nest in sodden trash;
Rawthey truculent, dingy.
Drudge at the mallet, the may is down,
fog on fells. Guilty of spring
and spring's ending
amputated years ache after
the bull is beef, love a convenience.
It is easier to die than to remember.
Name and date
split in soft slate
a few months obliterate.

STEVIE SMITH (1902–1971)

Stevie Smith was born in Hull in 1902 and lived from the age of three in London, where she worked as a secretary. Her first collection of poetry was A Good Time Was Had By All, *published in 1937, a year after her prose book* Novel on Yellow Paper *had brought her to prominence. Six other books of poetry were to follow, including* Selected Poems *in 1964, and her work is well known for the cartoon illustrations drawn by the author herself to accompany the poems.* Collected Poems *was published in 1975, four years after her death.*

Do Take Muriel Out

Do take Muriel out
She is looking so glum
Do take Muriel out
All her friends have gone.

And after too much pressure
Looking for them in the Palace
She goes home to too much leisure
And this is what her life is.

All her friends are gone
And she is alone
And she looks for them where they have never been
And her peace is flown.

Her friends went into the forest
And across the river
And the desert took their footprints
And they went with a believer.

Ah they are gone they were so beautiful
And she can not come to them
And she kneels in her room at night
Crying, Amen.

Do take Muriel out
Although your name is Death
She will not complain
When you dance her over the blasted heath.

Not Waving but Drowning

Nobody heard him, the dead man,
But still he lay moaning:
I was much further out than you thought
And not waving but drowning.

Poor chap, he always loved larking
And now he's dead
It must have been too cold for him his heart gave way,
They said.

Oh, no no no, it was too cold always
(Still the dead one lay moaning)
I was much too far out all my life
And not waving but drowning.

The Jungle Husband

Dearest Evelyn, I often think of you
Out with the guns in the jungle stew
Yesterday I hittapotamus
I put the measurements down for you but they got lost in the fuss
It's not a good thing to drink out here
You know, I've practically given it up dear.
Tomorrow I am going alone a long way
Into the jungle. It is all gray
But green on top
Only sometimes when a tree has fallen
The sun comes down plop, it is quite appalling.
You never want to go in a jungle pool
In the hot sun, it would be the act of a fool
Because it's always full of anacondas, Evelyn, not looking ill-fed
I'll say. So no more now, from your loving husband, Wilfred.

Piggy to Joey

Piggy to Joey,
Piggy to Joe,
Yes, that's what I was –
Piggy to Joe.

Will he come back again?
Oh no, no, no.
Oh how I wish I hadn't been
Piggy to Joe.

PATRICK KAVANAGH (1904–1967)

Patrick Kavanagh was born in Inniskeen, County Monaghan, in 1904, and first worked as a cobbler and a farmer. He published his first book, Ploughman and other Poems, *in 1936, and in 1939 moved to Dublin, where he published* The Great Hunger *in 1942. Often concerned with the plight of the rural population in Ireland, he created controversy through his arguments and legal battles with the literary establishment in Dublin. Following ill-health in the early fifties he entered a more settled period of his life, and married in 1967, the same year as his death. He also wrote a number of prose works, and his* Collected Poems *was published in 1972.*

A Christmas Childhood

I

One side of the potato-pits was white with frost –
How wonderful that was, how wonderful!
And when we put our ears to the paling-post
The music that came out was magical.

The light between the ricks of hay and straw
Was a hole in Heaven's gable. An apple tree
With its December-glinting fruit we saw –
O you, Eve, were the world that tempted me

To eat the knowledge that grew in clay
And death the germ within it! Now and then
I can remember something of the gay
Garden that was childhood's. Again

The tracks of cattle to a drinking-place,
A green stone lying sideways in a ditch
Or any common sight the transfigured face
Of a beauty that the world did not touch.

II

My father played the melodeon
Outside at our gate;
There were stars in the morning east
And they danced to his music.

Across the wild bogs his melodeon called
To Lennons and Callans.
As I pulled on my trousers in a hurry
I knew some strange thing had happened.

Outside in the cow-house my mother
Made the music of milking;
The light of her stable-lamp was a star
And the frost of Bethlehem made it twinkle.

A water-hen screeched in the bog,
Mass-going feet
Crunched the wafer-ice on the pot-holes,
Somebody wistfully twisted the bellows wheel.

My child poet picked out the letters
On the grey stone,
In silver the wonder of a Christmas townland,
The winking glitter of a frosty dawn.

Cassiopeia was over
Cassidy's hanging hill,
I looked and three whin bushes rode across
The horizon – the Three Wise Kings.

An old man passing said:
'Can't he make it talk' –
The melodeon. I hid in the doorway
And tightened the belt of my box-pleated coat.

I nicked six nicks on the door-post
With my penknife's big blade –
There was a little one for cutting tobacco.
And I was six Christmases of age.

My father played the melodeon,
My mother milked the cows,
And I had a prayer like a white rose pinned
On the Virgin Mary's blouse.

The Long Garden

It was the garden of the golden apples,
A long garden between a railway and a road,
In the sow's rooting where the hen scratches
We dipped our fingers in the pockets of God.

In the thistly hedge old boots were flying sandals
By which we travelled through the childhood skies,
Old buckets rusty-holed with half-hung handles
Were drums to play when old men married wives.

The pole that lifted the clothes-line in the middle
Was the flag-pole on a prince's palace when
We looked at it through fingers crossed to riddle
In evening sunlight miracles for men.

It was the garden of the golden apples,
And when the Carrick train went by we knew
That we could never die till something happened
Like wishing for a fruit that never grew,

Or wanting to be up on Candle-Fort
Above the village with its shops and mill.
The racing cyclists' gasp-gapped reports
Hinted of pubs where life can drink his fill.

And when the sun went down into Drumcatton
And the New Moon by its little finger swung
From the telegraph wires, we knew how God had happened
And what the blackbird in the whitehorn sang.

It was the garden of the golden apples,
The half-way house where we had stopped a day
Before we took the west road to Drumcatton
Where the sun was always setting on the play.

JOHN BETJEMAN (1906–1984)

*John Betjeman was born in Highgate, London, in 1906, and studied at Oxford.
He worked as a writer with* Architectural Review, *as a journalist and with
various government departments during the war, and thereafter lived by his writing
and media engagements. His first book of poems was published in 1931, eventually
leading to the hugely successful* Collected Poems *(1958) containing much of his
best and most famous work. His verse-autobiography,* Summoned by Bells, *was
published in 1960. He received a knighthood in 1969 and was Poet Laureate from
1972 until his death in 1984.*

A Subaltern's Love-Song

Miss J. Hunter Dunn, Miss J. Hunter Dunn,
Furnish'd and burnish'd by Aldershot sun,
What strenuous singles we played after tea,
We in the tournament – you against me!

Love-thirty, love-forty, oh! weakness of joy,
The speed of a swallow, the grace of a boy,
With carefullest carelessness, gaily you won,
I am weak from your loveliness, Joan Hunter Dunn.

Miss Joan Hunter Dunn, Miss Joan Hunter Dunn,
How mad I am, sad I am, glad that you won.
The warm-handled racket is back in its press,
But my shock-headed victor, she loves me no less.

Her father's euonymus shines as we walk,
And swing past the summer-house, buried in talk,
And cool the verandah that welcomes us in
To the six-o'clock news and a lime-juice and gin.

The scent of the conifers, sound of the bath,
The view from my bedroom of moss-dappled path.
As I struggle with double-end evening tie,
For we dance at the Golf Club, my victor and I.

On the floor of her bedroom lie blazer and shorts
And the cream-coloured walls are be-trophied with sports,
And westering, questioning settles the sun
On your low-leaded window, Miss Joan Hunter Dunn.

The Hillman is waiting, the light's in the hall,
The pictures of Egypt are bright on the wall,
My sweet, I am standing beside the oak stair
And there on the landing's the light on your hair.

By roads 'not adopted', by woodlanded ways,
She drove to the club in the late summer haze,
Into nine-o'clock Camberley, heavy with bells
And mushroomy, pine-woody, evergreen smells.

Miss Joan Hunter Dunn, Miss Joan Hunter Dunn,
I can hear from the car park the dance has begun.
Oh! full Surrey twilight! importunate band!
Oh! strongly adorable tennis-girl's hand!

Around us are Rovers and Austins afar,
Above us, the intimate roof of the car,
And here on my right is the girl of my choice,
With the tilt of her nose and the chime of her voice,

And the scent of her wrap, and the words never said,
And the ominous, ominous dancing ahead.
We sat in the car park till twenty to one
And now I'm engaged to Miss Joan Hunter Dunn.

I. M.
Walter Ramsden
ob. March 26, 1947
Pembroke College, Oxford

Dr Ramsden cannot read *The Times* obituary to-day
   He's dead.
Let monographs on silk worms by other people be
   Thrown away
   Unread
For he who best could understand and criticize them, he
   Lies clay
   In bed.

The body waits in Pembroke College where the ivy taps the panes
   All night;
That old head so full of knowledge, that good heart that kept the brains
   All right,
Those old cheeks that faintly flushed as the port suffused the veins,
   Drain'd white.

Crocus in the Fellows' Garden, winter jasmine up the wall
   Gleam gold.
Shadows of Victorian chimneys on the sunny grassplot fall
   Long, cold.
Master, Bursar, Senior Tutor, these, his three survivors, all
   Feel old.

They remember, as the coffin to its final obsequations
   Leaves the gates,
Buzz of bees in window boxes on their summer ministrations,

Kitchen din,
  Cups and plates,
And the getting of bump suppers for the long-dead generations
  Coming in,
   From Eights.

Executive

I am a young executive. No cuffs than mine are cleaner;
I have a Slimline brief-case and I use the firm's Cortina.
In every roadside hostelry from here to Burgess Hill
The *màitres d'hôtel* all know me well and let me sign the bill.

You ask me what it is I do. Well actually, you know,
I'm partly a liaison man and partly P. R. O.
Essentially I integrate the current export drive
And basically I'm viable from ten o'clock till five.

For vital off-the-record work – that's talking transport-wise –
I've a scarlet Aston-Martin – and does she go? She flies!
Pedestrians and dogs and cats – we mark them down for slaughter.
I also own a speed-boat which has never touched the water.

She's built of fibre-glass, of course. I call her 'Mandy Jane'
After a bird I used to know – No soda, please, just plain –
And how did I acquire her? Well to tell you about that
And to put you in the picture I must wear my other hat.

I do some mild developing. The sort of place I need
Is a quiet country market town that's rather run to seed.
A luncheon and a drink or two, a little *savoir faire* –
I fix the Planning Officer, the Town Clerk and the Mayor.

And if some preservationist attempts to interfere
A 'dangerous structure' notice from the Borough Engineer
Will settle any buildings that are standing in our way –
The modern style, sir, with respect, has really come to stay.

LOUIS MacNEICE (1907–1963)

Louis MacNeice was born in 1907 in Belfast and educated in England, where he studied classics and philosophy at Oxford. He taught for some time, but much of his working life was as a producer for BBC radio, making radio features. He came to prominence in the 1930s along with his university contemporaries Auden, Day Lewis and Spender, and his reputation as a writer was made with the publication of Autumn Journal *in 1939. MacNeice wrote a great deal over the next twenty or so years, and his last two books are considered amongst his best work:* Solstices, *published in 1961, and* The Burning Perch, *published just days after his death in 1963.*

All Over Again

As if I had known you for years drink to me only if
Those frontiers have never changed on the mad map of the years
And all our tears were earned and this were the first cliff
From which we embraced the sea and these were the first words
We spread to lure the birds that nested in our day
As if it were always morning their dawnsong theirs and ours
And waking no one else me and you only now
Under the brow of a blue and imperturbable hill
Where still time stands and plays his bland and hemlock pipe
And the ripe moment tugs yet declines to fall and all
The years we had not met forget themselves in this
One kiss ingathered world and outward rippling bell
To the rim of the cup of the sky and leave it only there
Near into far blue into blue all over again
Notwithstanding unique all over all again
Of which to speak requires new fires of the tongue some trick
Of the light in the dark of the muted voice of the turning wild
World yet calm in her storm gay in her ancient rocks
To preserve today one kiss in this skybound timeless cup
Nor now shall I ask for anything more of future or past
This being last and first sound sight on eyes and ears

And each long then and there suspended on this cliff
Shining and slicing edge that reflects the sun as if
This one Between were All and we in love for years.

Soap Suds

This brand of soap has the same smell as once in the big
House he visited when he was eight: the walls of the bathroom open
To reveal a lawn where a great yellow ball rolls back through a hoop
To rest at the head of a mallet held in the hands of a child.

And these were the joys of that house: a tower with a telescope;
Two great faded globes, one of the earth, one of the stars;
A stuffed black dog in the hall; a walled garden with bees;
A rabbit warren; a rockery; a vine under glass; the sea.

To which he has now returned. The day of course is fine
And a grown-up voice cries Play! The mallet slowly swings,
Then crack, a great gong booms from the dog-dark hall and the ball
Skims forward through the hoop and then through the next and then

Through hoops where no hoops were and each dissolves in turn
And the grass has grown head-high and an angry voice cries Play!
But the ball is lost and the mallet slipped long since from the hands
Under the running tap that are not the hands of a child.

The Suicide

And this, ladies and gentlemen, whom I am not in fact
Conducting, was his office all those minutes ago,
This man you never heard of. There are the bills
In the intray, the ash in the ashtray, the grey memoranda stacked
Against him, the serried ranks of the box-files, the packed
Jury of his unanswered correspondence
Nodding under the paperweight in the breeze

From the window by which he left; and here is the cracked
Receiver that never got mended and here is the jotter
With his last doodle which might be his own digestive tract
Ulcer and all or might be the flowery maze
Through which he had wandered deliciously till he stumbled
Suddenly finally conscious of all he lacked
On a manhole under the hollyhocks. The pencil
Point had obviously broken, yet, when he left this room
By catdrop sleight-of-foot or simple vanishing act,
To those who knew him for all that mess in the street
This man with the shy smile has left behind
Something that was intact.

The Taxis

In the first taxi he was alone tra-la.
No extras on the clock. He tipped ninepence
But the cabby, while he thanked him, looked askance
As though to suggest someone had bummed a ride.

In the second taxi he was alone tra-la
But the clock showed sixpence extra; he tipped according
And the cabby from out his muffler said: 'Make sure
You have left nothing behind tra-la between you.'

In the third taxi he was alone tra-la
But the tip-up seats were down and there was an extra
Charge of one-and-sixpence and an odd
Scent that reminded him of a trip to Cannes.

As for the fourth taxi, he was alone
Tra-la when he hailed it but the cabby looked
Through him and said: 'I can't tra-la well take
So many people, not to speak of the dog.'

W. H. AUDEN (1907–1973)

W. H. Auden was born in Yorkshire in 1907. He was educated at Oxford, and during the 1930s worked as a schoolteacher as well as travelling extensively, including visits to Iceland with Louis MacNeice and to China with Christopher Isherwood. He emigrated to the United States in 1938, becoming a naturalized citizen in 1946. In 1953 he was elected Professor of Poetry at Oxford, and in his later years lived on the island of Ischia and in Austria. His vast output began in 1930 with Poems, *and numerous volumes were to follow as well as verse plays, libretti and critical writings, in addition to which he was the editor of several anthologies. His* Collected Poems *was published in 1976, and there are several versions of his collected and selected works. He died in 1973.*

The Fall of Rome

for Cyril Connolly

The piers are pummelled by the waves;
In a lonely field the rain
Lashes an abandoned train:
Outlaws fill the mountain caves.

Fantastic grow the evening gowns;
Agents of the Fisc pursue
Absconding tax-defaulters through
The sewers of provincial towns.

Private rites of magic send
The temple prostitutes to sleep;
All the literati keep
An imaginary friend.

Cerebrotonic Cato may
Extol the Ancient Disciplines,
But the muscle-bound Marines
Mutiny for food and pay.

Caesar's double-bed is warm
As an unimportant clerk
Writes *I DO NOT LIKE MY WORK*
On a pink official form.

Unendowed with wealth or pity,
Little birds with scarlet legs,
Sitting on their speckled eggs,
Eye each flu-infected city.

Altogether elsewhere, vast
Herds of reindeer move across
Miles and miles of golden moss,
Silently and very fast.

The Shield of Achilles

She looked over his shoulder
    For vines and olive trees,
Marble well-governed cities
    And ships upon untamed seas,
But there on the shining metal
    His hands had put instead
An artificial wilderness
    And a sky like lead.

A plain without a feature, bare and brown,
    No blade of grass, no sign of neighborhood,
Nothing to eat and nowhere to sit down,
    Yet, congregated on its blankness, stood
    An unintelligible multitude,
A million eyes, a million boots in line,
Without expression, waiting for a sign.

Out of the air a voice without a face
    Proved by statistics that some cause was just
In tones as dry and level as the place:

No one was cheered and nothing was discussed;
  Column by column in a cloud of dust
They marched away enduring a belief
Whose logic brought them, somewhere else, to grief.

> She looked over his shoulder
>   For ritual pieties,
> White flower-garlanded heifers,
>   Libation and sacrifice,
> But there on the shining metal
>   Where the altar should have been,
> She saw by his flickering forge-light
>   Quite another scene.

Barbed wire enclosed an arbitrary spot
  Where bored officials lounged (one cracked a joke)
And sentries sweated for the day was hot:
  A crowd of ordinary decent folk
  Watched from without and neither moved nor spoke
As three pale figures were led forth and bound
To three posts driven upright in the ground.

The mass and majesty of this world, all
  That carries weight and always weighs the same
Lay in the hands of others; they were small
  And could not hope for help and no help came:
  What their foes liked to do was done, their shame
Was all the worst could wish; they lost their pride
And died as men before their bodies died.

> She looked over his shoulder
>   For athletes at their games,
> Men and women in a dance
>   Moving their sweet limbs
> Quick, quick, to music,
>   But there on the shining shield
> His hands had set no dancing-floor
>   But a weed-choked field.

A ragged urchin, aimless and alone.
   Loitered about that vacancy; a bird
Flew up to safety from his well-aimed stone:
   That girls are raped, that two boys knife a third,
   Were axioms to him, who'd never heard
Of any world where promises were kept,
Or one could weep because another wept.

   The thin-lipped armorer,
      Hephaestos, hobbled away,
   Thetis of the shining breasts
      Cried out in dismay
   At what the god had wrought
      To please her son, the strong
   Iron-hearted man-slaying Achilles
      Who would not live long.

First Things First

Woken, I lay in the arms of my own warmth and listened
To a storm enjoying its storminess in the winter dark
Till my ear, as it can when half-asleep or half-sober,
Set to work to unscramble that interjectory uproar,
Construing its airy vowels and watery consonants
Into a love-speech indicative of a Proper Name.

Scarcely the tongue I should have chosen, yet, as well
As harshness and clumsiness would allow, it spoke in your praise,
Kenning you a god-child of the Moon and the West Wind
With power to tame both real and imaginary monsters,
Likening your poise of being to an upland county,
Here green on purpose, there pure blue for luck.

Loud though it was, alone as it certainly found me,
It reconstructed a day of peculiar silence
When a sneeze could be heard a mile off, and had me walking

On a headland of lava beside you, the occasion as ageless
As the stare of any rose, your presence exactly
So once, so valuable, so there, so now.

This, moreover, at an hour when only too often
A smirking devil annoys me in beautiful English,
Predicting a world where every sacred location
Is a sand-buried site all cultured Texans do,
Misinformed and thoroughly fleeced by their guides,
And gentle hearts are extinct like Hegelian Bishops.

Grateful, I slept till a morning that would not say
How much it believed of what I said the storm had said
But quietly drew my attention to what had been done
– So many cubic metres the more in my cistern
Against a leonine summer –, putting first things first:
Thousands have lived without love, not one without water.

In Praise of Limestone

If it form the one landscape that we, the inconstant ones,
    Are consistently homesick for, this is chiefly
Because it dissolves in water. Mark these rounded slopes
    With their surface fragrance of thyme and, beneath,
A secret system of caves and conduits; hear the springs
    That spurt out everywhere with a chuckle,
Each filling a private pool for its fish and carving
    Its own little ravine whose cliffs entertain
The butterfly and the lizard; examine this region
    Of short distances and definite places:
What could be more like Mother or a fitter background
    For her son, the flirtatious male who lounges
Against a rock in the sunlight, never doubting
    That for all his faults he is loved; whose works are but
Extensions of his power to charm? From weathered outcrop
    To hill-top temple, from appearing waters to

Conspicuous fountains, from a wild to a formal vineyard,
  Are ingenious but short steps that a child's wish
To receive more attention than his brothers, whether
  By pleasing or teasing, can easily take.

Watch, then, the band of rivals as they climb up and down
  Their steep stone gennels in twos and threes, at times
Arm in arm, but never, thank God, in step; or engaged
  On the shady side of a square at midday in
Voluble discourse, knowing each other too well to think
  There are any important secrets, unable
To conceive a god whose temper-tantrums are moral
  And not to be pacified by a clever line
Or a good lay: for, accustomed to a stone that responds,
  They have never had to veil their faces in awe
Of a crater whose blazing fury could not be fixed;
  Adjusted to the local needs of valleys
Where everything can be touched or reached by walking,
  Their eyes have never looked into infinite space
Through the lattice-work of a nomad's comb; born lucky,
  Their legs have never encountered the fungi
And insects of the jungle, the monstrous forms and lives
  With which we have nothing, we like to hope, in common.
So, when one of them goes to the bad, the way his mind works
  Remains comprehensible: to become a pimp
Or deal in fake jewellery or ruin a fine tenor voice
  For effects that bring down the house, could happen to all
But the best and the worst of us . . .
                              That is why, I suppose,
  The best and worst never stayed here long but sought
Immoderate soils where the beauty was not so external,
  The light less public and the meaning of life
Something more than a mad camp. 'Come!' cried the granite wastes,
  'How evasive is your humor, how accidental
Your kindest kiss, how permanent is death.' (Saints-to-be
  Slipped away sighing.) 'Come!' purred the clays and gravels,

'On our plains there is room for armies to drill; rivers
    Wait to be tamed and slaves to construct you a tomb
In the grand manner: soft as the earth is mankind and both
    Need to be altered.' (Intendant Caesars rose and
Left, slamming the door.) But the really reckless were fetched
    By an older colder voice, the oceanic whisper:
'I am the solitude that asks and promises nothing;
    That is how I shall set you free. There is no love;
There are only the various envies, all of them sad.'

    They were right, my dear, all those voices were right
And still are; this land is not the sweet home that it looks.
    Nor its peace the historical calm of a site
Where something was settled once and for all: A backward
    And dilapidated province, connected
To the big busy world by a tunnel, with a certain
    Seedy appeal, is that all it is now? Not quite:
It has a worldly duty which in spite of itself
    It does not neglect, but calls into question
All the Great Powers assume; it disturbs our rights. The poet,
    Admired for his earnest habit of calling
The sun the sun, his mind Puzzle, is made uneasy
    By these marble statues which so obviously doubt
His antimythological myth; and these gamins,
    Pursuing the scientist down the tiled colonnade
With such lively offers, rebuke his concern for Nature's
    Remotest aspects: I, too, am reproached, for what
And how much you know. Not to lose time, not to get caught,
    Not to be left behind, not, please! to resemble
The beasts who repeat themselves, or a thing like water
    Or stone whose conduct can be predicted, these
Are our Common Prayer, whose greatest comfort is music
    Which can be made anywhere, is invisible,
And does not smell. In so far as we have to look forward
    To death as a fact, no doubt we are right: But if

Sins can be forgiven, if bodies rise from the dead,
  These modifications of matter into
Innocent athletes and gesticulating fountains,
  Made solely for pleasure, make a further point:
The blessed will not care what angle they are regarded from,
  Having nothing to hide. Dear, I know nothing of
Either, but when I try to imagine a faultless love
  Or the life to come, what I hear is the murmur
Of underground streams, what I see is a limestone landscape.

JOHN HEWITT (1907–1987)

John Hewitt was born in 1907 and grew up in Belfast. He worked in the Belfast Museum and Art Gallery and later as the director of the Herbert Museum in Coventry. His last fifteen years were spent in Belfast, where he died in 1987. His Collected Poems *was published in 1992.*

I Write For . . .

I write for my own kind,
I do not pitch my voice
that every phrase be heard
by those who have no choice:
their quality of mind
must be withdrawn and still,
as moth that answers moth
across a roaring hill.

The Scar

for Padraic Fiacc

There's not a chance now that I might recover
one syllable of what that sick man said,
tapping upon my great-grandmother's shutter,
and begging, I was told, a piece of bread;
for on his tainted breath there hung infection
rank from the cabins of the stricken west,
the spores from black potato-stalks, the spittle
mottled with poison in his rattling chest;
but she who, by her nature, quickly answered,
accepted in return the famine-fever;
and that chance meeting, that brief confrontation,
conscribed me of the Irishry for ever.

Though much I cherish lies outside their vision,
and much they prize I have no claim to share,
yet in that woman's death I found my nation;
the old wound aches and shews its fellow scar.

KATHLEEN RAINE (b.1908)

Kathleen Raine was born in London in 1908 and grew up in Northumberland. Her first volume, Stone and Flower, *was published in 1943. As well as several more books of poetry she has published autobiography and literary criticism, and is well-known for her scholarship on Blake. Her* Collected Poems *was published in 1981 and* Selected Poems *in 1988.*

Air

Element that utters doves, angels and cleft flames,
The bees of Helicon and the cloudy houses,
Impulse of music and the word's equipoise,

Dancer that never wearies of the dance
That prints in the blown dust eternal wisdom
Or carves its abstract sculptures in the snow,
The wind unhindered passes beyond its trace.

But from a high fell on a summer day
Sometimes below you may see the air like water,
The dazzle of the light upon its waves
That flow unbroken to the end of the world.

The bird of god descends between two moments
Like silence into music, opening a way through time.

The Pythoness

for John Hayward

I am that serpent-haunted cave
Whose navel breeds the fates of men.
All wisdom issues from a hole in the earth:
The gods form in my darkness, and dissolve again.

From my blind womb all kingdoms come,
And from my grave seven sleepers prophesy.
No babe unborn but wakens to my dream,
No lover but at last entombed in me shall lie.

I am that feared and longed-for burning place
Where man and phoenix are consumed away,
And from my low polluted bed arise
New sons, new suns, new skies.

ROBERT GARIOCH (1909–1981)

Robert Garioch Sutherland (who wrote as Robert Garioch) was born in 1909 in Edinburgh and began publishing poetry in the 1930s in newspapers. He shared a joint publication in 1940 with Sorley MacLean. He was conscripted in 1941 and spent most of the Second World War as a prisoner, then after 1946 worked for many years as a teacher. He wrote in Scots and in English, and also published translations, reviews and memoirs. He died in 1981, and his Complete Poetical Works *appeared in 1983.*

The Wire

This day I saw ane endless muir
wi sad horizon, like the sea
around some uncouth landless globe
whaur waters flauchter endlessly.

Heather bell and blaeberry
grow on this muir; reid burns rin
in clear daylicht; the luift is free
frae haar, and yet there is nae sun.

Gossamers glint in aa the airts,
criss-cross about the lang flure-heids
of girss and thristles here, and there
amang the purpie willow-weeds.

Bog-myrtle scent is in the air
heavy wi hinnie-sap and peat
whiles mellit like uneasy thochts
wi something human, shairn or sweit.

Nou guns gaun aff, and pouther-reik
and yappin packs of foetid dugs,
and blobs of cramosie, like blebs
of bluid squeezed frae vanilla bugs

pash suddenlike intill the licht
that dings on this unshadowed muir
frae ilka airt, and syne are gane
like tourbillions of twisted stour.

The criss-cross gossamers, the while,
twang owre the heather, ticht and real;
I ken, houever jimp they seem,
that they are spun frae strands of steel.

And they are barbed wi twisted spikes
wi scant a handsbreidth space atween,
and reinforced wi airn rods
and hung about wi bits of tin

that hing in pairs alang the Wire,
ilkane three-cornered like a fang:
clashin thegither at a touch
they break aukwart the lairick's sang.

Heich in their sentry-posts, the guairds
wha daurna sleep, on pain of daith,
watch throu the graticules of guns,
cruel and persecuted, baith.

This endless muir is thrang wi folk
that hirple aye aa airts at aince
wi neither purport nor content
nor rest, in fidgan impotence.

They gae in danger of the Wire
but staucher on anither mile
frae line to line of spider steel
to loup anither deidlie stile.

A man trips up: the Wire gaes ding,
tins clash, the guaird lifts up his heid;
fu slaw he traverses his gun
and blatters at him till he's deid.

The dugs loup on him, reivan flesh.
crunchin the bane as they were wud;
swith they come and swith are gane,
syne nocht is left but pools of bluid.

Bluid dreipan doun amang the roots
is soukit up the vampire stem
and suin the gaudy felloun flures
begowk the man that nourished them.

Some pairts the Wires close in and leave
smaa space whaur men may freely gang,
and ilka step is taen in dreid:
there flures and men maist thickly thrang.

A man gets taiglit on a barb,
endlang his wame the cauld fear creeps:
he daurna muve, the hert beats hard,
but beats awa. The sentry sleeps.

Aye! his virr comes back in spate,
as some auld trout this man is slee;
he hauds himsel still as a stane,
back comes his ain self-maistery.

Cannily he sets to wark,
warp by warp his sleeve is free,
it hings nou by a single threid:
loud clash the tins and bullets flee.

Forrit and back and in and out
they darn in waesome figure-dance;
bydin still they canna thole
and ilk man warks his ain mischance.

They see the Wire, and weill they ken
whilk wey it warks. In middle-air
the glintan guns are clear in sicht,
tho nae man kens wha set them there.

Impersonal in uniform,
the guairds are neither freins nor faes;
nane ettles to propitiate
nor fashes them wi bribes or praise.

Efficient and predictable,
they cairry out their orders stricht;
here naething happens unforeseen;
it is jist sae, no wrang nor richt.

On this dour mechanistic muir
wi nae land's end, and endless day,
whaur nae thing thraws a shadow, here
the truth is clear, and it is wae.

The crouds that thrang the danger–spots
weill ken what wey their warld's wrocht,
but aye the mair they pauchle on
to win release frae nigglin thocht.

Some pairts the pattern of the Wire
leaves clear for fifty yairds and mair
whaur soil has crined to desert stuir
wi scroggie bussels puir and bare.

Here some folk wycer nor the lave
or maybe suiner gien to skar
tether theirsels wi chains to stakes,
sae they may gang, but no owre far.

Birlan in wretchedness aroun
their safe lives' centre, they maun dree
temptation sair to break their chains
for aye they ettle to gang free.

Some stark and strang stravaig their yird
like shelties that hae never taen
the bit; mere smeddum drives them on,
their lives are short, but are their ain.

A wheen in orra ill-faur'd airts
on barren streitches of the muir
gae whaur nae bluid is ever shed
to drouk the dreich unslockent stour.

Within a pentagon of wire
they gang alane, or twae by twae,
thole the condition of their life
and dree the weird as best they may.

Alane in thon hale fremmit globe
thae slaw-gaun folk hae in their een
some sapience, as gin their looks
refleckit ferlies they hae seen

in their ain thochts, the nucleus
of man himsel is keethit there.
Expressed in terms of happiness
are premises of pure despair.

Thae guidlie folk are nae great men;
the best of men are unco smaa
whan in the autumn of despair
irrelevance has dwined awa.

Their syllogisms widdershins
wither the petal; syne the leaf
and stem crine in as life gaes doun
intill a corm of prime belief.

Wi utmaist pouer of forcy thocht
they crine their life within its core,
and what they ken wi certainty
is kent inby the bracken-spore.

And aye alane or twae by twae
they gang unhurt amang the noy
of thon fell planet, and their een
lowe wi the licht of inwart joy.

Outwartly they seem at rest,
binna the glint of hidden fires.
Their warld shaks, but they bide still
as nodal points on dirlan wires.

In ither airts, whaur folk are thrang,
the Wire vibrates, clash gae the tins,
flures blume frae bluidie marl, dugs
yowl throu the blatter of the guns.

I saw thon planet slawlie birl;
I saw it as ane endless muir
in daylicht, and I saw a few
guid men bide still amang the stour.

NORMAN MacCAIG (1910–1996)

Norman MacCaig was born in Edinburgh in 1910 and read Classics at Edinburgh University. Except for a period during the Second World War when he was a conscientious objector, he spent most of his working life as a schoolteacher, up until 1970 when he became a lecturer and then Reader in Poetry at the University of Stirling. He began publishing poetry in the 1940s, though became disillusioned with his early style of writing and nothing from his first two collections found its way into Collected Poems *(1990). That volume takes in thirteen previous books, as well as previously uncollected work. Norman MacCaig died in 1996.*

Summer farm

Straws like tame lightnings lie about the grass
And hang zigzag on hedges. Green as glass
The water in the horse-trough shines.
Nine ducks go wobbling by in two straight lines.

A hen stares at nothing with one eye,
Then picks it up. Out of an empty sky
A swallow falls and, flickering through
The barn, dives up again into the dizzy blue.

I lie, not thinking, in the cool, soft grass,
Afraid of where a thought might take me – as
This grasshopper with plated face
Unfolds his legs and finds himself in space.

Self under self, a pile of selves I stand
Threaded on time, and with metaphysic hand
Lift the farm like a lid and see
Farm within farm, and in the centre, me.

July evening

A bird's voice chinks and tinkles
Alone in the gaunt reedbed –
        Tiny silversmith
Working late in the evening.

I sit and listen. The rooftop
With a quill of smoke stuck in it
        Wavers against the sky
In the dreamy heat of summer.

Flowers' closing time: bee lurches
Across the hayfield, singing
        And feeling its drunken way
Round the air's invisible corners.

And grass is grace. And charlock
Is gold of its own bounty.
        The broken chair by the wall
Is one with immortal landscapes.

Something has been completed
That everything is part of,
    Something that will go on
Being completed forever.

Aunt Julia

Aunt Julia spoke Gaelic
very loud and very fast.
I could not answer her –
I could not understand her.

She wore men's boots
when she wore any.
– I can see her strong foot,
stained with peat,
paddling with the treadle of the spinningwheel
while her right hand drew yarn
marvellously out of the air.

Hers was the only house
where I've lain at night
in the absolute darkness
of a box bed, listening to
crickets being friendly.

She was buckets
and water flouncing into them.
She was winds pouring wetly
round house-ends.
She was brown eggs, black skirts
and a keeper of threepennybits
in a teapot.

Aunt Julia spoke Gaelic
very loud and very fast.
By the time I had learned

a little, she lay
silenced in the absolute black
of a sandy grave
at Luskentyre.
But I hear her still, welcoming me
with a seagull's voice
across a hundred yards
of peatscrapes and lazybeds
and getting angry, getting angry
with so many questions
unanswered.

Toad

Stop looking like a purse. How could a purse
squeeze under the rickety door and sit,
full of satisfaction, in a man's house?

You clamber towards me on your four corners –
right hand, left foot, left hand, right foot.

I love you for being a toad,
for crawling like a Japanese wrestler,
and for not being frightened.

I put you in my purse hand, not shutting it,
and set you down outside directly under
every star.

A jewel in your head? Toad,
you've put one in mine,
a tiny radiance in a dark place.

Small boy

He picked up a pebble
and threw it into the sea.

And another, and another.
He couldn't stop.

He wasn't trying to fill the sea.
He wasn't trying to empty the beach.

He was just throwing away,
nothing else but.

Like a kitten playing
he was practising for the future

when there'll be so many things
he'll want to throw away

if only his fingers will unclench
and let them go.

SOMHAIRLE MacGILL-EAIN
SORLEY MacLEAN (1911–1996)

Somhairle MacGill-Eain / Sorley MacLean was born on the Scottish island of Raasay in 1911, into a Gaelic-speaking family. He studied English at Edinburgh University and during the Second World War served in North Africa, where he was wounded on three separate occasions, in one case severely. His first book of poems was published in Gaelic in 1943, and he is recognized as being an important figure in the renaissance of the Gaelic language through his work. O Choille gu Bearradh / From Wood to Ridge – Collected Poems in Gaelic and English was published in 1989. In his later years, he lived on the Isle of Skye; he died in 1996. The English translations here are by the poet.

Soluis

Nuair laigheas an ceann ruadh seo
air mo ghualainn 's air mo bhroilleach
fosglaidh camhanaich na buaidhe
air cho gruamach 's a tha 'n doilleir.

Solus anns an Aird an Earraidheas,
an Sealgair thar beinn na Gréige,
solus anns an Aird an Iaras,
Bhénus thar Cuilithionn na féile.

Nuair tha mo bhilean air a gruaidhean
boillsgidh uachdarain ra-dorcha,
mìle solus shìos is shuas ann,
falt ruadh is sùilean gorma.

Lights

When this auburn head lies
on my shoulder and my breast
the dawn of triumph opens
however gloomy the darkness.

A light in the South-East,
Orion over the Greek Mountain,
a light in the South-West,
Venus over the generous Cuillin.

When my lips are on her cheeks
the inter-lunar lords are shining
a thousand lights low and high,
auburn head and blue eyes.

Hallaig

'Tha tìm, am fiadh, an coille Hallaig'

Tha bùird is tàirnean air an uinneig
troimh 'm faca mi an Aird an Iar
's tha mo ghaol aig Allt Hallaig
'na craoibh bheithe, 's bha i riamh

eadar an t-Inbhir 's Poll a' Bhainne,
thall 's a bhos mu Bhaile-Chùirn:
tha i 'na beithe, 'na calltuinn,
'na caorunn dhìreach sheang ùir.

Ann an Screapadal mo chinnidh,
far robh Tarmad 's Eachunn Mór,
tha 'n nigheanan 's am mic 'nan coille
ag gabhail suas ri taobh an lóin.

Uaibhreach a nochd na coilich ghiuthais
ag gairm air mullach Cnoc an Rà,
dìreach an druim ris a' ghealaich –
chan iadsan coille mo ghràidh.

Fuirichidh mi ris a' bheithe
gus an tig i mach an Càrn,
gus am bi am bearradh uile
o Bheinn na Lice f' a sgàil.

Mura tig 's ann theàrnas mi a Hallaig
a dh' ionnsaigh sàbaid nam marbh,
far a bheil an sluagh a' tathaich,
gach aon ghinealach a dh' fhalbh.

Tha iad fhathast ann a Hallaig,
Clann Ghill-Eain's Clann MhicLeòid,
na bh' ann ri linn Mhic Ghille-Chaluim:
Chunnacas na mairbh beò.

Na fir 'nan laighe air an lianaig
aig ceann gach taighe a bh' ann,
na h-igheanan 'nan coille bheithe,
dìreach an druim, crom an ceann.

Eadar an Leac is na Feàrnaibh
tha 'n rathad mór fo chóinnich chiùin,
's na h-igheanan 'nam badan sàmhach
a' dol a Chlachan mar o thùs.

Agus a' tilleadh as a' Chlachan,
á Suidhisnis 's á tir nam beò;
a chuile té òg uallach
gun bhristeadh cridhe an sgeòil.

O Allt na Feàrnaibh gus an fhaoilinn
tha soilleir an dìomhaireachd nam beann
chan eil ach coimhthional nan nighean
ag cumail na coiseachd gun cheann.

A' tilleadh a Hallaig anns an fheasgar,
anns a' chamhanaich bhalbh bheò,
a' lìonadh nan leathadan casa,
an gàireachdaich 'nam chluais 'na ceò,

's am bòidhche 'na sgleò air mo chridhe
mun tig an ciaradh air na caoil,
's nuair theàrnas grian air cùl Dhùn Cana
thig peileir dian á gunna Ghaoil;

's buailear am fiadh a tha 'na thuaineal
a' snòtach nan làraichean feòir;
thig reothadh air a shùil 'sa' choille:
chan fhaighear lorg air fhuil ri m' bheò.

Hallaig

'*Time, the deer, is in the wood of Hallaig*'

The window is nailed and boarded
through which I saw the West
and my love is at the Burn of Hallaig,
a birch tree, and she has always been

between Inver and Milk Hollow,
here and there about Baile-chuirn:
she is a birch, a hazel,
a straight, slender young rowan.

In Screapadal of my people
where Norman and Big Hector were,
their daughters and their sons are a wood
going up beside the stream.

Proud tonight the pine cocks
crowing on the top of Cnoc an Ra,
straight their backs in the moonlight —
they are not the wood I love.

I will wait for the birch wood
until it comes up by the cairn,
until the whole ridge from Beinn na Lice
will be under its shade.

If it does not, I will go down to Hallaig,
to the Sabbath of the dead,
where the people are frequenting,
every single generation gone.

They are still in Hallaig,
MacLeans and MacLeods,
all who were there in the time of Mac Gille Chaluim
the dead have been seen alive.

The men lying on the green
at the end of every house that was,
the girls a wood of birches,
straight their backs, bent their heads.

Between the Leac and Fearns
the road is under mild moss
and the girls in silent bands
go to Clachan as in the beginning,

and return from Clachan
from Suisnish and the land of the living;
each one young and light-stepping,
without the heartbreak of the tale.

From the Burn of Fearns to the raised beach
that is clear in the mystery of the hills,
there is only the congregation of the girls
keeping up the endless walk,

coming back to Hallaig in the evening,
in the dumb living twilight,
filling the steep slopes,
their laughter a mist in my ears,

and their beauty a film on my heart
before the dimness comes on the kyles,
and when the sun goes down behind Dun Cana
a vehement bullet will come from the gun of Love;

and will strike the deer that goes dizzily,
sniffing at the grass-grown ruined homes;
his eye will freeze in the wood,
his blood will not be traced while I live.

A' Bheinn air Chall

Tha bheinn ag éirigh os cionn na coille
air chall anns a' choille th' air chall,
is bhristeadh sinn air clàr ar gréine
on a tha na speuran teann.

Air chall ann an aomadh na coille
iomhaighean iomadhathach ar spéis
a chionn 's nach téid na sràidean ciùrrte
's a' choille mhaoth an cochur réidh.

A chionn 's gu bheil Vietnam's Uladh
'nan torran air Auschwitz nan cnàmh
agus na craobhan saoibhir ùrar
'nam prìneachan air beanntan cràidh.

Dé 'n t-sìorruidheachd inntinn 's an cuirear
Aimeireaga mu Dheas no Belsen,
agus 'a ghrian air Sgurr Urain
's a bhearraidhean geàrrte 'san t-sneachda?

Tha 'm bristeadh cridhe mu na beanntan
's anns na coilltean air am bòidhche
ged tha 'n fhuil mhear gu luaineach
air mire bhuadhar' san òigridh.

Sìorruidheachd Dhante is Dhùghaill
'n seann solus ùr aig beagan
agus neoini ghlas na h-ùrach
'na comhfhurtachd chrìon phrann aig barrachd.

Pàrras gun phàrras a chuideachd,
imcheist a' ghiullain Shaoir-Chléirich
a ghearan is a dhiùltadh sàmhach
'nan toibheum an amhaich Sineubha;

agus an amhaich na Ròimhe
– ged tha Purgadair nas ciùine –
an robair eile air a' chrann
is Spartacus le armailt chiùrrte.

The Lost Mountain

The mountain rises above the wood,
lost in the wood that is lost,
and we have been broken on the board of our sun
since the skies are tight.

Lost in the decline of the wood
the many-coloured images of our aspiration
since the tortured streets will not go
in the wood in a smooth synthesis.

Because Vietnam and Ulster are
heaps on Auschwitz of the bones,
and the fresh rich trees
pins on mountains of pain.

In what eternity of the mind
will South America or Belsen be put
with the sun on Sgurr Urain
and its ridges cut in snow?

Heartbreak is about the mountains
and in the woods for all their beauty,
though the restless sportive blood
rages triumphantly in the young.

The eternity of Dante and of Dugald Buchanan
an old new light to a few,
and the grey nonentity of the dust
a withered brittle comfort to more.

Paradise without the paradise of his own people,
the perplexity of the little Free Presbyterian boy:
his complaint and silent refusal
blasphemy in the throat of Geneva;

and in the throat of Rome
– though Purgatory is gentler –
the other robber on the tree
and Spartacus with his tortured army.

ROY FULLER (1912–1991)

Roy Fuller was born in 1912 in Lancashire. A qualified solicitor, he worked for the
Woolwich Building Society, becoming a director in 1969, and at one time served as a
governor of the BBC. In 1970 he received the Queen's Gold Medal for Poetry and the
CBE. He published novels, children's books, memoirs and criticism written during his
term as Oxford Professor of Poetry. New and Collected Poems 1934–1984 *was*
followed by further collections. He died in 1991.

1948

Reading among the crumbs of leaves upon
The lawn, beneath the thin October sun,
I hear behind the words
And noise of birds
The drumming aircraft; and am blind till they have gone.

The feeling that they give is now no more
That of the time when we had not reached war:
It is as though the lease
Of crumbling peace
Had run already and that life was as before.

For this is not the cancer or the scream,
A grotesque interlude, but what will seem
On waking to us all
Most natural –
The gnawed incredible existence of a dream.

GEORGE BARKER (1913–1991)

George Barker was born in Loughton, Essex, in 1913, and published his first poetry at the age of twenty. With the exception of occasional teaching appointments in Britain and abroad, he worked as a full-time writer for all his life, and caused controversy in Parliament when his True Confessions of George Barker *was broadcast by the BBC.* Collected Poems *was published in 1987, four years before his death.*

On a Friend's Escape from Drowning off the Norfolk Coast

Came up that cold sea at Cromer like a running grave
    Beside him as he struck
Wildly towards the shore, but the blackcapped wave
    Crossed him and swung him back,
And he saw his son digging in the castled dirt that could save.
    Then the farewell rock
Rose a last time to his eyes. As he cried out
    A pawing gag of the sea
Smothered his cry and he sank in his own shout
    Like a dying airman. Then she
Deep near her son asleep on the hourglass sand
    Was awakened by whom
Save the Fate who knew that this was the wrong time:
    And opened her eyes

On the death of her son's begetter. Up she flies
   Into the hydra-headed
Grave as he closes his life upon her who for
   Life has so richly bedded him.
But she drove through his drowning like Orpheus and tore
   Back by the hair
Her escaping bridegroom. And on the sand their son
   Stood laughing where
He was almost an orphan. Then the three lay down
   On that cold sand,
Each holding the other by a living hand.

from Villa Stellar

XLVII

Hand of my hand, rest.
Heart of my heart, sleep.
Bright eye of childhood count
the lambs and not the sheep:
may the shepherd keep
a watch over your bed
till every lamb and you
rest a dreaming head.

The monsters of the day
have fled to other fields,
and now the mothering one
her milk of moonlight yields
and the great hunter wields
his wonders in the sky:
may all the monsters of
night and the nightmare fly.

From the foal and from
the kitten, child and kid
as they dream within
the eye and shuttered lid
our shoddy world is hid:
may a Mary of dreams
show them it is not
as monstrous as it seems.

R. S. THOMAS (b.1913)

R. S. Thomas was born in Cardiff in 1913 and brought up in Holyhead. He trained in theology and practised as an Anglican priest until his retirement from the Church in 1978. He has written prose work in Welsh, including his autobiography Neb *(1985), but his published poetry is in English and* Collected Poems, *published to coincide with his eightieth birthday in 1993, contained work from more than twenty volumes written over five decades. He has received numerous awards for his work including the Queen's Gold Medal for Poetry in 1964. He lives in Gwynedd.*

A Peasant

Iago Prytherch his name, though, be it allowed,
Just an ordinary man of the bald Welsh hills,
Who pens a few sheep in a gap of cloud.
Docking mangels, chipping the green skin
From the yellow bones with a half-witted grin
Of satisfaction, or churning the crude earth
To a stiff sea of clouds that glint in the wind –
So are his days spent, his spittled mirth
Rarer than the sun that cracks the cheeks
Of the gaunt sky perhaps once in a week.

And then at night see him fixed in his chair
Motionless, except when he leans to gob in the fire.
There is something frightening in the vacancy of his mind.
His clothes, sour with years of sweat
And animal contact, shock the refined,
But affected, sense with their stark naturalness.
Yet this is your prototype, who, season by season
Against siege of rain and the wind's attrition,
Preserves his stock, an impregnable fortress
Not to be stormed even in death's confusion.
Remember him, then, for he, too, is a winner of wars,
Enduring like a tree under the curious stars.

Because

I praise you because
I envy your ability to
See these things: the blind hands
Of the aged combing sunlight
For pity; the starved fox and
The obese pet; the way the world
Digests itself and the thin flame
Scours. The youth enters
The brothel, and the girl enters
The nunnery, and a bell tolls.
Viruses invade the blood.
On the smudged empires the dust
Lies and in the libraries
Of the poets. The flowers wither
On love's grave. This is what
Life is, and on it your eye
Sets tearless, and the dark
Is dear to you as the light.

Concession

Not that he brought flowers
Except for the eyes' blue,
Perishable ones, or that his hands,
Famed for kindness were put then
To such usage; but rather that, going
Through flowers later, she yet could feel
These he spared perhaps for my sake.

The Coming

And God held in his hand
A small globe. Look, he said.
The son looked. Far off,
As through water, he saw
A scorched land of fierce
Colour. The light burned
There; crusted buildings
Cast their shadows; a bright
Serpent, a river
Uncoiled itself, radiant
With slime.
                On a bare
Hill a bare tree saddened
The sky. Many people
Held out their thin arms
To it, as though waiting
For a vanished April
To return to its crossed
Boughs. The son watched
Them. Let me go there, he said.

The Way of It

With her fingers she turns paint
into flowers, with her body
flowers into a remembrance
of herself. She is at work
always, mending the garment
of our marriage, foraging
like a bird for something
for us to eat. If there are thorns
in my life, it is she who
will press her breast to them and sing.

Her words, when she would scold,
are too sharp. She is busy
after for hours rubbing smiles
into the wounds. I saw her,
when young, and spread the panoply
of my feathers instinctively
to engage her. She was not deceived,
but accepted me as a girl
will under a thin moon
in love's absence as someone
she could build a home with
for her imagined child.

Gift

Some ask the world
    and are diminished
in the receiving
    of it. You gave me

only this small pool
     that the more I drink
from, the more overflows
     me with sourceless light.

DYLAN THOMAS (1914–1953)

Dylan Thomas was born in Swansea in 1914, worked as a journalist, broadcaster and freelance writer, and died in 1953 in the United States during one of his hugely popular and notorious reading tours. During his life he wrote radio scripts; prose, including Portrait of the Artist as a Young Dog *(1940); and radio plays, the most notable being* Under Milk Wood *(1954).* Eighteen Poems *published in 1934 was followed by three subsequent collections, and* Collected Poems 1934–1953 *was published in 1988, supplemented by* The Notebook Poems 1930–1934, *published in 1989.*

In my craft or sullen art

In my craft or sullen art
Exercised in the still night
When only the moon rages
And the lovers lie abed
With all their griefs in their arms.
I labour by singing light
Not for ambition or bread
Or the strut and trade of charms
On the ivory stages
But for the common wages
Of their most secret heart.

Not for the proud man apart
From the raging moon I write
On these spindrift pages
Nor for the towering dead

With their nightingales and psalms
But for the lovers, their arms
Round the griefs of the ages,
Who pay no praise or wages
Nor heed my craft or art.

Lie still, sleep becalmed

Lie still, sleep becalmed, sufferer with the wound
In the throat, burning and turning. All night afloat
On the silent sea we have heard the sound
That came from the wound wrapped in the salt sheet.

Under the mile off moon we trembled listening
To the sea sound flowing like blood from the loud wound
And when the salt sheet broke in a storm of singing
The voices of all the drowned swam on the wind.

Open a pathway through the slow sad sail,
Throw wide to the wind the gates of the wandering boat
For my voyage to begin to the end of my wound,
We heard the sea sound sing, we saw the salt sheet tell.
Lie still, sleep becalmed, hide the mouth in the throat,
Or we shall obey, and ride with you through the drowned.

Do not go gentle into that good night

Do not go gentle into that good night,
Old age should burn and rave at close of day;
Rage, rage against the dying of the light.

Though wise men at their end know dark is right,
Because their words had forked no lightning they
Do not go gentle into that good night.

Good men, the last wave by, crying how bright
Their frail deeds might have danced in a green bay,
Rage, rage against the dying of the light.

Wild men who caught and sang the sun in flight,
And learn, too late, they grieved it on its way,
Do not go gentle into that good night.

Grave men, near death, who see with blinding sight
Blind eyes could blaze like meteors and be gay,
Rage, rage against the dying of the light.

And you, my father, there on the sad height,
Curse, bless, me now with your fierce tears, I pray.
Do not go gentle into that good night.
Rage, rage against the dying of the light.

Fern Hill

Now as I was young and easy under the apple boughs
About the lilting house and happy as the grass was green,
    The night above the dingle starry,
        Time let me hail and climb
    Golden in the heydays of his eyes,
And honoured among wagons I was prince of the apple towns
And once below a time I lordly had the trees and leaves
        Trail with daisies and barley
    Down the rivers of the windfall light.

And as I was green and carefree, famous among the barns
About the happy yard and singing as the farm was home,
    In the sun that is young once only,
        Time let me play and be
    Golden in the mercy of his means,
And green and golden I was huntsman and herdsman, the calves

Sang to my horn, the foxes on the hills barked clear and cold,
    And the sabbath rang slowly
  In the pebbles of the holy streams.

All the sun long it was running, it was lovely, the hay
Fields high as the house, the tunes from the chimneys, it was air
    And playing, lovely and watery
      And fire green as grass.
    And nightly under the simple stars
As I rode to sleep the owls were bearing the farm away,
All the moon long I heard, blessed among stables, the nightjars
    Flying with the ricks, and the horses
      Flashing into the dark.

And then to awake, and the farm, like a wanderer white
With the dew, come back, the cock on his shoulder: it was all
    Shining, it was Adam and maiden,
      The sky gathered again
    And the sun grew round that very day.
So it must have been after the birth of the simple light
In the first, spinning place, the spellbound horses walking warm
    Out of the whinnying green stable
      On to the fields of praise.

And honoured among foxes and pheasants by the gay house
Under the new made clouds and happy as the heart was long,
    In the sun born over and over,
      I ran my heedless ways,
    My wishes raced through the house high hay
And nothing I cared, at my sky blue trades, that time allows
In all his tuneful turning so few and such morning songs
    Before the children green and golden
      Follow him out of grace,

Nothing I cared, in the lamb white days, that time would take me
Up to the swallow thronged loft by the shadow of my hand,
    In the moon that is always rising,
      Nor that riding to sleep

I should hear him fly with the high fields
And wake to the farm forever fled from the childless land.
Oh as I was young and easy in the mercy of his means,
    Time held me green and dying
  Though I sang in my chains like the sea.

A Refusal to Mourn the Death, by Fire, of a Child in London

Never until the mankind making
Bird beast and flower
Fathering and all humbling darkness
Tells with silence the last light breaking
And the still hour
Is come of the sea tumbling in harness

And I must enter again the round
Zion of the water bead
And the synagogue of the ear of corn
Shall I let pray the shadow of a sound
Or sow my salt seed
In the least valley of sackcloth to mourn

The majesty and burning of the child's death.
I shall not murder
The mankind of her going with a grave truth
Nor blaspheme down the stations of the breath
With any further
Elegy of innocence and youth.

Deep with the first dead lies London's daughter.
Robed in the long friends,
The grains beyond age, the dark veins of her mother,
Secret by the unmourning water
Of the riding Thames.
After the first death, there is no other.

NORMAN NICHOLSON (1914–1987)

Norman Nicholson was born in 1914 in Millom, Cumbria, and lived there in the same house for almost all of his life. He wrote prose works about the Lake District, two novels and a number of verse plays. He was awarded the Queen's Gold Medal for Poetry in 1977 and the OBE in 1981. He died in 1987, and his Collected Poems *was published posthumously in 1994.*

The Tame Hare

She came to him in dreams – her ears
Diddering like antennae, and her eyes
Wide as dark flowers where the dew
Holds and dissolves a purple hoard of shadow.
The thunder clouds crouched back, and the world opened
Tiny and bright as a celandine after rain.
A gentle light was on her, so that he
Who saw the talons in the vetch
Remembered now how buttercup and daisy
Would bounce like springs when a child's foot stepped off them.
Oh, but never dared he touch –
Her fur was still electric to the fingers.

Yet of all the beasts blazoned in gilt and blood
In the black-bound missal of his mind,
Pentecostal dove and paschal lamb,
Eagle, lion, serpent, she alone
Lived also in the noon of ducks and sparrows;
And the cleft-mouthed kiss which plugged the night with fever
Was sweetened by a lunch of docks and lettuce.

The Shape of Clouds

Clouds are not dreams, but dreams
Take the shape of clouds.

Up glass stems of air
The steaming saps rise
To bloom as cumulus:
Meadowsweet and white
Elderflower and may.

Turned like cups of clay,
Pummelled and thumbed by the wind,
Like bubbles bent on a sigh,
They stream along the air.

Every breath we draw
Modifies the sky, adjusts
Temperature and pressure,
Shapes and directs the clouds,
And the warm draught from a kitchen fire
Stirs its spoon among the stars.

The shape we see
Is a shape we dream,
Forming a firmament
In retina and brain;
But the true shape
We neither see nor know –
A barometric order
Beyond the knack of eye,
The gauge of mercury.

Dreams are not clouds, but clouds
Take the shape of dreams.

SYDNEY GOODSIR SMITH (1915–1975)

Sydney Goodsir Smith was born in New Zealand, educated in England and settled in Edinburgh. He wrote verse drama, criticism, memoirs, and was also an artist and cartoonist. In 1966 he edited A Choice of Burns's Poems and Songs. *He wrote poetry in Scots, and* Collected Poems *was published in 1975, the same year as his death.*

The Grace of God and the Meth-Drinker

There ye gang, ye daft
And doitit dotterel, ye saft
Crazed outland skalrag saul
In your bits and ends o winnockie duds
Your fyled and fozie-fousome clouts
As fou 's a fish, crackt and craftie-drunk
Wi bleerit reid-rimmed
Ee and slaveran crozie mou
Dwaiblan owre the causie like a ship
Storm-toss't i' the Bay of Biscay O
At-sea indeed and hauf-seas-owre
Up-til-the-thrapple's-pap
Or up-til-the-crosstrees-sunk –
   Wha kens? Wha racks?
Hidderie-hetterie stouteran in a dozie dwaum
O' ramsh reid-biddie – Christ!
      The stink
O' jake ahint him, a mephitic
Rouk o miserie, like some unco exotic
Perfume o the Orient no juist sae easilie tholit
By the bleak barbarians o the Wast
But subtil, acrid, jaggan the nebstrous
Wi 'n owrehailan ugsome guff, maist delicat,
Like in scent til the streel o a randie gib . . .
     O-hone-a-ree!

His toothless gums, his lips, bricht cramasie
A schere-bricht slash o bluid
A schene like the leaman gleid o rubies
Throu the gray-white stibble
O' his blank unrazit chafts, a hangman's
Heid, droolie wi gob, the bricht een
Sichtless, cannie, blythe, and slee – *Unkennan.*

Ay,
    Puir gangrel!
                There
– But for the undeemous glorie and grace
O a mercifu omnipotent majestic God
Superne eterne and sceptred in the firmament
Whartil the praises o the leal rise
Like incense aye about Your throne,
Ayebydan, thochtless, and eternallie hauf-drunk
Wi nectar, Athole-brose, ambrosia – nae jake for
    You –
          God there –
But for the 'bunesaid unsocht grace, unprayed-for,
Undeserved
        Gangs,
            Unregenerate,
                Me.

GAVIN EWART (1916–1995)

Gavin Ewart was born in 1916 and began publishing poems while still at school. He served in the Royal Artillery during the Second World War and worked later for the British Council and in advertising. Ewart's humour and satire remained constant throughout his publications up until his death in 1995. Selected Poems 1933–1993 was one of several retrospective collections published towards the end of his life.

The Dildo

The Dildo is a big heavy cumbersome sort of bird,
Supposed extinct for many years but its voice is often heard
Booming and blasting over the marshes and moors
With the harsh note of Lesbos and the great outdoors.
The Dildo wears tweed skirts and Twenties elastic-thighed knickers
And smokes black cheroots and still calls films 'the flickers'.
It wears pork-pie hats and is really one of the boys,
It has initiated many pretty girls into forbidden joys.

It has an eye-glass in one eye, and its bad-taste jokes are myriad,
Such as the one about Emily Bronte's Last Period,
And a good many others that are best left unsaid,
Buried in the old laughter, as the dead bury the dead.

The Dildo is quite frankly worshipped by some members of the
   community,
Who consider that even its name cannot be taken in vain with
   impunity
As it hops heavily about on its one wooden leg –
But most real Nature-lovers think it should be taken down a peg.

Crimewatch

In some quite ordinary bathrooms and kitchens
have been committed the most marvellous murders
such as, witnessed by sadists,
would have made their upright members like girders!

In sinks and coppers and wash-basins and bath-tubs
the victimised corpses have been dismembered
and there are thousands of real life crime books
that take good care that this is remembered.

Radio commentators, like black-fairy-story-tellers,
have gloated over the execution of Crippen and others
without for a moment thinking
that in a way he and they are brothers . . .

I believe the deep psychological fact is
that what they admire is the man with the nerve
to put some great cruelty into practice –
like Genghis Khan or Hitler, who would never swerve

or show weakness over Jews, gypsies,
liberals, psychopaths or reds.
After every battle Genghis had to have his
fixed quota of a thousand heads.

All of these determined lunatics
fascinate the meek and mild
who could never quite screw up their courage
to murder a child,

and perhaps even less to saw up a body
or hack one to pieces;
so these murderers act as a sort of safety-valve.
That is my thesis.

CHARLES CAUSLEY (b.1917)

Charles Causley was born in Launceston, Cornwall, in 1917, and returned to live there after serving in the Royal Navy during the Second World War. His first book of poems appeared in 1951, and he has received a number of accolades for his work, including the Queen's Gold Medal for Poetry. In 1986 he was appointed CBE. His Collected Poems was published in 1992.

My Friend Maloney

My friend Maloney, eighteen,
    Swears like a sentry,
Got into trouble two years back
    With the local gentry.

Parson and squire's sons
    Informed a copper.
The magistrate took one look at Maloney.
    Fixed him proper.

Talked of the crime of youth,
    The innocent victim.
Maloney never said a blind word
    To contradict him.

Maloney of Gun Street,
    Back of the Nuclear Mission,
Son of the town whore,
    Blamed television.

Justice, as usual, triumphed.
    Everyone felt fine.
Things went deader.
    Maloney went up the line.

Maloney learned one lesson:
    Never play the fool
With the products of especially a minor
    Public school.

Maloney lost a thing or two
    At that institution.
First shirt, second innocence,
    The old irresolution.

Found himself a girlfriend,
　Sharp suit, sharp collars.
Maloney on a moped,
　Pants full of dollars.

College boys on the corner
　In striped, strait blazers
Look at old Maloney,
　Eyes like razors.

'You don't need talent,' says Maloney.
　'You don't need looks.
All I got you got, fellers.
　You can keep your thick books.'

Parson got religion,
　Squire, in the end, the same.
The magistrate went over the wall.★
　'Life,' said Maloney, ''s a game.'

Consider then the case of Maloney,
　College boys, parson, squire, beak.
Who was the victor and who was the victim?
　Speak.

Loss of an Oil Tanker

Over our heads the missiles ran
Through skies more desolate than the sea.
In jungles, where man hides from man,
Leaves fell, in springtime, from the tree.

★ *over the wall*: to gaol; sentenced to detention barracks.

A cracked ship on the Seven Stones lies
Dying in resurrection weather.
With squalid hands we hold our prize:
A drowned fish and a sea-bird's feather.

W. S. GRAHAM (1918–1986)

W. S. Graham was born in Greenock in 1918, and worked for a time as a structural engineer. His first book of poems, Cage without Grievance, *was published in 1942; there were six subsequent volumes up until* Collected Poems 1942–1977 *and two posthumous collections following his death in 1986. He gave readings of his work throughout Britain and America, and for most of his life lived in Cornwall.*

Listen. Put On Morning

Listen. Put on morning.
Waken into falling light.
A man's imagining
Suddenly may inherit
The handclapping centuries
Of his one minute on earth.
And hear the virgin juries
Talk with his own breath
To the corner boys of his street.
And hear the Black Maria
Searching the town at night.
And hear the playropes caa
The sister Mary in.
And hear Willie and Davie
Among bracken of Narnain
Sing in a mist heavy
With myrtle and listeners.
And hear the higher town

Weep a petition of fears
At the poorhouse close upon
The public heartbeat.
And hear the children tig
And run with my own feet
Into the netting drag
Of a suiciding principle.
Listen. Put on lightbreak.
Waken into miracle.
The audience lies awake
Under the tenements
Under the sugar docks
Under the printed moments.
The centuries turn their locks
And open under the hill
Their inherited books and doors
All gathered to distil
Like happy berry pickers
One voice to talk to us.
Yes listen. It carries away
The second and the years
Till the heart's in a jacket of snow
And the head's in a helmet white
And the song sleeps to be wakened
By the morning ear bright.
Listen. Put on morning.
Waken into falling light.

Malcolm Mooney's Land

I

Today, Tuesday, I decided to move on
Although the wind was veering. Better to move
Than have them at my heels, poor friends

I buried earlier under the printed snow.
From wherever it is I urge these words
To find their subtle vents, the northern dazzle
Of silence cranes to watch. Footprint on foot
Print, word on word and each on a fool's errand.
Malcolm Mooney's Land. Elizabeth
Was in my thoughts all morning and the boy.
Wherever I speak from or in what particular
Voice, this is always a record of me in you.
I can record at least out there to the west
The grinding bergs and, listen, further off
Where we are going, the glacier calves
Making its sudden momentary thunder.
This is as good a night, a place as any.

2

From the rimed bag of sleep, Wednesday,
My words crackle in the early air.
Thistles of ice about my chin,
My dreams, my breath a ruff of crystals.
The new ice falls from canvas walls.
O benign creature with the small ear-hole,
Submerger under silence, lead
Me where the unblubbered monster goes
Listening and makes his play.
Make my impediment mean no ill
And be itself a way.

A fox was here last night (Maybe Nansen's,
Reading my instruments.) the prints
All round the tent and not a sound.
Not that I'd have him call my name.
Anyhow how should he know? Enough
Voices are with me here and more
The further I go. Yesterday

I heard the telephone ringing deep
Down in a blue crevasse.
I did not answer it and could
Hardly bear to pass.

Landlice, always my good bedfellows,
Ride with me in my sweaty seams.
Come bonny friendly beasts, brother
To the grammarsow and the word-louse,
Bite me your presence, keep me awake
In the cold with work to do, to remember
To put down something to take back.
I have reached the edge of earshot here
And by the laws of distance
My words go through the smoking air
Changing their tune on silence.

3

My friend who loves owls
Has been with me all day
Walking at my ear
And speaking of old summers
When to speak was easy.
His eyes are almost gone
Which made him hear well.
Under our feet the great
Glacier drove its keel.
What is to read there
Scored out in the dark?

Later the north-west distance
Thickened towards us.
The blizzard grew and proved
Too filled with other voices
High and desperate

For me to hear him more.
I turned to see him go
Becoming shapeless into
The shrill swerving snow.

4

Today, Friday, holds the white
Paper up too close to see
Me here in a white-out in this tent of a place
And why is it there has to be
Some place to find, however momentarily
To speak from, some distance to listen to?

Out at the far-off edge I hear
Colliding voices, drifted, yes
To find me through the slowly opening leads.
Tomorrow I'll try the rafted ice.
Have I not been trying to use the obstacle
Of language well? It freezes round us all.

5

Why did you choose this place
For us to meet? Sit
With me between this word
And this, my furry queen.
Yet not mistake this
For the real thing. Here
In Malcolm Mooney's Land
I have heard many
Approachers in the distance
Shouting. Early hunters
Skittering across the ice
Full of enthusiasm
And making fly and,
Within the ear, the yelling

Spear steepening to
The real prey, the right
Prey of the moment.
The honking choir in fear
Leave the tilting floe
And enter the sliding water.
Above the bergs the foolish
Voices are lighting lamps
And all their sounds make
This diary of a place
Writing us both in.

Come and sit. Or is
It right to stay here
While, outside the tent
The bearded blinded go
Calming their children
Into the ovens of frost?
And what's the news? What
Brought you here through
The spring leads opening?

Elizabeth, you and the boy
Have been with me often
Especially on those last
Stages. Tell him a story.
Tell him I came across
An old sulphur bear
Sawing his log of sleep
Loud beneath the snow.
He puffed the powdered light
Up on to this page
And here his reek fell
In splinters among
These words. He snored well.
Elizabeth, my furry
Pelted queen of Malcolm

Mooney's Land, I made
You here beside me
For a moment out
Of the correct fatigue.

I have made myself alone now.
Outside the tent endless
Drifting hummock crests.
Words drifting on words.
The real unabstract snow.

I Leave This at Your Ear

for Nessie Dunsmuir

I leave this at your ear for when you wake,
A creature in its abstract cage asleep.
Your dreams blindfold you by the light they make.

The owl called from the naked-woman tree
As I came down by the Kyle farm to hear
Your house silent by the speaking sea.

I have come late but I have come before
Later with slaked steps from stone to stone
To hope to find you listening for the door.

I stand in the ticking room. My dear, I take
A moth kiss from your breath. The shore gulls cry.
I leave this at your ear for when you wake.

Greenock at Night I Find You

I

As for you loud Greenock long ropeworking
Hide and seeking rivetting town of my child
Hood, I know we think of us often mostly
At night. Have you ever desired me back
Into the set-in bed at the top of the land
In One Hope Street? I am myself lying
Half-asleep hearing the rivetting yards
And smelling the bone-works with no home
Work done for Cartsburn School in the morning.

At night. And here I am descending and
The welding lights in the shipyards flower blue
Under my hopeless eyelids as I lie
Sleeping conditioned to hide from happy.

2

So what did I do? I walked from Hope Street
Down Lyndoch Street between the night's words
To Cartsburn Street and got to the Cartsburn Vaults
With half an hour to go. See, I am back.

3

See, I am back. My father turned and I saw
He had the stick he cut in Sheelhill Glen.
Brigit was there and Hugh and double-breasted
Sam and Malcolm Mooney and Alastair Graham.
They all were there in the Cartsburn Vaults shining
To meet me but I was only remembered.

PATRICIA BEER (b.1919)

Patricia Beer was born into a Plymouth Brethren family in Exmouth in 1919. She taught English Literature at Padua University in Italy and at Goldsmith's College in London, before taking up full-time writing in 1968. Her Collected Poems *was published in 1988. She lives in Devon.*

The Fifth Sense

A sixty-five-year-old Cypriot Greek shepherd, Nicolis Loizou, was wounded by security forces early today. He was challenged twice; when he failed to answer, troops opened fire. A subsequent hospital examination showed that the man was deaf. NEWS ITEM, December 30th, 1957.

Lamps burn all the night
Here, where people must be watched and seen,
And I, a shepherd, Nicolis Loizou,
Wish for the dark, for I have been
Sure-footed in the dark, but now my sight
Stumbles among these beds, scattered white boulders,
As I lean towards my far slumbering house
With the night lying upon my shoulders.

My sight was always good,
Better than others. I could taste wine and bread
And name the field they spattered when the harvest
Broke. I could coil in the red
Scent of the fox out of a maze of wood
And grass. I could touch mist, I could touch breath.
But of my sharp senses I had only four.
The fifth one pinned me to my death.

The soldiers must have called
The word they needed: Halt. Not hearing it,
I was their failure, relaxed against the winter
Sky, the flag of their defeat.

With their five senses they could not have told
That I lacked one, and so they had to shoot.
They would fire at a rainbow if it had
A colour less than they were taught.

Christ said that when one sheep
Was lost, the rest meant nothing any more.
Here in this hospital where others' breathing
Swings like a lantern in the polished floor
And squeezes those who cannot sleep,
I see how precious each thing is, how dear,
For I may never touch, smell, taste or see
Again, because I could not hear.

Head of a Snowdrop

After the north-east wind I carried
A snowdrop indoors. Taut as a bead
And bright, it lay in a bottle-top,
Nothing but petal from the wound up.

Its roots, stem, were still out of doors; strange
That away from them it could so change,
Normally opening into flower,
Wide as a primrose in one warm hour.

Human fingernails and hair move less
After death and lack naturalness.
Births after death – young Macduff – have such
Horror they can be used by a witch.

Anti-vivisectionists show men
Keeping dogs' heads alive, yapping even.
Schoolboys studying the Stuarts laugh
About Charles talking with his head off.

And I have this freak on my own hearth
Making me think about roots and birth
By false analogies and ignore
Its fulfilled purpose: an open flower.

EDWIN MORGAN (b.1920)

Edwin Morgan was born in 1920 in Glasgow and after military service in the Royal Army Medical Corps taught at the University of Glasgow until 1980. His first two collections were published in 1952, but it was The Second Life *(1968) which brought him to wider attention. Highly influential amongst a younger generation of Scottish writers, his* Collected Poems *was published in 1990, drawing on several volumes. He has also published dramatic work, libretti, critical essays and reviews, as well as translations — sometimes into Scots. He lives in Glasgow.*

Message Clear

```
    am              i
                          if
i am                  he
      he r        o
      h      ur   t
      the re            and
      he     re        and
      he re
    a                n   d
      the r                        e
i am      r                       ife
                      i n
            s        ion and
i                        d     i e
    am    e res    ect
    am    e res    ection
```

```
                    o              f
        the                        life
                    o              f
    m    e          n
            sur e
        the                  d    i e
i          s
            s      e t    and
i am the   sur              d
  a    t   res    t
                    o          life
i am  he r                      e
i a             ct
i       r   u       n
i   m   e e      t
i            t              i e
i          s     t    and
i am th            o        th
i am       r          a
i am the   su       n
i am the   s        on
i am the   e    rect on        e if
i am       re         n      t
i am       s          a         fe
i am       s      e   n      t
i      he e              d
i     t e s      t
i        re           a d
  a    th re           a d
  a         s     t on        e
  a    t   re           a d
  a    th r         on        e
i          resurrect
                    a          life
i am                i   n         life
```

i am   resurrection
i am the resurrection and
i am
i am the resurrection and the life

Canedolia

an off-concrete Scotch fantasia

oa! hoy! awe! ba! mey!

who saw?
rhu saw rum. garve saw smoo. nigg saw tain. lairg saw lagg.
rigg saw eigg. largs saw haggs. tongue saw luss. mull saw yell.
stoer saw strone. drem saw muck. gask saw noss. unst saw cults.
echt saw banff. weem saw wick. trool saw twatt.

how far?
from largo to lunga from joppa to skibo from ratho to shona from
ulva to minto from tinto to tolsta from soutra to marsco from
braco to barra from alva to stobo from fogo to fada from gigha to
gogo from kelso to stroma from hirta to spango.

what is it like there?
och it's freuchie, it's faifley, it's wamphray, it's frandy, it's
sliddery.

what do you do?
we foindle and fungle, we bonkle and meigle and maxpoffle. we
scotstarvit, armit, wormit, and even whifflet. we play at crossstobs,
leuchars, gorbals, and finfan. we scavaig, and there's aye a bit of
tilquhilly. if it's wet, treshnish and mishnish.

what is the best of the country?
blinkbonny! airgold! thundergay!

and the worst?
scrishven, shiskine, scrabster, and snizort.

listen! what's that?
catacol and wauchope, never heed them.

tell us about last night
well, we had a wee ferintosh and we lay on the quiraing. it was
pure strontian!

but who was there?
petermoidart and craigenkenneth and cambusputtock and
ecclemuchty and corriehulish and balladolly and altnacanny and
clauchanvrechan and stronachlochan and auchenlachar and
tighnacrankie and tilliebruaich and killieharra and invervannach
and achnatudlem and machrishellach and inchtamurchan and
auchterfechan and kinlochculter and ardnawhallie and
invershuggle.

and what was the toast?
schiehallion! schiehallion! schiehallion!

The First Men on Mercury

– We come in peace from the third planet.
Would you take us to your leader?

– Bawr stretter! Bawr. Bawr. Stretterhawl?

– This is a little plastic model
of the solar system, with working parts.
You are here and we are there and we
are now here with you, is this clear?

– Gawl horrop. Bawr. Abawrhannahanna!

– Where we come from is blue and white
with brown, you see we call the brown
here 'land', the blue is 'sea', and the white
is 'clouds' over land and sea, we live

on the surface of the brown land,
all round is sea and clouds. We are 'men'.
Men come –

– Glawp men! Gawrbenner menko. Menhawl?

– Men come in peace from the third planet
which we call 'earth'. We are earthmen.
Take us earthmen to your leader.

– Thmen? Thmen? Bawr. Bawrhossop.
Yuleeda tan hanna. Harrabost yuleeda.

– I am the yuleeda. You see my hands,
we carry no benner, we come in peace.
The spaceways are all stretterhawn.

– Glawn peacemen all horrabhanna tantko!
Tan come at'mstrossop. Glawp yuleeda!

– Atoms are peacegawl in our harraban.
Menbat worrabost from tan hannahanna.

– You men we know bawrhossoptant. Bawr.
We know yuleeda. Go strawg backspetter quick.

– We cantantabawr, tantingko backspetter now!

– Banghapper now! Yes, third planet back.
Yuleeda will go back blue, white, brown
nowhanna! There is no more talk.

– Gawl han fasthapper?

– No. You must go back to your planet.
Go back in peace, take what you have gained
but quickly.

– Stretterworra gawl, gawl . . .

– Of course, but nothing is ever the same,
now is it? You'll remember Mercury.

Cinquevalli

Cinquevalli is falling, falling.
The shining trapeze kicks and flirts free,
solo performer at last.
The sawdust puffs up with a thump,
settles on a tangle of broken limbs.
St Petersburg screams and leans.
His pulse flickers with the gas-jets. He lives.

Cinquevalli has a therapy.
In his hospital bed, in his hospital chair
he holds a ball, lightly, lets it roll round his hand,
or grips it tight, gauging its weight and resistance,
begins to balance it, to feel its life attached to his
by will and knowledge, invisible strings
that only he can see. He throws it
from hand to hand, always different,
always the same, always
different, always the
same.
His muscles learn to think, his arms grow very strong.

Cinquevalli in sepia
looks at me from an old postcard: bundle of enigmas.
Half faun, half military man; almond eyes, curly hair,
conventional moustache; tights, and a tunic loaded
with embroideries, tassels, chains, fringes; hand on hip
with a large signet-ring winking at the camera
but a bull neck and shoulders and a cannon-ball
at his elbow as he stands by the posing pedestal;
half reluctant, half truculent,
half handsome, half absurd,
but let me see you forget him: not to be done.

Cinquevalli is a juggler.
In a thousand theatres, in every continent,

he is the best, the greatest. After eight years perfecting
he can balance one billiard ball on another billiard ball
on top of a cue on top of a third billiard ball
in a wine-glass held in his mouth. To those
who say the balls are waxed, or flattened,
he patiently explains the trick will only work
because the spheres are absolutely true.
There is no deception in him. He is true.

Cinquevalli is juggling with a bowler,
a walking-stick, a cigar, and a coin.
Who foresees? How to please.
The last time round, the bowler
flies to his head, the stick sticks in his hand,
the cigar jumps into his mouth, the coin
lands on his foot – ah, but
is kicked into his eye
and held there as the miraculous monocle
without which the portrait would be incomplete.

Cinquevalli is practising.
He sits in his dressing-room talking to some friends,
at the same time writing a letter with one hand
and with the other juggling four balls.
His friends think of demons, but
'You could all do this,' he says,
sealing the letter with a billiard ball.

Cinquevalli is on the high wire in Odessa.
The roof cracks, he is falling, falling
into the audience, a woman breaks his fall,
he cracks her like a flea, but lives.

Cinquevalli broods in his armchair in Brixton Road.
He reads in the paper about the shells whining
at Passchendaele, imagines the mud and the dead.
He goes to the window and wonders through that dark evening
what is happening in Poland where he was born.

His neighbours call him a German spy.
'Kestner, Paul Kestner, that's his name!'
'Keep Kestner out of the British music-hall!'
He frowns; it is cold; his fingers seem stiff and old.

Cinquevalli tosses up a plate of soup
and twirls it on his forefinger; not a drop spills.
He laughs, and well may he laugh
who can do that. The astonished table
breathe again, laugh too, think the world
a spinning thing that spills, for a moment, no drop.

Cinquevalli's coffin sways through Brixton
only a few months before the Armistice.
Like some trick they cannot get off the ground
it seems to burden the shuffling bearers, all their arms
cross-juggle that displaced person, that man
of balance, of strength, of delights and marvels,
in his unsteady box at last into the earth.

D. J. ENRIGHT (b.1920)

D. J. Enright was born in Leamington, Warwickshire, in 1920, and spent many years teaching abroad in Egypt, Germany and the Far East. In 1981 he received the Queen's Gold Medal for Poetry, and his Selected Poems *published in 1990 drew on fourteen previous collections.*

Oyster Lament

We are a poor people, who
Cannot afford oysters any more.
The sea is a long way away
Nowadays.

Freedom we have in plenty,
Golden and tall it waves in the fields.
How lovingly somebody tilled the soil,
Manured it so richly!

But who can eat that much? What happened
To those overseas markets? Something is wrong
With the rate of exchange.

It makes such a rattle against the panes.
It is cracking the tarmac out in the streets.
They say it uses up the oxygen.

Freedom is a pearl, to be sure,
A pearl above price.
But so are oysters.
Often I think I would rather have oysters,
Their taste, their indefinable taste.

Entertaining Women

In a night-club in Hiroshima,
A combo playing noisily,
A girl asked sweetly, *Kohi shimaska?*:
Should they make coffee?
No, he replied, it kept him awake.
It was *koi*, it struck him later, not *kohi*:
It was love she had offered, not coffee.
The thought kept him awake.

Next day, as a guest of Rotary,
He conveyed (without authority)
Fraternal greetings from Cradley Heath.
Waiting outside was a victim
(Rotary does not entertain women),

A victim for him to see, to see him.
Him with his face still scarlet,
Her with her white scarred arms.

RUARAIDH MacTHÒMAIS/
DERICK THOMSON (b.1921)

Ruaraidh MacThòmais / Derick Thomson was born on the Isle of Lewis, educated in
Stornoway, then Aberdeen and Cambridge. He undertook an academic career at
universities in Scotland, becoming Professor of Celtic at Glasgow in 1964. His poetry,
written in Scottish Gaelic, covers the period 1951 to the present day, and his collected
poems, Creachadh na Clarsaich/Plundering the Harp *(1982), contains English*
translations of his work. The translations here are by the poet.

Clann-Nighean An Sgadain

An gàire mar chraiteachan salainn
ga fhroiseadh bho 'm beul,
an sàl 's am picil air an teanga,
's na miaran cruinne, goirid a dheanadh giullachd,
no a thogadh leanabh gu socair, cuimir,
seasgair, fallain,
gun mhearachd,
's na sùilean cho domhainn ri fèath.

B'e bun-os-cionn na h-eachdraidh a dh' fhàg iad
'nan tràillean aig ciùrairean cutach,
thall 's a-bhos air Galldachd 's an Sasainn.
Bu shaillte an duais a thàrr iad
ás na miltean bharaillean ud,
gaoth na mara geur air an craiceann,
is eallach a' bhochdainn 'nan ciste,
is mara b'e an gàire
shaoileadh tu gu robh an teud briste.

Ach bha craiteachan uaille air an cridhe,
ga chumail fallain,
is bheireadh cutag an teanga
slisinn á fanaid nan Gall –
agus bha obair rompa fhathast
nuair gheibheadh iad dhachaigh,
ged nach biodh maoin ac':
air oidhche robach gheamhraidh,
ma bha siud an dàn dhaibh,
dheanadh iad daoine.

The Herring Girls

Their laughter like a sprinkling of salt
showered from their lips,
brine and pickle on their tongues,
and the stubby short fingers that could handle fish,
or lift a child gently, neatly,
safely, wholesomely,
unerringly,
and the eyes that were as deep as a calm.

The topsy-turvy of history had made them
slaves to short-arsed curers,
here and there in the Lowlands, in England.
Salt the reward they won
from those thousands of barrels,
the sea-wind sharp on their skins,
and the burden of poverty in their kists,
and were it not for their laughter
you might think the harp-string was broken.

But there was a sprinkling of pride on their hearts,
keeping them sound,
and their tongues' gutting-knife
would tear a strip from the Lowlanders' mockery –

and there was work awaiting them
when they got home,
though they had no wealth:
on a wild winter's night,
if that were their lot,
they would make men.

Cisteachan-Laighe

Duin' àrd, tana
's fiasag bheag air,
's locair 'na làimh:
gach uair theid mi seachad
air bùth-shaoirsneachd sa' bhaile,
's a thig gu mo chuinnlean fàileadh na min-sàibh,
thig gu mo chuimhne cuimhne an àit ud,
le na cisteachan-laighe,
na h-ùird 's na tairgean,
na sàibh 's na sgeilbean,
is mo sheanair crom,
is sliseag bho shliseag ga locradh
bhon bhòrd thana lom.

Mus robh fhios agam dè bh' ann bàs;
beachd, bloigh fios, boillsgeadh
den dorchadas, fathann den t-sàmhchair.
'S nuair a sheas mi aig uaigh,
là fuar Earraich, cha dainig smuain
thugam air na cisteachan-laighe
a rinn esan do chàch:
'sann a bha mi 'g iarraidh dhachaigh,
far am biodh còmhradh, is tea, is blàths.

Is anns an sgoil eile cuideachd,
san robh saoir na h-inntinn a' locradh,
cha tug mi 'n aire do na cisteachan-laighe,

ged a bha iad 'nan suidhe mun cuairt orm;
cha do dh' aithnich mi 'm brèid Beurla,
an liomh Gallda bha dol air an fhiodh,
cha do leugh mi na facail air a' phràis,
cha do thuig mi gu robh mo chinneadh a' dol bàs.
Gus an dainig gaoth fhuar an Earraich-sa
a locradh a' chridhe;
gus na dh' fhairich mi na tairgean a' dol tromham,
's cha shlànaich tea no còmhradh an cràdh.

Coffins

A tall thin man
with a short beard,
and a plane in his hand:
whenever I pass
a joiner's shop in the city,
and the scent of sawdust comes to my nostrils,
memories return of that place,
with the coffins,
the hammers and nails,
saws and chisels,
and my grandfather, bent,
planing shavings
from a thin, bare plank.

Before I knew what death was;
or had any notion, a glimmering
of the darkness, a whisper of the stillness.
And when I stood at his grave,
on a cold Spring day, not a thought
came to me of the coffins
he made for others:
I merely wanted home
where there would be talk, and tea, and warmth.

And in the other school also,
where the joiners of the mind were planing,
I never noticed the coffins,
though they were sitting all round me;
I did not recognise the English braid,
the Lowland varnish being applied to the wood,
I did not read the words on the brass,
I did not understand that my race was dying.
Until the cold wind of this Spring came
to plane the heart;
until I felt the nails piercing me,
and neither tea nor talk will heal the pain.

GEORGE MACKAY BROWN (1921–1996)

George Mackay Brown was born in Stromness, Orkney, and lived there almost all of his life. Editor, playwright and novelist, his first book of poems, Loaves and Fishes, *was published in 1959, and was followed by ten further volumes before his death in 1996. Selected Poems 1954–1992, a revised and expanded edition of an earlier selection, was published in 1992.*

The Old Women

Go sad or sweet or riotous with beer
Past the old women gossiping by the hour,
They'll fix on you from every close and pier
An acid look to make your veins run sour.

'No help,' they say, 'his grandfather that's dead
Was troubled with the same dry-throated curse,
And many a night he made the ditch his bed.
This blood comes welling from the same cracked source.'

On every kind of merriment they frown.
But I have known a gray-eyed sober boy
Sail to the lobsters in a storm, and drown.
Over his body dripping on the stones
Those same old hags would weave into their moans
An undersong of terrible holy joy.

Kirkyard

A silent conquering army,
The island dead,
Column on column, each with a stone banner
Raised over his head.

A green wave full of fish
Drifted far
In wavering westering ebb-drawn shoals beyond
Sinker or star.

A labyrinth of celled
And waxen pain.
Yet I come to the honeycomb often, to sip the finished
Fragrance of men.

Taxman

Seven scythes leaned at the wall.
Beard upon golden beard
The last barley load
Swayed through the yard.
The girls uncorked the ale.
Fiddle and feet moved together.
Then between stubble and heather
A horseman rode.

from Stations of the Cross

3   *The Stone Cross*

At dawn Havard sighted a hill in Ulster.
'A point to west,' said the helmsman. 'There the hive is.
There the barren kingdom of drones.'

We sailed past cave and cormorant and curragh.
We anchored under a stone cross at noon.

Creatures came down to meet us
With stony heads, voices like insects, raised hands.

They murmured, 'Mother', 'Sancta Maria', 'Our Lady'
But that hostess was not to be seen.

Brother Simon drew me from sea to rock.
He made a cross of gray air between us.

It was a household of men only.
A boy offered to wipe salt from our foreheads.

'Havard, it is time to make a start now.'
Havard flashed his axe in the face of a brother.

Then women began to screech from the crag above,
Gaelic keenings and cursings.

A dozen eunuchs fell beside the porch.
The boy made a dove of his two hands.

We entered a cave of wax and perfumes.
Mund took a silver cup from a niche.

Cold tinklings like nails
Took us to nothing – a crust, a red splash.

Soon that hive was all smoke and stickiness.

We brought a fair cargo down to the *Skua*.
The abbot had called that treasure 'moth-food'.

Sunset. Sharing of spoils. A harp-stroke.
Soon I drifted into the stone of sleep.

DONALD DAVIE (1922–1995)

*Donald Davie was born in Barnsley in 1922, educated at Cambridge and served in the
Royal Navy in the Second World War. He held a number of lectureships in Eastern
Europe, and was a professor for most of his life in this country and the United States.
He edited a number of anthologies and was a prominent literary commentator, publishing
books of criticism and literary theory, as well as translations and adaptations of European
poetry.* Collected Poems *brought together work from over four decades and was
published in 1990. He died in 1995.*

The Priory of St Saviour, Glendalough

A carving on the jamb of an embrasure,
'Two birds affronted with a human head
Between their beaks' is said to be
'Uncertain in its significance but
A widely known design.' I'm not surprised.

For the guidebook cheats: the green road it advises
In fact misled; and a ring of trees
Screened in the end the level knoll on which
St Saviour's, like a ruin on a raft,
Surged through the silence.

I burst through brambles, apprehensively
Crossed an enormous meadow. I was there.
Could holy ground be such a foreign place?
I climbed the wall, and shivered. There flew out
Two birds affronted by my human face.

Revulsion

Angry and ashamed at
Having not to look,
I have lived constricted
Among occasions
Of nausea, like this book
That I carefully leave on the train.

My strongest feeling all
My life has been,
I recognize, revulsion
From the obscene;
That more than anything
My life-consuming passion.

That so much more reaction
Than action should have swayed
My life and rhymes
Must be the heaviest charge
That can be brought against
Me, or my times.

PHILIP LARKIN (1922–1985)

Philip Larkin was born in Coventry in 1922 and educated at Oxford. He worked in various libraries before becoming librarian of the Brynmor Jones Library at the University of Hull, and also wrote regular jazz reviews for a daily newspaper. His books include The North Ship *(1945),* The Less Deceived *(1955),* The Whitsun Weddings *(1964) and* High Windows *(1974). He also wrote two novels, literary criticism and edited* The Oxford Book of Twentieth Century Verse *(1973). His* Collected Poems *appeared in 1988, and a controversial collection of his letters was published in 1992. He died in 1985.*

The Whitsun Weddings

That Whitsun, I was late getting away:
   Not till about
One-twenty on the sunlit Saturday
Did my three-quarters-empty train pull out,
All windows down, all cushions hot, all sense
Of being in a hurry gone. We ran
Behind the backs of houses, crossed a street
Of blinding windscreens, smelt the fish-dock; thence
The river's level drifting breadth began,
Where sky and Lincolnshire and water meet.

All afternoon, through the tall heat that slept
   For miles inland,
A slow and stopping curve southwards we kept.
Wide farms went by, short-shadowed cattle, and
Canals with floatings of industrial froth;
A hothouse flashed uniquely: hedges dipped
And rose: and now and then a smell of grass
Displaced the reek of buttoned carriage-cloth
Until the next town, new and nondescript,
Approached with acres of dismantled cars.

At first, I didn't notice what a noise
   The weddings made
Each station that we stopped at: sun destroys
The interest of what's happening in the shade,
And down the long cool platforms whoops and skirls
I took for porters larking with the mails,
And went on reading. Once we started, though,
We passed them, grinning and pomaded, girls
In parodies of fashion, heels and veils,
All posed irresolutely, watching us go,

As if out on the end of an event
   Waving goodbye
To something that survived it. Struck, I leant
More promptly out next time, more curiously,
And saw it all again in different terms:
The fathers with broad belts under their suits
And seamy foreheads; mothers loud and fat;
An uncle shouting smut; and then the perms,
The nylon gloves and jewellery-substitutes,
The lemons, mauves, and olive-ochres that

Marked off the girls unreally from the rest.
   Yes, from cafés
And banquet-halls up yards, and bunting-dressed
Coach-party annexes, the wedding-days
Were coming to an end. All down the line
Fresh couples climbed aboard: the rest stood round;
The last confetti and advice were thrown,
And, as we moved, each face seemed to define
Just what it saw departing: children frowned
At something dull; fathers had never known

Success so huge and wholly farcical;
   The women shared
The secret like a happy funeral;
While girls, gripping their handbags tighter, stared
At a religious wounding. Free at last,
And loaded with the sum of all they saw,
We hurried towards London, shuffling gouts of steam.
Now fields were building-plots, and poplars cast
Long shadows over major roads, and for
Some fifty minutes, that in time would seem

Just long enough to settle hats and say
   I nearly died,
A dozen marriages got under way.
They watched the landscape, sitting side by side

– An Odeon went past, a cooling tower,
And someone running up to bowl – and none
Thought of the others they would never meet
Or how their lives would all contain this hour.
I thought of London spread out in the sun,
Its postal districts packed like squares of wheat:

There we were aimed. And as we raced across
   Bright knots of rail
Past standing Pullmans, walls of blackened moss
Came close, and it was nearly done, this frail
Travelling coincidence; and what it held
Stood ready to be loosed with all the power
That being changed can give. We slowed again,
And as the tightened brakes took hold, there swelled
A sense of falling, like an arrow-shower
Sent out of sight, somewhere becoming rain.

Here

Swerving east, from rich industrial shadows
And traffic all night north; swerving through fields
Too thin and thistled to be called meadows,
And now and then a harsh-named halt, that shields
Workmen at dawn; swerving to solitude
Of skies and scarecrows, haystacks, hares and pheasants,
And the widening river's slow presence,
The piled gold clouds, the shining gull-marked mud,

Gathers to the surprise of a large town:
Here domes and statues, spires and cranes cluster
Beside grain-scattered streets, barge-crowded water,
And residents from raw estates, brought down
The dead straight miles by stealing flat-faced trolleys,

Push through plate-glass swing doors to their desires –
Cheap suits, red kitchen-ware, sharp shoes, iced lollies,
Electric mixers, toasters, washers, driers –

A cut-price crowd, urban yet simple, dwelling
Where only salesmen and relations come
Within a terminate and fishy-smelling
Pastoral of ships up streets, the slave museum,
Tattoo-shops, consulates, grim head-scarfed wives;
And out beyond its mortgaged half-built edges
Fast-shadowed wheat-fields, running high as hedges,
Isolate villages, where removed lives

Loneliness clarifies. Here silence stands
Like heat. Here leaves unnoticed thicken,
Hidden weeds flower, neglected waters quicken,
Luminously-peopled air ascends;
And past the poppies bluish neutral distance
Ends the land suddenly beyond a beach
Of shapes and shingle. Here is unfenced existence:
Facing the sun, untalkative, out of reach.

This Be The Verse

They fuck you up, your mum and dad.
   They may not mean to, but they do.
They fill you with the faults they had
   And add some extra, just for you.

But they were fucked up in their turn
   By fools in old-style hats and coats,
Who half the time were soppy-stern
   And half at one another's throats.

Man hands on misery to man.
   It deepens like a coastal shelf.
Get out as early as you can,
   And don't have any kids yourself.

Sad Steps

Groping back to bed after a piss
I part thick curtains, and am startled by
The rapid clouds, the moon's cleanliness.

Four o'clock: wedge-shadowed gardens lie
Under a cavernous, a wind-picked sky.
There's something laughable about this,

The way the moon dashes through clouds that blow
Loosely as cannon-smoke to stand apart
(Stone-coloured light sharpening the roofs below)

High and preposterous and separate —
Lozenge of love! Medallion of art!
O wolves of memory! Immensements! No,

One shivers slightly, looking up there.
The hardness and the brightness and the plain
Far-reaching singleness of that wide stare

Is a reminder of the strength and pain
Of being young; that it can't come again,
But is for others undiminished somewhere.

Water

If I were called in
To construct a religion
I should make use of water.

Going to church
Would entail a fording
To dry, different clothes;

My liturgy would employ
Images of sousing,
A furious devout drench,

And I should raise in the east
A glass of water
Where any-angled light
Would congregate endlessly.

DANNIE ABSE (b.1923)

Dannie Abse was born into a Jewish family in Cardiff in 1923 and has worked as a doctor in London for much of his life. White Coat, Purple Coat, Collected Poems 1948–1988 *contained the work of seven previous collections, and there have been several books since. Dannie Abse is also the editor of* Twentieth Century Anglo Welsh Poetry *(1997).*

White Balloon

Dear love, Auschwitz made me
more of a Jew than Moses did.
But the world's not always with us.
Happiness enters here again tonight
like an unexpected guest
with no memory of the future either;

enters with such an italic emphasis,
jubilant, announcing triumphantly
hey presto and here I am and opening
the June door into our night living room

where, under the lampshade's ciliate,
an armchair's occupied by a white balloon.
As if there'd been a party.

Of course, Happiness, uninhibited,
will pick it up, his stroking thumb
squeaking a little as he leads us to the hall.
And we shall follow him, too,
when he climbs the lit staircase
towards the landing's darkness,
bouncing bouncing the white balloon
from hand to hand.

It's bedtime; soon we must dream
separately – but what does it matter now
as the white balloon is thrown up high?
Quiet, so quiet, the moon above Masada
and closed, abandoned for the night,
the icecream van at Auschwitz.

DENISE LEVERTOV (b.1923)

Denise Levertov was born in Ilford, Essex, in 1923, and worked as a nurse in London during the Second World War. She published her first book of poems in England in 1946. In 1948 she emigrated to the United States, becoming an American citizen in 1955, and has taught at many US universities including Stanford, where she was a professor of English. Her prose books are The Poet in the World *(1973) and* Light Up the Cave *(1981). She has published more than a dozen separate volumes of poetry, including* Selected Poems *(1986) and* Breathing the Water *(1988).*

Casselden Road, NW10

for Marya

The wind would fan the life-green fires that smouldered
under the lamps, and from the glistening road
draw out deep shades of rain, and we would hear
the beat of rain on darkened panes, the sound
of night and no one stirring but ourselves,
leaning still from the window. No one else
will remember this. No one else will remember.

Shadows of leaves like riders hurried by
upon the wall within. The street would fill
with phantasy, the night become
a river or an ocean where the tree
and silent lamp were sailing; the wind would fail
and sway towards the light. And no one else
will remember this. No one else will remember.

The Rainwalkers

An old man whose black face
shines golden-brown as wet pebbles
under the streetlamp, is walking
two mongrel dogs of dis-
proportionate size, in the rain,
in the relaxed early-evening avenue.

The small sleek one wants to stop,
docile to the imploring soul of the trashbasket,
but the young tall curly one
wants to walk on; the glistening sidewalk
entices him to arcane happenings.

Increasing rain. The old bareheaded man
smiles and grumbles to himself.
The lights change; the avenue's
endless nave echoes notes of
liturgical red. He drifts

between his dogs' desires.
The three of them are enveloped –
turning now to go crosstown – in their
sense of each other, of pleasure,
of weather, of corners,
of leisurely tensions between them
and private silence.

A Map of the Western Part of the County of Essex in England

Something forgotten for twenty years: though my fathers
and mothers came from Cordova and Vitepsk and Caernarvon,
and though I am a citizen of the United States and less a
stranger here than anywhere else, perhaps,
I am Essex-born:
Cranbrook Wash called me into its dark tunnel,
the little streams of Valentines heard my resolves,
Roding held my head above water when I thought it was
drowning me; in Hainault only a haze of thin trees
stood between the red doubledecker buses and the boar-hunt,
the spirit of merciful Phillipa glimmered there.
Pergo Park knew me, and Clavering, and Havering-atte-Bower,
Stanford Rivers lost me in osier beds, Stapleford Abbots
sent me safe home on the dark road after Simeon-quiet evensong
Wanstead drew me over and over into its basic poetry,
in its serpentine lake I saw bass-viols among the golden dead leaves,
through its trees the ghost of a great house. In
Ilford High Road I saw the multitudes passing pale under the

light of flaring sundown, seven kings
in somber starry robes gathered at Seven Kings
the place of law
where my birth and marriage are recorded
and the death of my father. Woodford Wells
where an old house was called The Naked Beauty (a white
statue forlorn in its garden)
saw the meeting and parting of two sisters,
(forgotten? and further away
the hill before Thaxted? where peace befell us? not once
but many times?).
All the Ivans dreaming of their villages
all the Marias dreaming of their walled cities,
picking up fragments of New World slowly,
not knowing how to put them together nor how to join
image with image, now I know how it was with you, an old map
made long before I was born shows ancient
rights of way where I walked when I was ten burning with desire
for the world's great splendors, a child who traced voyages
indelibly all over the atlas, who now in a far country
remembers the first river, the first
field, bricks and lumber dumped in it ready for building,
that new smell, and remembers
the walls of the garden, the first light.

Psalm Concerning the Castle

Let me be at the place of the castle.
Let the castle be within me.
Let it rise foursquare from the moat's ring.
Let the moat's waters reflect green plumage of ducks, let the
    shells of swimming turtles break the surface or be seen through
    the rippling depths.
Let horsemen be stationed at the rim of it, and a dog, always alert on
    the brink of sleep.

Let the space under the first storey be dark, let the water lap the stone
   posts, and vivid green slime glimmer upon them; let a boat be
   kept there.
Let the caryatids of the second storey be bears upheld on beams that
   are dragons.
On the parapet of the central room, let there be four archers, looking
   off to the four horizons. Within, let the prince be at home, let him
   sit in deep thought, at peace, all the windows open to the loggias.

Let the young queen sit above, in the cool air, her child in her arms;
   Let her look with joy at the great circle, the pilgrim shadows, the
   work of the sun and the play of the wind. Let her walk to and fro.
   Let the columns uphold the roof, let the storeys uphold the
   columns, let there be dark space below the lowest floor, let the
   castle rise foursquare out of the moat, let the moat be a ring and
   the water deep, let the guardians guard it, let there be wide lands
   around it, let that country where it stands be within me, let me be
   where it is.

KAREN GERSHON (1923–1993)

*Karen Gershon was born into a Jewish, German-speaking family in 1923 and was saved
at the last moment from the Nazis, though her parents were left behind to die. After
settling in England, she published several collections including* Selected Poems *(1966)
and* Legacies and Encounters *(1972). Her* Collected Poems *was published in 1990.
She died in Jerusalem.*

I Was Not There

The morning they set out from home
I was not there to comfort them
the dawn was innocent with snow

in mockery – it is not true
the dawn was neutral was immune
their shadows threaded it too soon
they were relieved that it had come
I was not there to comfort them

One told me that my father spent
a day in prison long ago
he did not tell me that he went
what difference does it make now
when he set out when he came home
I was not there to comfort him
and now I have no means to know
of what I was kept ignorant

Both my parents died in camps
I was not there to comfort them
I was not there they were alone
my mind refuses to conceive
the life the death they must have known
I must atone because I live
I could not have saved them from death
the ground is neutral underneath

Every child must leave its home
time gathers life impartially
I could have spared them nothing since
I was too young – it is not true
they might have lived to succour me
and none shall say in my defence
had I been there to comfort them
it would have made no difference

JOHN ORMOND (1923–1990)

John Ormond was born in 1923 in Dunvant near Swansea, and was a journalist on the
Picture Post *before joining the BBC in Wales. His* Selected Poems *(1987) contained*
work from Requiem and Celebration *(1969) and* Definition of a Waterfall *(1973),*
as well as new and unpublished work. He died in 1990.

Design for a Quilt

First let there be a tree, roots taking ground
In bleached and soft blue fabric.
Into the well-aired sky branches extend
Only to bend away from the turned-back
Edge of linen where day's horizons end;

Branches symmetrical, not over-flaunting
Their leaves (let ordinary swansdown
Be their lining), which in the summertime
Will lie lightly upon her, the girl
This quilt's for, this object of designing;

But such too, when deep frosts veneer
Or winds prise at the slates above her,
Or snows lie in the yard in a black sulk,
That the embroidered cover, couched
And applied with pennants of green silk,

Will still be warm enough that should she stir
To draw a further foliage about her
The encouraged shoots will quicken
And, at her breathing, midnight's spring
Can know new season as they thicken.

Feather-stitch on every bough
A bird, one neat French-knot its eye,
To sing a silent night-long lullaby

And not disturb her or disbud her.
See that the entwining motives run

In and about themselves to bring
To bed the sheens and mossy lawns of Eden;
For I would have a perfect thing
To echo if not equal Paradise
As garden for her true temptation:

So that in future times, recalling
The pleasures of past falling, she'll bequeath it
To one or other of the line,
Bearing her name or mine,
With luck I'll help her make beneath it.

JAMES BERRY (b.1924)

James Berry was born in 1924 in Boston, Jamaica, and has lived in Britain since 1948. For over twenty-five years he worked for Post Office International Telegraphs before becoming a full-time writer in 1977. He also edited the anthologies of Caribbean poetry Bluefoot Traveller *and* News for Babylon. *His collections include* Hot Earth Cold Earth, *published in 1995. He lives in Brighton.*

Folk Proverbs Found Poems

1

Stump-a-foot★ man can't kick
with his good foot.

2

Tiger wants to eat a child, tiger says
he could swear it was a puss.

★ *stump-a-foot*: stumpy or one-legged.

3
Is a blessing me come me see you:
eye-to-eye joy is a love.

4
Is better to walk for nothing
than sit down for so-so.

5
A man with half-a-foot
must dance near his door.

6
Good-friend you can't buy.
Cheap bargain takes money.

7
Better go heaven a pauper
than go hell a rector.

8
If ants waller too much in fat,
fat will drown ants.

9
Stretch your hand and give
it's a God own grace.

ELIZABETH BARTLETT (b.1924)

Elizabeth Bartlett was born in Kent in 1924, and lives in Burgess Hill, Sussex. She has worked as a medical secretary, and later in the home-help service and as a tutor. Her first collection, A Lifetime of Dying, was not published until 1979 and contained poems written over thirty-seven years. Two Women Dancing, New and Selected Poems was published in 1995.

Charlotte, Her Book

I am Charlotte. I don't say hello
to people and sometimes I bite.
Although I am dead I still jump
out of bed and wake them up at night.

This is my mother. Her hair is blue
and I have drawn her with no eyes
and arms like twigs. I don't do
what I'm told and I tell lies.

This is my father. He has a mouth
under his left ear. I'm fed up
with drawing people, so I scribble
smoke and cover his head right up.

I am a brat kid, fostered out because
my mother is sick in the head,
and I would eat her if I could,
and make her good and dead.

Although I am only four I went away
so soon they hardly knew me,
and stars sprang out of my eyes,
and cold winds blew me.

My mother always says she loves me.
My father says he loves me too.
I love Charlotte. A car ran
over Charlotte. This is her book.

IAN HAMILTON FINLAY (b.1925)

Ian Hamilton Finlay was born in Nassau, Bahamas, but grew up in Scotland. He served in the Royal Army Service Corps in the Second World War, then worked as a shepherd in Perthshire and on Rousay, Orkney. After publishing a number of short stories, Finlay published such poetry collections as The Dancers Inherit the Party *(1960) and* Glasgow Beasts, an a Burd *(1961). During the 1960s Finlay became an important member of the international Concrete poetry movement. In 1966 he settled at Stonypath, Lanarkshire, in a small shepherd's cottage with four acres of land where with the help of Sue Finlay he began creating a garden, later renamed Little Sparta, in which he installed poems and texts carved in stone, ceramic and wood.*

from Stonechats

THE CLOUD'S ANCHOR

swallow

Evening – Sail

EVEN
–ING
WILL
COME

THEY
WILL
SEW
THE
BLUE
SAIL

'Star/Steer'

'Acrobats'

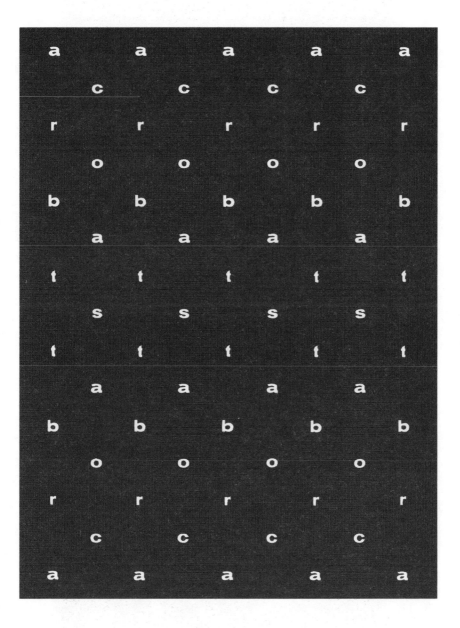

from SF★

★ In this sequence, as in the earlier 'Footnotes to an essay' (Catalogue of the Ian Hamilton Finlay Serpentine Gallery exhibition, 1977), and the print-variation on Bernini's 'Apollo and Daphne' (1977), the notorious Nazi-German organisation, the SS, is equated with Nature. That is to say, it signifies the ultimate 'wildness' in a scale whose other, 'cultivated' extreme is the eighteenth century. In tracing the progression (or descent) from the civilised script of this period – in which 'f's were customarily susbstituted for 's's – to the runic rendering or double lightning stroke of the SS uniform and banners, we therefore follow the gradation between 'Culture' and 'Nature'. We must ourselves 'allegorise' the letter-forms of the stages which intervene.

ELIZABETH JENNINGS (b.1926)

Elizabeth Jennings was born in Boston, Lincolnshire, in 1926. Before full-time writing she worked in advertising, then in Oxford City Library and briefly in publishing. Since Collected Poems *(1986), drawing on seventeen volumes and containing 'all the work she wishes to preserve', she has continued to write, and* Times and Seasons *was published in 1992. She lives in Oxford.*

Lazarus

It was the amazing white, it was the way he simply
Refused to answer our questions, it was the cold pale glance
Of death upon him, the smell of death that truly
Declared his rising to us. It was no chance
Happening, as a man may fill a silence
Between two heart-beats, seem to be dead and then
Astonish us with the closeness of his presence;
This man was dead, I say it again and again.
All of our sweating bodies moved towards him
And our minds moved too, hungry for finished faith.
He would not enter our world at once with words
That we might be tempted to twist or argue with:
Cold like a white root pressed in the bowels of earth
He looked, but also vulnerable – like birth.

The Diamond Cutter

Not what the light will do but how he shapes it
And what particular colours it will bear,

And something of the climber's concentration
Seeing the white peak, setting the right foot there.

Not how the sun was plausible at morning
Nor how it was distributed at noon,

And not how much the single stone could show
But rather how much brilliance it would shun;

Simply a paring down, a cleaving to
One object, as the star-gazer who sees

One single comet polished by its fall
Rather than countless, untouched galaxies.

My Grandmother

She kept an antique shop – or it kept her.
Among Apostle spoons and Bristol glass,
The faded silks, the heavy furniture,
She watched her own reflection in the brass
Salvers and silver bowls, as if to prove
Polish was all, there was no need of love.

And I remember how I once refused
To go out with her, since I was afraid.
It was perhaps a wish not to be used
Like antique objects. Though she never said
That she was hurt, I still could feel the guilt
Of that refusal, guessing how she felt.

Later, too frail to keep a shop, she put
All her best things in one long narrow room.
The place smelt old, of things too long kept shut,
The smell of absences where shadows come
That can't be polished. There was nothing then
To give her own reflection back again.

And when she died I felt no grief at all,
Only the guilt of what I once refused.
I walked into her room among the tall
Sideboards and cupboards – things she never used
But needed; and no finger-marks were there,
Only the new dust falling through the air.

CHRISTOPHER LOGUE (b.1926)

*Christopher Logue was born in 1926 in Portsmouth. He served as a private in the Black
Watch in the forties and spent sixteen months in an army prison. He has written a
pornographic novel, and his poetry collections include his adaptations of Homer's* Iliad:
War Music *(1981),* Kings *(1991) and* The Husbands *(1994). Selected Poems was
published in 1996. He lives in Camberwell, London.*

The Song of the Dead Soldier

For seven years at school I named
   Our kings, their wars (if these were won)
A boy trained simple as we come,
   I read of an island in the sun,
   Where the Queen of Love was born.

At seventeen the postman brought,
   Into the room (my place of birth)
Some correspondence from the Crown,
   Demanding that with guns I earn
   The modern shilling I was worth.

Lucky for me that I could read,
   Lucky for me our captain said:
'You'll see the world for free my son,
   You're posted to an island, John,
   Where the Queen of Love was born.'

So twenty weeks went by and by
   My back was straightened out my eye
Dead true as any button shone,
   And nine white-bellied porpoise led
   Our ship of shillings through the sun.

We landed with our drums and clad
   In war suits worth ten well-taxed pounds
(The costliest I ever had)
   Our foreign shoulders crossed the town,
   The Queen of Love our flag.

And three by three through our curfew,
   Mother we marched like black and tan,
Singing to match our captain's cheers.
   Then I drank my eyes out of my head
   And wet Her shilling with my fears.

When morning came our captain bold
   Said: 'The island shaped like an ass's skin
Must be kept calm, must be patrolled,
   For outposts are the heart and soul
   Of empire, love, and lawful rule.'

I did not know to serve meant kill.
   I did not see the captain fall.
As my life went out through a bullet hole:
   'Mother,' I said, 'my life is gone –
   Did they spend your English shilling well?'

And then I saw a hag whose eyes
   Were big as medals, grey as lead,
I called my rifle but it was dead,
   Our captain roared but my ears were dud,
   The hag kissed warm, we met in blood,
   English shilling, Queen of Love.

CHRISTOPHER MIDDLETON (b.1926)

Christopher Middleton was born in Truro, Cornwall, read German and French at Oxford, has taught in Zurich and London, and emigrated in 1965 when he became a professor at the University of Texas. He has published many translations of both poetry and prose, as well as literary criticism. His Selected Writings *was published in 1989.*

A Forge in Darkness

They hadn't forgotten his name
Or whereabouts the forge was,
The brick oven, hot glow
Of charcoal, the hammer floats
Up, held in mid-air now, and
What beer the old man drank.

A heart isn't like that. A heart
Won't wait until the dark
Comes to cool things off a bit.
It works through the blinding
Noon heat, careless of sparks,
Of hoofs clipclopping uphill.

Boys came by. Owls looked on.
A horse tail flicked at bluebottles,
Under the canopy of this pecan.
This hill – part of the night then,
A slope, that's all, crested with a forge,
Like a wave flecked with red foam.

What a letdown for her, hitched
To that limping, fretful man,
The reek of sweat and charcoal on him –
And her arms could take a whole sky in,
Her thumbs govern long ships or fondle lambs,
Yet she slid from her wave and under him.

It was here, right here, where I came
To be living. She's gone, he's gone.
I cook chicken where the forge
Must have been. In the dark I
Pour out more wine to remember
The little old lives of them.

Taking a chance, I think
That's where she must have gone:
Into the artifice of not forgetting
A name and what went on,
When the boys watched and owls
Heard the hammer come down.

RICHARD MURPHY (b.1927)

Richard Murphy was born in County Galway in 1927, and was brought up in Ceylon (Sri Lanka), where his father was the last British Mayor of Colombo. His first book, Sailing to an Island, *was published in 1963, followed by six other volumes, leading to* New Selected Poems *in 1989. He lives near Dublin.*

Slate

Slate I picked from a nettlebed
Had history, my neighbour said.

To quarry it, men had to row
Five miles, twelve centuries ago.

An inch thick, it hung watertight
Over monks' litany by candlelight:

Till stormed by Viking raids, it slipped.
Four hundred years overlapped.

Pirates found it and roofed a fort
A mile west, commanding the port.

Red-clawed choughs perched on it saw
Guards throw priests to the sea's jaw.

Repaired to succour James the Shit
The battle of Aughrim shattered it.

Through centuries of penal gale
Hedge-scholars huddled where it fell.

Pegged above a sea-wormed rafter
It rattled over landlord's laughter.

Windy decades pined across
Barrack roof, rebellion, moss.

This week I paved my garden path
With slate St Colman nailed on lath.

CHARLES TOMLINSON (b.1927)

Charles Tomlinson was born in Stoke-on-Trent in 1927, and published his first collection,
Seeing is Believing, in 1958 in the US. He has published criticism and translations,
and in 1980 edited the Oxford Book of Verse in English Translation. From 1957 he
taught at the University of Bristol, becoming Professor of English Literature. He is also
known as a visual artist. His Collected Poems was published in 1985.

A Given Grace

Two cups,
a given grace,
afloat and white
on the mahogany pool
of table. They unclench

the mind, filling it
with themselves.
Though common ware,
these rare reflections,
coolness of brown
so strengthens and refines
the burning of their white,
you would not wish
them other than they are –
you, who are challenged
and replenished by
those empty vessels.

The Blade

I looked to the west:
I saw it thrust
a single blade
between the shadows:
a lean stiletto-shard
tapering to its tip
yellowed along greensward,
lit on a roof that lay
mid-way across its path
and then outran it:
it was so keen,
it seemed to go
right through and cut
in two the land
it was lancing. Then
as I stood,
the shaft shifted,
fading across grass,
withdrew as visibly as the sand
down the throat of an hour-glass:

you could see time
trickle out, a grainy
lesion, and the green
filter back to fill
the crack in creation.

THOMAS KINSELLA (b.1928)

Thomas Kinsella was born in 1928 in Dublin, worked in the Irish Civil Service until 1965, has been the director of a number of poetry presses and has taught at various universities in the United States. His first collection was The Starlit Eye, *published in 1952, and his work also includes translations of early Irish poetry, such as* The Tain *(1969). In 1986 he edited* The New Oxford Book of Irish Verse. *His* Poems 1956–1973 *has been followed by further individual collections.*

Ancestor

I was going up to say something,
and stopped. Her profile against the curtains
was old, and dark like a hunting bird's.

It was the way she perched on the high stool,
staring into herself, with one fist
gripping the side of the barrier around her desk
– or her head held by something, from inside.
And not caring for anything around her
or anyone there by the shelves.
I caught a faint smell, musky and queer.

I may have made some sound – she stopped rocking
and pressed her fist in her lap; then she stood up
and shut down the lid of the desk, and turned the key.
She shoved a small bottle under her aprons
and came toward me, darkening the passageway.

Ancestor . . . among sweet- and fruit-boxes.
Her black heart . . .
                              Was that a sigh?
– brushing by me in the shadows,
with her heaped aprons, through the red hangings
to the scullery, and down to the back room.

IAIN MAC A'GHOBHAINN/
IAIN CRICHTON SMITH (b.1928)

Iain Mac a' Ghobhainn / Iain Crichton Smith was born in 1928 and brought up on the Isle of Lewis. A speaker of both English and Gaelic, he served in the British Army Education Corps and was a schoolteacher up until 1977, when he retired to write full-time. As well as poetry, he has written novels, stories, plays and reviews, and in 1980 received the OBE. He is the author of many volumes of poetry in English and / or Gaelic; his Collected Poems *(in English) was published in 1992. He lives in Taynuilt, Argyll.*

Old Woman

And she, being old, fed from a mashed plate
as an old mare might droop across a fence
to the dull pastures of its ignorance.
Her husband held her upright while he prayed

to God who is all-forgiving to send down
some angel somewhere who might land perhaps
in his foreign wings among the gradual crops.
She munched, half dead, blindly searching the spoon.

Outside, the grass was raging. There I sat
imprisoned in my pity and my shame
that men and women having suffered time
should sit in such a place, in such a state

and wished to be away, yes, to be far away
with athletes, heroes, Greek or Roman men
who pushed their bitter spears into a vein
and would not spend an hour with such decay.

'Pray God,' he said, 'we ask you, God,' he said.
The bowed back was quiet. I saw the teeth
tighten their grip around a delicate death.
And nothing moved within the knotted head

but only a few poor veins as one might see
vague wishless seaweed floating on a tide
of all the salty waters where had died
too many waves to mark two more or three.

Na h-eilthirich

A liuthad soitheach a dh'fhàg ar dùthaich
le sgiathan geala a'toirt Chanada orra.
Tha iad mar neapaigearan 'nar cuimhne
's an sàl mar dheòirean.
's anns na crainn aca seòladairean a' seinn
mar eòin air gheugan.
Muir a' Mhàigh ud gu gorm a' ruith,
gealach air an oidhche, grian air an latha,
ach a' ghealach mar mheas buidhe,
mar thruinnsear air balla,
ris an tog iad an làmhan,
neo mar mhagnet airgeadach
le gathan goirte
a' sruthadh do'n chridhe.

The Exiles*

The many ships that left our country
with white wings for Canada.
They are like handkerchiefs in our memories
and the brine like tears
and in their masts sailors singing
like birds on branches.
That sea of May running in such blue,
a moon at night, a sun at daytime,
and the moon like a yellow fruit,
like a plate on a wall
to which they raise their hands
like a silver magnet
with piercing rays
streaming into the heart.

Owl and Mouse

The owl wafts home with a mouse in its beak.
The moon is stunningly bright in the high sky.

Such a gold stone, such a brilliant hard light.
Such large round eyes of the owl among the trees.

All seems immortal but for the dangling mouse,
an old hurt string among the harmony

of the masterful and jewelled orchestra
which shows no waste soundlessly playing on.

* *Trans. from the author's own Gaelic.*

Gaelic Stories

1
A fisherman in wellingtons
and his sweetheart
and his mother.

2
A story
about an old man
and a seal.

3
A woman
reading a Bible for seven years
waiting for a sailor.

4
A melodeon.
A peat stack.
An owl.

5
A croft.
Two brothers.
A plate with potatoes.

6
A girl from Glasgow
wearing a mini
in church.

7
The sea
and a drifter,
the Golden Rose.

8

A man who was in Australia
coming home
on a wedding night.

9

A romance
between cheese
and milk.

10

Glasgow
in a world of nylons
and of neon.

11

Two women
talking
in a black house.

12

A monster
rising from the sea,
'Will you take tea?'

13

A comedy
in a kitchen,
with jerseys.

14

A conversation
between a loaf and
cheese.

15

A conversation
between a wellington
and a herring.

16
A conversation
between fresh butter
and a cup.

17
A conversation
between Yarmouth
and Garrabost.

18
A moon
hard and high
above a marsh.

BOBI JONES (b.1929)

Bobi Jones was born in Cardiff in 1929 into an English-speaking family. He learnt Welsh at school, studied the subject at university, and after working as a teacher and lecturer, retired from his post of Professor of Welsh at the University College of Wales, Aberystwyth in 1996. He has written literary criticism and prose as well as poetry. Bobi Jones: Selected Poems, with translations into English by Joseph P. Clancy, was published in 1986.

Merch Siop

Mae petalau'i lliw
Yn geiniog goch.
A phan â-hi adref
Ni chlywir sawr
Ar ei threigladau.
Ni ŵyr yn iawn
Sut mae plygu

Yn awel y pentref:
Hi a'i hewinedd tref
A'i gwefusau tref.

Cloncia'i phetalau
Fel ar gownter.
Gadawodd Sir Gâr
Lle na chaiff ddŵr pibau,
A dim ond clawdd
(Neu fwced mewn cwt pren
Ym mhen draw'r ardd
I'r ymwelwyr.)
Ac nid yw mwy
Yn Lili Ann.

Eto, pe gwelit hi
Ar ei gwely
A gwyn ei nwydau'n
Flodyn agored led ceg
Yn tynnu cleddyf neu bastwn
Tua'i chalon
Fe wyddit mai yn y wlad
Y gwreiddiwyd ei chyhyrau.
Yno gwelit sglein
Ar ei ffolennau trist.

Shop Girl★

Her petals of colour
Are a copper penny.
And when she's off home
No relish is taken
In her mutations.
She does not rightly

★ Trans. by Joseph P. Clancy.

Know how to bend
In the village breeze:
Her and her town nails
And her town lips.

Her petals clank
As on a counter.
She left Carmarthenshire
Where there's no indoor plumbing,
Nothing but a ditch
(Or a bucket in a wooden hut
At the far end of the garden
For visitors).
And she's no longer
Lili Ann.

Still, if you saw her
Upon her bed,
The white of her passions
In open-mouthed bloom,
Pulling a sword or a cudgel
Towards her heart,
You'd know her sinews
Were rooted in the country.
There you'd see a shine
On her sad buttocks.

Aber-porth

Yn y gaeaf

Mae-hi bron yn normal drachefn ond bod syrffed o dai,
Hylciau hyll hyd ddistyll. Y mae'r swnd yn loyw
A'r tonnau'n deintio diden binc y traethell fel babanod
Fel pe na bai roced na rhyfel, caffe, hysbysiad
Am gyfarfod y Lleng Brydeinig, eglwys siabi. Diolch nad oes neb

Heblaw gwylanod (ni saethwyd eto'r rheini) a'r tonnau gwib
Mor ddydd arhosol – heb ronyn o groen oren na phecyn sigaréd –
Yn fythol ifainc. Yna fe blygais uwchben cenllysgen gron . . .

Uwch ei ffrwyth teimlais fel edn a ollyngwyd i berllan berlau
Wedi bod noson mewn cysgodle tanddaearol rhag ofn y bomiad
A'r lle'n llawn dop o smygu i ladd amser, neu fel dyn
Fu'n troi mewn breuddwyd wyllt am oriau, yna dihuno
A chael y bore'n oer ond hynod fyw . . . Yng nghrisial nen
Gwelwn wyneb yr Un sy'n caru ar bob ochr, o'r môr, o'r lan,
O'r awyr: yn y glôb mân ar lawr gwyliwn
Ysbryd sy'n ceisio torri'r gwydr, hud yn Aber-porth
Am ddod i maes o'r purdeb belen, er ein gwarth.

Ym mhob geni mae darganfod. Fe fydd byd neu wlad
A'i tyn ei hun o'r gwacter yn debyg i greadur twp
Sy'n hwpo ei ben llysnafeddog o ddyfroedd y dechreuad
Gan ganfod y coed nas gwelodd neb o'r blaen,
Gan ddelwi wrth y pridd. Darganfyddaf mewn strydoedd cefn
Werin o hyd, ac yn y gair a leferir allwedd gwyrth, –
Cof. Allwedd palasau crisial hen ar lawr yn Aber-porth:
Wele, o'r cwmwl du daeth cenllysgen wen.

Aber-Porth*

in winter

It is almost normal again except for a surfeit of houses,
Ugly hulks along the tide-line. The sand is bright
And the waves are nibbling the strand's pink nipple like babies
As though there were neither rocket nor war, a café, an announcement
Of a meeting of the British Legion, a shabby church. Thank goodness there's
*   no one*

---

* Trans. by Joseph P. Clancy.

Except the gulls (those haven't yet been shot) and the darting, so day lasting
Waves – not a shred of orange peel or a cigarette packet –
Eternally young. Then I bent above a round hailstone . . .

Over its fruit I felt like a bird let loose in an orchard of pearls
After a night in an underground shelter for fear of the bombing,
The place chock full of smoking to kill time, or like a man
Who has tossed in a wild dream for hours, then wakens
And finds the morning cold but strangely alive . . . In heaven's crystal
I saw the face of the One who loves on all sides, from the sea, from the shore,
From the sky: in the tiny globe on the ground I watched
A spirit trying to break the glass, magic in Aber-porth
Striving to emerge from the pellet pureness, despite our disgrace.

In every birth is discovery. A world or a land
That pulls itself from the void is like a stupid creature
Thrusting its slimy head from the waters of beginning,
Perceiving the trees that no one has seen before,
Numb with staring at the soil. I discover in the back streets
A people still, and in the word that is spoken a miracle's key –
Memory. Old crystal palaces' key on the ground in Aber-porth:
Look, from the black cloud has come a white hailstone.

Mynwent Bilbo

Ar ôl y rhyfel cartref daeth gorchymyn o Fadrid i ddileu
a thynnu'r enwau Basg oddi ar feddau mewn mynwentydd

Bu'r beddau'n bygwth.
Gallet ti eu gweld nhw
Ar noson loergan yn enwedig.
Fe gripiai'u henwau Basg
Oddi ar eu cerrig
Ac ysgyrnygu ar glustiau
Sbaenig yn Gwernigaidd.
Doedd dim amdani

Ond hwylio â chŷn a morthwyl
I'w llunio nhw'n llawnach eu llonydd.
Beiddgar fydd beddau.
Myn rhai frathu'r llaw
Sy'n eu porthi.

Bilbao Cemetery★

After the civil war an order came from Madrid to delete
and remove the Basque names from graves in cemeteries

The graves were threatening.
You could see them especially
On a moonlight evening.
Their Basque names
Would creep from their stones
And Guernically snarl
At Spanish ears.
There was nothing for it
But to set out with hammer and chisel
And make their stillness stiller.
Graves are bold.
Some will insist on biting
The hand that feeds them.

U. A. FANTHORPE (b.1929)

U. A. Fanthorpe was born in Kent in 1929 and educated at Oxford. She has worked as a
clerk in a Bristol hospital and also as a teacher. Her first collection of poems, Side Effects,
did not appear until 1978, since when she has published a number of books, including
Selected Poems *in 1986. She lives in Gloucestershire.*

★ Trans. by Joseph P. Clancy.

The Poet's Companion

Must be in mint condition, not disposed
To hayfever, headaches, hangovers, hysteria, these being
The Poet's prerogative.

Typing and shorthand desirable. Ability
To function on long walks and in fast trains an advantage.
Must be visible/invisible

At the drop of a dactyl. Should be either
A mobile dictionary, thesaurus and encyclopaedia,
Or have instant access to same.

Cordon bleu and accountancy skills essential,
Also cooking of figures and instant recall of names
Of once-met strangers.

Should keep a good address book. In public will lead
The laughter, applause, the unbearably moving silence.
Must sustain with grace

The role of Muse, with even more grace the existence
Of another eight or so, also camera's curious peeping
When the Poet is reading a particularly

Randy poem about her, or (worse) about someone else.
Ability to endure reproaches for forgetfulness, lack of interest,
Heart, is looked for,

Also instant invention of convincing excuses for what the Poet
Does not want to do, and long-term ability to remember
Precise detail of each.

Must be personable, not beautiful. The Poet
Is not expected to waste time supervising
The Companion. She will bear

Charming, enchanted children, all of them
Variations on the Poet theme; and
Impossibly gifted.

Must travel well, be fluent in the more aesthetic
European languages; must be a Finder
Of nasty scraps of paper

And the miscellany of junk the Poet loses
And needs *this minute, now.* Must be well-read,
Well-earthed, well able

To forget her childhood's grand trajectory,
And sustain with undiminished poise
That saddest dedication: *lastly my wife,*

Who did the typing.

PETER PORTER (b.1929)

Peter Porter was born in Brisbane, Australia, in 1929, and came to England in 1951.
He worked in an advertising agency, has held a number of residencies at British and
Australian universities and since 1968 has been a full-time writer and broadcaster.
His Collected Poems *published in 1983 contained poetry from eight previous volumes*
written over twenty years and won the Duff Cooper Memorial Prize. A Porter Selected
was published six years later, and there have been further volumes in recent years.
He lives in London.

Annotations of Auschwitz

I

When the burnt flesh is finally at rest,
The fires in the asylum grates will come up
And wicks turn down to darkness in the madman's eyes.

2

My suit is hairy, my carpet smells of death,
My toothbrush handle grows a cuticle.
I have six million foulnesses of breath.
Am I mad? The doctor holds my testicles
While the room fills with the zyklon B I cough.

3

On Piccadilly underground I fall asleep –
I shuffle with the naked to the steel door,
Now I am only ten from the front – I wake up –
We are past Gloucester Rd, I am not a Jew,
But scratches web the ceiling of the train.

4

Around staring buildings the pale flowers grow;
The frenetic butterfly, the bee made free by work,
Rouse and rape the pollen pads, the nectar stoops.
The rusting railway ends here. The blind end in Europe's gut.
Touch one piece of unstrung barbed wire –
Let it taste blood: let one man scream in pain,
Death's Botanical Gardens can flower again.

5

A man eating his dressing in the hospital
Is lied to by his stomach. It's a final feast to him
Of beef, blood pudding and black bread.
The orderly can't bear to see this mimic face
With its prim accusing picture after death.
On the stiff square a thousand bodies
Dig up useless ground – he hates them all,
These lives ignoble as ungoverned glands.
They fatten in statistics everywhere
And with their sick, unkillable fear of death
They crowd out peace from executioners' sleep.

6

Forty thousand bald men drowning in a stream –
The like of light on all those bobbing skulls
Has never been seen before. Such death, says the painter,
Is worthwhile – it makes a colour never known.
It makes a sight that's unimagined, says the poet.
It's nothing to do with me, says the man who hates
The poet and the painter. Six million deaths can hardly
Occur at once. What do they make? Perhaps
An idiot's normalcy. I need never feel afraid
When I salt the puny snail – cruelty's grown up
And waits for time and men to bring into its hands
The snail's adagio and all the taunting life
Which has not cared about or guessed its tortured scope.

7

London is full of chickens on electric spits,
    Cooking in windows where the public pass.
This, say the chickens, is their Auschwitz,
    And all poultry eaters are psychopaths.

Eat Early Earthapples

There were boys at my Prep. School my own age
And three stone heavier, who made fifty pounds
Over the holidays selling kangaroo hides
They'd skinned and pegged out themselves
On their fathers' stations. Many shaved, several
Slept with the maids – one I remember
Running his hand up the Irish maid's leg
At breakfast not ten feet away
From the Headmaster's enormous armature of head.
Then there were those marathon journeys home

In the train for the holidays, without sleepers,
And the carriages full of Glennie and Fairholme
Girls sitting up all night – some crying
In the lavatory, some sipping sweet sherry
From dark label-less bottles passed them in the dark,
Some knowing what to do and spattered
By Queensland Railways' coal dust trying
To do it on the floor, their black lisle
Stockings changed for wartime rayon. There were
So many ways of losing a troublesome innocence
But so many ways of keeping it too. Being troubled,
I found a sophistication which drove me mad
Sitting out dances, a viewed humiliation,
Walking through waltzes on boracic'd floors,
(Chopped horsehair rising, said to make girls sexy).
The girls were nicer than I needed, the Headmaster
Led the Jolly Miller, the knowing athletes
Waited for the Gypsy Tap, their stories next day
Full of what they'd managed on the dark verandah.
My schooldays when I was so eagerly unhappy
Have me back among them when I sleep
Freely associating with those baffled fears.
The lascivious miler, the confident three-quarter
Are thick men now with kids and problems.
There is no way back into their wormy Eden,
Ripe with girls, esplanaded with sex,
To stuff myself to sickness and forget
(Taking their chances, my old wounds averted)
The boy with something wrong reading a book
While the smut-skeined train goes homeward
Carrying the practised to the sensual city.

Soliloquy at Potsdam

There are always the poor –
Getting themselves born in crowded houses,
Feeding on the parish, losing their teeth early
And learning to dodge blows, getting
Strong bodies – cases for the warped nut of the mind.
The masterful cat-o'-nine-tails, the merciful
Discipline of the hours of drill – better
Than being poor in crowded Europe, the swan-swept
Waters where the faces dredge for bread
And the soggy dead are robbed on their way to the grave.
I can hear it from this window, the musket-drill
On the barrack square. Later today I'll visit
The punishment block. Who else in Europe
Could take these verminous, clutching creatures
And break them into men? What of the shredded back
And the broken pelvis, when the side-drum sounds,
When the uniformed wave tilts and overwhelms
The cheese-trading burghers' world, the aldermanic
Principalities. The reformers sit at my table,
They talk well but they've never seen a battle
Or watched the formed brain in the flogged body
Marching to death on a bellyful of soup and orders.
There has to be misery so there can be discipline.
People will have to die because I cannot bear
Their clinging to life. Why are the best trumpeters
Always French? Watch the west, the watershed
Of revolution. Now back to Quantz. I like to think
That in an afternoon of three sonatas
A hundred regiments have marched more miles
Than lie between here and Vienna and not once
Has a man broken step. Who would be loved
If he could be feared and hated, yet still
Enjoy his lust, eat well and play the flute?

An Exequy

In wet May, in the months of change,
In a country you wouldn't visit, strange
Dreams pursue me in my sleep,
Black creatures of the upper deep –
Though you are five months dead, I see
You in guilt's iconography,
Dear Wife, lost beast, beleaguered child,
The stranded monster with the mild
Appearance, whom small waves tease,
(Andromeda upon her knees
In orthodox deliverance)
And you alone of pure substance,
The unformed form of life, the earth
Which Piero's brushes brought to birth
For all to greet as myth, a thing
Out of the box of imagining.

This introduction serves to sing
Your mortal death as Bishop King
Once hymned in tetrametric rhyme
His young wife, lost before her time;
Though he lived on for many years
His poem each day fed new tears
To that unreaching spot, her grave,
His lines a baroque architrave
The Sunday poor with bottled flowers
Would by-pass in their mourning hours,
Esteeming ragged natural life
('Most dearly loved, most gentle wife'),
Yet, looking back when at the gate
And seeing grief in formal state
Upon a sculpted angel group,
Were glad that men of god could stoop
To give the dead a public stance
And freeze them in their mortal dance.

The words and faces proper to
My misery are private – you
Would never share your heart with those
Whose only talent's to suppose,
Nor from your final childish bed
Raise a remote confessing head –
The channels of our lives are blocked,
The hand is stopped upon the clock,
No one can say why hearts will break
And marriages are all opaque:
A map of loss, some posted cards,
The living house reduced to shards,
The abstract hell of memory,
The pointlessness of poetry –
These are the instances which tell
Of something which I know full well,
I owe a death to you – one day
The time will come for me to pay
When your slim shape from photographs
Stands at my door and gently asks
If I have any work to do
Or will I come to bed with you.
O scala enigmatica,
I'll climb up to that attic where
The curtain of your life was drawn
Some time between despair and dawn –
I'll never know with what halt steps
You mounted to this plain eclipse
But each stair now will station me
A black responsibility
And point me to that shut-down room,
'This be your due appointed tomb.'

I think of us in Italy:
Gin-and-chianti-fuelled, we
Move in a trance through Paradise,

Feeding at last our starving eyes,
Two people of the English blindness
Doing each masterpiece the kindness
Of discovering it – from Baldovinetti
To Venice's most obscure jetty.
A true unfortunate traveller, I
Depend upon your nurse's eye
To pick the altars where no Grinner
Puts us off our tourists' dinner
And in hotels to bandy words
With Genevan girls and talking birds,
To wear your feet out following me
To night's end and true amity,
And call my rational fear of flying
A paradigm of Holy Dying –
And, oh my love, I wish you were
Once more with me, at night somewhere
In narrow streets applauding wines,
The moon above the Apennines
As large as logic and the stars,
Most middle-aged of avatars,
As bright as when they shone for truth
Upon untried and avid youth.

The rooms and days we wandered through
Shrink in my mind to one – there you
Lie quite absorbed by peace – the calm
Which life could not provide is balm
In death. Unseen by me, you look
Past bed and stairs and half-read book
Eternally upon your home,
The end of pain, the left alone.
I have no friend, or intercessor,
No psychopomp or true confessor
But only you who know my heart
In every cramped and devious part –

Then take my hand and lead me out,
The sky is overcast by doubt,
The time has come, I listen for
Your words of comfort at the door,
O guide me through the shoals of fear –
'Fürchte dich nicht, ich bin bei dir.'

THOM GUNN (b.1929)

Thom Gunn was born in Gravesend in 1929. After national service he read English at Cambridge and his first book of poems, Fighting Terms, *was published while he was still an undergraduate in 1954. In the same year he moved to North California, and now lives in San Francisco and teaches half of each year at Berkeley. He has published two books of criticism, and in 1993 published* Collected Poems, *which contained eight previous volumes, along with* The Man with Night Sweats, *his first volume for ten years, which included a set of poems about the deaths of friends from AIDS and won the 1992 Forward Prize for Poetry.*

The Unsettled Motorcyclist's Vision of his Death

Across the open countryside,
Into the walls of rain I ride.
It beats my cheek, drenches my knees,
But I am being what I please.

The firm heath stops, and marsh begins.
Now we're at war: whichever wins
My human will cannot submit
To nature, though brought out of it.
The wheels sink deep; the clear sound blurs:
Still, bent on the handle-bars,
I urge my chosen instrument
Against the mere embodiment.
The front wheel wedges fast between

Two shrubs of glazed insensate green
– Gigantic order in the rim
Of each flat leaf. Black eddies brim
Around my heel which, pressing deep,
Accelerates the waiting sleep.

I used to live in sound, and lacked
Knowledge of still or creeping fact,
But now the stagnant strips my breath,
Leant on my cheek in weight of death.
Though so oppressed I find I may
Through substance move. I pick my way,
Where death and life in one combine,
Through the dark earth that is not mine,
Crowded with fragments, blunt, unformed;
While past my ear where noises swarmed
The marsh plant's white extremities,
Slow without patience, spread at ease
Invulnerable and soft, extend
With a quiet grasping toward their end.

And though the tubers, once I rot,
Reflesh my bones with pallid knot,
Till swelling out my clothes they feign
This dummy is a man again,
It is as servants they insist,
Without volition that they twist;
And habit does not leave them tired,
By men laboriously acquired.
Cell after cell the plants convert
My special richness in the dirt:
All that they get, they get by chance.

And multiply in ignorance.

Touch

You are already
asleep. I lower
myself in next to
you, my skin slightly
numb with the restraint
of habits, the patina of
self, the black frost
of outsideness, so that even
unclothed it is
a resilient chilly
hardness, a superficially
malleable, dead
rubbery texture.

You are a mound
of bedclothes, where the cat
in sleep braces
its paws against your
calf through the blankets,
and kneads each paw in turn.

Meanwhile and slowly
I feel a is it
my own warmth surfacing or
the ferment of your whole
body that in darkness beneath
the cover is stealing
bit by bit to break
down that chill.

        You turn and
hold me tightly, do
you know who
I am or am I

your mother or
the nearest human being to
hold on to in a
dreamed pogrom.

What I, now loosened,
sink into is an old
big place, it is
there already, for
you are already
there, and the cat
got there before you, yet
it is hard to locate.
What is more, the place is
not found but seeps
from our touch in
continuous creation, dark
enclosing cocoon round
ourselves alone, dark
wide realm where we
walk with everyone.

The Discovery of the Pacific

They lean against the cooling car, backs pressed
Upon the dust of a brown continent,
And watch the sun, now Westward of their West,
Fall to the ocean. Where it led they went.

Kansas to California. Day by day
They travelled emptier of the things they knew.
They improvised new habits on the way,
But lost the occasions, and then lost them too.

One night, no one and nowhere, she had woken
To resin-smell and to the firs' slight sound,
And through their sleeping-bag had felt the broken
Tight-knotted surfaces of the naked ground.

Only his lean quiet body cupping hers
Kept her from it, the extreme chill. By degrees
She fell asleep. Around them in the firs
The wind probed, tiding through forked estuaries.

And now their skin is caked with road, the grime
Merely reflecting sunlight as it fails.
They leave their clothes among the rocks they climb,
Blunt leaves of iceplant nuzzle at their soles.

Now they stand chin-deep in the sway of ocean,
Firm West, two stringy bodies face to face,
And come, together, in the water's motion,
The full caught pause of their embrace.

The Man with Night Sweats

I wake up cold, I who
Prospered through dreams of heat
Wake to their residue,
Sweat, and a clinging sheet.

My flesh was its own shield:
Where it was gashed, it healed.

I grew as I explored
The body I could trust
Even while I adored
The risk that made robust,

A world of wonders in
Each challenge to the skin.

I cannot but be sorry
The given shield was cracked,
My mind reduced to hurry,
My flesh reduced and wrecked.

I have to change the bed,
But catch myself instead

Stopped upright where I am
Hugging my body to me
As if to shield it from
The pains that will go through me,

As if hands were enough
To hold an avalanche off.

ELAINE FEINSTEIN (b.1930)

Elaine Feinstein was born in 1930 in Liverpool, has worked for Cambridge University Press and has taught at the University of Essex. She has written fiction, biography and radio plays, and made translations of Russian poets including Marina Tsvetayeva. Unease and Angels: Selected Poems was published in 1977, since when there have been several further poetry collections. She lives in London.

Father

The wood trade in his hands
at sixtyone back at the sawbench,
my stubborn father sands and planes
birchwood for kitchen chairs.

All my childhood he was a rich man
unguarded purchaser
of salmon trout, off-season strawberries
and spring in Switzerland.

Bully to prudish aunts
whose niggard habits taught them to assess
honest advantage, without rhetoric:
his belly laughter overbore their tutting.

Still boss of his own shop
he labours in the chippings without grudge
loading the heavy tables,
shabby and powerful as an old bus.

Mother Love

You eat me, your
nights eat me.
Once you took
haemoglobin and bone
out of my blood,

now my head
sleeps forward on my neck
holding you.

In the morning my
skin shines hot
and you are happy
banging your fat hands.

I kiss your
soft feet mindless:
delicately

your shit slides out
yellow and
smelling of curd cheese.

ROY FISHER (b.1930)

*Roy Fisher was born in Handsworth, Birmingham, in 1930, and has worked as
a teacher, a lecturer in American studies, and in later years as a freelance writer and
musician. Jazz is often cited as an influence on his composition, and his books include*
Collected Poems: The Ghost of a Paper Bag *(1969),* Poems 1959−1980 *(1980)*
and Poems 1955−1987 *(1988).*

The Entertainment of War

I saw the garden where my aunt had died
And her two children and a woman from next door;
It was like a burst pod filled with clay.

A mile away in the night I had heard the bombs
Sing and then burst themselves between cramped houses
With bright soft flashes and sounds like banging doors;

The last of them crushed the four bodies into the ground,
Scattered the shelter, and blasted my uncle's corpse
Over the housetop and into the street beyond.

Now the garden lay stripped and stale; the iron shelter
Spread out its separate petals around a smooth clay saucer,
Small, and so tidy it seemed nobody had ever been there.

When I saw it, the house was blown clean by blast and care:
Relations had already torn out the new fireplaces;
My cousin's pencils lasted me several years.

And in his office notepad that was given me
I found solemn drawings in crayon of blondes without dresses.
In his lifetime I had not known him well.

Those were the things I noticed at ten years of age:
Those, and the four hearses outside our house,
The chocolate cakes, and my classmates' half-shocked envy.

But my grandfather went home from the mortuary
And for five years tried to share the noises in his skull,
Then he walked out and lay under a furze-bush to die.

When my father came back from identifying the daughter
He asked us to remind him of her mouth.
We tried. He said 'I think it was the one'.

These were marginal people I had met only rarely
And the end of the whole household meant that no grief was seen;
Never have people seemed so absent from their own deaths.

This bloody episode of four whom I could understand better dead
Gave me something I needed to keep a long story moving;
I had no pain of it; can find no scar even now.

But had my belief in the fiction not been thus buoyed up
I might, in the sigh and strike of the next night's bombs
Have realized a little what they meant, and for the first time been
    afraid.

Report on August

How do I sleep? Well, but
the dreams are bad:

filled with accusations
small but just.

These slack summer dawns
that fail of sunrise

there's a relief at falling
awake and into comfort,

becoming once again
four people, watching

from pillow level
my boys' khaki heads bustle about.

Over breakfast I see,
staring at the garden,

how the times have fed:
under heavy leaves and low sky

in profile the bold woodpigeon
walks the lawn.

Beats of a shadowy fanblade
tick through from behind,

time going; ignored,
nobody measuring time, so much

constant, the weather unchanging,
the work I do filling days

so that they seem one day,
a firm framework, made

of the window where I sit
(or lie, slumped, feet on the desk,

waved to by passers-by
like a paraplegic)

a window-shaped guise of myself
that holds what few events come round

like slides, and in what seems
capricious sequence.

ANTHONY THWAITE (b.1930)

*Anthony Thwaite was born in Chester in 1930 and grew up in Yorkshire and the US.
He has worked as a literary editor, BBC producer and broadcaster, and taught at a number
of foreign universities. In 1988 he edited Philip Larkin's* Collected Poems *and in 1992
Larkin's* Selected Letters. Poems 1953–1988 *brings together several previous
collections, and more recent volumes include* The Dust of the World, *published in 1994.
He lives in Norfolk.*

Mr Cooper

Two nights in Manchester: nothing much to do,
One of them I spent partly in a pub,
Alone, quiet, listening to people who
Didn't know me. *So I told the bloody sub-
Manager what he could do with it . . . Mr Payne
Covers this district – you'll have met before?*
Caught short, I looked for the necessary door
And moved towards it; could hear, outside, the rain.

The usual place, with every surface smooth
To stop, I suppose, the aspirations of
The man with pencil stub and dreams of YOUTH
AGED 17. And then I saw, above
The stall, a card, a local jeweller's card
Engraved with name, JEWELLER AND WATCHMENDER
FOR FIFTY YEARS, address, telephone number.
I heard the thin rain falling in the yard.

The card was on a sort of shelf, just close
Enough to let me read this on the front.
Not, I'd have said, the sort of words to engross
Even the keenest reader, nothing to affront

The public decency of Manchester.
And yet I turned it over. On the back
Were just three words in rather smudgy black
Soft pencil: MR COPPER – DEAD. The year

Grew weakly green outside, in blackened trees,
Wet grass by statues. It was ten to ten
In March in Manchester. Now, ill at ease
And made unsure of sense and judgement when
Three words could throw me, I walked back into
The bar, where nothing much had happened since
I'd left. A man was trying to convince
Another man that somehow someone knew

Something that someone else had somehow done.
Two women sat and drank the lagers they
Were drinking when I'd gone. If anyone
Knew I was there, or had been, or might stay,
They didn't show it. *Good night*, I almost said,
Went out to find the rain had stopped, walked back
To my hotel, and felt the night, tall, black,
Above tall roofs. And Mr Cooper dead.

TED HUGHES (b.1930)

Ted Hughes was born in 1930 in Mytholmroyd, West Yorkshire, and lives in Devon. His first book of poems, The Hawk in the Rain, *made an immediate impact when it was published in 1967. He has gone on to write over a dozen further collections, plus theatre works, books for children and critical studies such as* Shakespeare and the Goddess of Complete Being *(1992). All of the poems that consolidated his reputation are contained within* New Selected Poems 1957–1994. *Hughes has won many literary awards, and in 1984 he was appointed Poet Laureate.*

The Thought-Fox

I imagine this midnight moment's forest:
Something else is alive
Beside the clock's loneliness
And this blank page where my fingers move.

Through the window I see no star:
Something more near
Though deeper within darkness
Is entering the loneliness:

Cold, delicately as the dark snow
A fox's nose touches twig, leaf;
Two eyes serve a movement, that now
And again now, and now, and now

Sets neat prints into the snow
Between trees, and warily a lame
Shadow lags by stump and in hollow
Of a body that is bold to come

Across clearings, an eye,
A widening deepening greenness,
Brilliantly, concentratedly,
Coming about its own business

Till, with a sudden sharp hot stink of fox
It enters the dark hole of the head.
The window is starless still; the clock ticks,
The page is printed.

Wind

This house has been far out at sea all night,
The woods crashing through darkness, the booming hills,
Winds stampeding the fields under the window
Floundering black astride and blinding wet

Till day rose; then under an orange sky
The hills had new places, and wind wielded
Blade-light, luminous black and emerald,
Flexing like the lens of a mad eye.

At noon I scaled along the house-side as far as
The coal-house door. Once I looked up –
Through the brunt wind that dented the balls of my eyes
The tent of the hills drummed and strained its guyrope,

The fields quivering, the skyline a grimace,
At any second to bang and vanish with a flap:
The wind flung a magpie away and a black-
Back gull bent like an iron bar slowly. The house

Rang like some fine green goblet in the note
That any second would shatter it. Now deep
In chairs, in front of the great fire, we grip
Our hearts and cannot entertain book, thought,

Or each other. We watch the fire blazing,
And feel the roots of the house move, but sit on,
Seeing the window tremble to come in,
Hearing the stones cry out under the horizons.

Full Moon and Little Frieda

A cool small evening shrunk to a dog bark and the clank of a bucket –

And you listening.
A spider's web, tense for the dew's touch.
A pail lifted, still and brimming – mirror
To tempt a first star to a tremor.

Cows are going home in the lane there, looping the hedges with their
warm wreaths of breath –
A dark river of blood, many boulders,
Balancing unspilled milk.

'Moon!' you cry suddenly, 'Moon! Moon!'

The moon has stepped back like an artist gazing amazed at a work

That points at him amazed.

February 17th

A lamb could not get born. Ice wind
Out of a downpour dishclout sunrise. The mother
Lay on the mudded slope. Harried, she got up
And the blackish lump bobbed at her back-end
Under her tail. After some hard galloping,
Some manoeuvring, much flapping of the backward
Lump head of the lamb looking out,
I caught her with a rope. Laid her, head uphill
And examined the lamb. A blood-ball swollen
Tight in its black felt, its mouth gap
Squashed crooked, tongue stuck out, black-purple,
Strangled by its mother. I felt inside,
Past the noose of mother-flesh, into the slippery
Muscled tunnel, fingering for a hoof,
Right back to the port-hole of the pelvis.

But there was no hoof. He had stuck his head out too early
And his feet could not follow. He should have
Felt his way, tip-toe, his toes
Tucked up under his nose
For a safe landing. So I kneeled wrestling
With her groans. No hand could squeeze past
The lamb's neck into her interior
To hook a knee. I roped that baby head
And hauled till she cried out and tried
To get up and I saw it was useless. I went
Two miles for the injection and a razor.
Sliced the lamb's throat-strings, levered with a knife
Between the vertebrae and brought the head off
To stare at its mother, its pipes sitting in the mud
With all earth for a body. Then pushed
The neck-stump right back in, and as I pushed
She pushed. She pushed crying and I pushed gasping.
And the strength
Of the birth push and the push of my thumb
Against that wobbly vertebra were deadlock,
A to-fro futility. Till I forced
A hand past and got a knee. Then like
Pulling myself to the ceiling with one finger
Hooked in a loop, timing my effort
To her birth push groans, I pulled against
The corpse that would not come. Till it came.
And after it the long, sudden, yolk-yellow
Parcel of life
In a smoking slither of oils and soups and syrups —
And the body lay born, beside the hacked-off head.

17 February 1974

The Last of the 1st/5th Lancashire Fusiliers

A Souvenir of the Gallipoli Landings

The father capers across the yard cobbles
Look, like a bird, a water-bird, an ibis going over pebbles
We laughed, like warships fluttering bunting.

Heavy-duty design, deep-seated in ocean-water
The warships flutter bunting.
A fiesta day for the warships
Where war is only an idea, as drowning is only an idea
In the folding of a wave, in the mourning
Funeral procession, the broadening wake
That follows a ship under power.

War is an idea in the muzzled calibre of the big guns.
In the grey, wolvish outline.
War is a kind of careless health, like the heart-beat
In the easy bodies of sailors, feeling the big engines
Idling between emergencies.

It is what has left the father
Who has become a bird.
Once he held war in his strong pint mugful of tea
And drank at it, heavily sugared.
It was all for him
Under the parapet, under the periscope, the look-out
Under Achi Baba and the fifty billion flies.

Now he has become a long-billed, spider-kneed bird
Bow-backed, finding his footing, over the frosty cobbles
A wader, picking curiosities from the shallows.

His sons don't know why they laughed, watching him through the
    window
Remembering it, remembering their laughter
They only want to weep

As after the huge wars

Senseless huge wars

Huge senseless weeping.

SYLVIA PLATH (1932–1963)

Sylvia Plath was born in Boston, Massachusetts, in 1932, and began writing while at college in America. She came to England in 1955 and the following year married the poet Ted Hughes. Her prose fiction includes The Bell Jar *(1963), and she also wrote for children. Her first poetry collection,* The Colossus, *was published in 1961, and there followed three more separate volumes, concluding with* Ariel, *published posthumously after her suicide in 1963. Sylvia Plath's letters were presented in the book* Letters Home: Correspondence 1950–1963, *edited by her mother, and* Collected Poems *was published in 1981.*

You're

Clownlike, happiest on your hands,
Feet to the stars, and moon-skulled,
Gilled like a fish. A common-sense
Thumbs-down on the dodo's mode.
Wrapped up in yourself like a spool,
Trawling your dark as owls do.
Mute as a turnip from the Fourth
Of July to All Fools' Day,
O high-riser, my little loaf.

Vague as fog and looked for like mail.
Farther off than Australia.
Bent-backed Atlas, our traveled prawn.
Snug as a bud and at home

Like a sprat in a pickle jug.
A creel of eels, all ripples.
Jumpy as a Mexican bean.
Right, like a well-done sum.
A clean slate, with your own face on.

The Arrival of the Bee Box

I ordered this, this clean wood box
Square as a chair and almost too heavy to lift.
I would say it was the coffin of a midget
Or a square baby
Were there not such a din in it.

The box is locked, it is dangerous.
I have to live with it overnight
And I can't keep away from it.
There are no windows, so I can't see what is in there.
There is only a little grid, no exit.

I put my eye to the grid.
It is dark, dark,
With the swarmy feeling of African hands
Minute and shrunk for export,
Black on black, angrily clambering.

How can I let them out?
It is the noise that appalls me most of all,
The unintelligible syllables.
It is like a Roman mob,
Small, taken one by one, but my god, together!

I lay my ear to furious Latin.
I am not a Caesar.
I have simply ordered a box of maniacs.
They can be sent back.
They can die, I need feed them nothing, I am the owner.

I wonder how hungry they are.
I wonder if they would forget me
If I just undid the locks and stood back and turned into a tree.
There is the laburnum, its blond colonnades,
And the petticoats of the cherry.

They might ignore me immediately
In my moon suit and funeral veil.
I am no source of honey
So why should they turn on me?
Tomorrow I will be sweet God, I will set them free.

The box is only temporary.

Daddy

You do not do, you do not do
Any more, black shoe
In which I have lived like a foot
For thirty years, poor and white,
Barely daring to breathe or Achoo.

Daddy, I have had to kill you.
You died before I had time——
Marble-heavy, a bag full of God,
Ghastly statue with one gray toe
Big as a Frisco seal

And a head in the freakish Atlantic
Where it pours bean green over blue
In the waters off beautiful Nauset.
I used to pray to recover you.
Ach, du.

In the German tongue, in the Polish town
Scraped flat by the roller
Of wars, wars, wars.
But the name of the town is common.
My Polack friend

Says there are a dozen or two.
So I never could tell where you
Put your foot, your root,
I never could talk to you.
The tongue stuck in my jaw.

It stuck in a barb wire snare.
Ich, ich, ich, ich,
I could hardly speak.
I thought every German was you.
And the language obscene

An engine, an engine
Chuffing me off like a Jew.
A Jew to Dachau, Auschwitz, Belsen.
I began to talk like a Jew.
I think I may well be a Jew.

The snows of the Tyrol, the clear beer of Vienna
Are not very pure or true.
With my gipsy ancestress and my weird luck
And my Taroc pack and my Taroc pack
I may be a bit of a Jew.

I have always been scared of *you*,
With your Luftwaffe, your gobbledygoo.
And your neat mustache
And your Aryan eye, bright blue.
Panzer-man, panzer-man, O You——

Not God but a swastika
So black no sky could squeak through.
Every woman adores a Fascist,
The boot in the face, the brute
Brute heart of a brute like you.

You stand at the blackboard, daddy,
In the picture I have of you,
A cleft in your chin instead of your foot
But no less a devil for that, no not
Any less the black man who

Bit my pretty red heart in two.
I was ten when they buried you.
At twenty I tried to die
And get back, back, back to you.
I thought even the bones would do.

But they pulled me out of the sack,
And they stuck me together with glue.
And then I knew what to do.
I made a model of you,
A man in black with a Meinkampf look

And a love of the rack and the screw.
And I said I do, I do.
So daddy, I'm finally through.
The black telephone's off at the root,
The voices just can't worm through.

If I've killed one man, I've killed two——
The vampire who said he was you
And drank my blood for a year,
Seven years, if you want to know.
Daddy, you can lie back now.

There's a stake in your fat black heart
And the villagers never liked you.
They are dancing and stamping on you.
They always *knew* it was you.
Daddy, daddy, you bastard, I'm through.

Edge

The woman is perfected.
Her dead

Body wears the smile of accomplishment,
The illusion of a Greek necessity

Flows in the scrolls of her toga,
Her bare

Feet seem to be saying:
We have come so far, it is over.

Each dead child coiled, a white serpent,
One at each little

Pitcher of milk, now empty.
She has folded

Them back into her body as petals
Of a rose close when the garden

Stiffens and odors bleed
From the sweet, deep throats of the night flower.

The moon has nothing to be sad about,
Staring from her hood of bone.

She is used to this sort of thing.
Her blacks crackle and drag.

JENNY JOSEPH (b.1932)

Jenny Joseph was born in Birmingham in 1932. She has worked as a journalist, a teacher and a publican, and for a time lived in South Africa. Her first collection of poetry, The Unlooked-for Season *(1960), was followed by four other volumes as well as an experimental poem-novel,* Persephone *(1985).* Selected Poems *(1992) contains the poem* Warning, *once voted the 'nation's most popular poem'.*

The lost sea

You have stood on a quayside in the flat grey morning
Watching the rotting pierhead swim to view
Through mist on the estuary, as if it moved,
As if the sea still rose beneath its boards.
And heard at noon the brittle seaweed crunch
Under the slipping shoes of a tired child
Shortcutting from the village, along the path
Salt has not lined for many a high tide now.

The little railway faltered long ago
Waving antennae over the mud banks
That turned it back in smooth indifference.
With nothing on the other side to reach
It settles now for grass and butterflies.

Ships must have called here often, for on the pier
Shreds of tyres still cling that once stove off
The vulnerable white sides of pleasure boats.
Among the stinking debris in that hut
Beneath the swarm of flies on a dead cat
Remains of nets lie rolled.

Family men in inland garden suburbs
Collected maybe pebbles and precious glass
From what was once a shore.

And knew the names of birds flown South long since,
And cadged sweets from the trippers when they came
And owned the place again when they had gone.

Nobody bombed the place. There was no army
Trampled its heart out. Nor did the nearby town
Account for this desertion.
                    Merely it was:
The land built up here, or the sea receded.
Over the years the fish bypassed the shallows
And those that came the fishermen could not get,
High tide beyond their reach; and the cold moon
Hauled only over mud.

                    The sea forsook.
Nothing to do that would not have been useless.

                    So we did nothing
But watch that shore die as the sea receded.

GEOFFREY HILL (b.1932)

Geoffrey Hill was born in 1932 in Bromsgrove, Worcestershire, where his father was a police constable. He taught for many years at Leeds University, later at Cambridge, and in 1988 moved to the US where he is a member of the University Professors Program at Boston University. He has published six collections of poetry and two collections of critical essays, plus a version of Ibsen's Brand, *commissioned by the National Theatre in 1978. His* New & Collected Poems 1952–1992 *was published in 1994, and recent volumes include* Caanan *(1996).*

Genesis

I

Against the burly air I strode
Crying the miracles of God.

And first I brought the sea to bear
Upon the dead weight of the land;
And the waves flourished at my prayer,
The rivers spawned their sand.

And where the streams were salt and full
The tough pig-headed salmon strove,
Ramming the ebb, in the tide's pull,
To reach the steady hills above.

II

The second day I stood and saw
The osprey plunge with triggered claw,
Feathering blood along the shore,
To lay the living sinew bare.

And the third day I cried: 'Beware
The soft-voiced owl, the ferret's smile,
The hawk's deliberate stoop in air,
Cold eyes, and bodies hooped in steel,
Forever bent upon the kill.'

III

And I renounced, on the fourth day,
This fierce and unregenerate clay,
Building as a huge myth for man
The watery Leviathan,

And made the long-winged albatross
Scour the ashes of the sea
Where Capricorn and Zero cross,
A brooding immortality –
Such as the charmed phoenix has
In the unwithering tree.

IV

The phoenix burns as cold as frost;
And, like a legendary ghost,
The phantom-bird goes wild and lost,
Upon a pointless ocean tossed.

So, the fifth day, I turned again
To flesh and blood and the blood's pain.

V

On the sixth day, as I rode
In haste about the works of God,
With spurs I plucked the horse's blood.

By blood we live, the hot, the cold,
To ravage and redeem the world:
There is no bloodless myth will hold.

And by Christ's blood are men made free
Though in close shrouds their bodies lie
Under the rough pelt of the sea;

Though Earth has rolled beneath her weight
The bones that cannot bear the light.

Two Formal Elegies

for the Jews in Europe

I

Knowing the dead, and how some are disposed:
Subdued under rubble, water, in sand graves,
In clenched cinders not yielding their abused
Bodies and bonds to those whom war's chance saves
Without the law: we grasp, roughly, the song.
Arrogant acceptance from which song derives
Is bedded with their blood, makes flourish young
Roots in ashes. The wilderness revives,

Deceives with sweetness harshness. Still beneath
Live skin stone breathes, about which fires but play,
Fierce heart that is the iced brain's to command
To judgment – studied reflex, contained breath –
Their best of worlds since, on the ordained day,
This world went spinning from Jehovah's hand.

II

For all that must be gone through, their long death
Documented and safe, we have enough
Witnesses (our world being witness-proof).
The sea flickers, roars, in its wide hearth.
Here, yearly, the pushing midlanders stand
To warm themselves; men, brawny with life,
Women who expect life. They relieve
Their thickening bodies, settle on scraped sand.

Is it good to remind them, on a brief screen,
Of what they have witnessed and not seen?
(Deaths of the city that persistently dies . . . ?)
To put up stones ensures some sacrifice.
Sufficient men confer, carry their weight.
(At whose door does the sacrifice stand or start?)

Ovid In The Third Reich

non peccat, quaecumque potest peccasse negare,
solaque famosam culpa professa facit.
(AMORES, III, xiv)

I love my work and my children. God
Is distant, difficult. Things happen.
Too near the ancient troughs of blood
Innocence is no earthly weapon.

I have learned one thing: not to look down
So much upon the damned. They, in their sphere,
Harmonize strangely with the divine
Love. I, in mine, celebrate the love-choir.

September Song

born 19.6.32 – deported 24.9.42

Undesirable you may have been, untouchable
you were not. Not forgotten
or passed over at the proper time.

As estimated, you died. Things marched,
sufficient, to that end.
Just so much Zyklon and leather, patented
terror, so many routine cries.

(I have made
an elegy for myself it
is true)

September fattens on vines. Roses
flake from the wall. The smoke
of harmless fires drifts to my eyes.

This is plenty. This is more than enough.

from Mercian Hymns

I

King of the perennial holly-groves, the riven sandstone: overlord of the
M5: architect of the historic rampart and ditch, the citadel at Tamworth,
the summer hermitage in Holy Cross: guardian of the Welsh Bridge
and the Iron Bridge: contractor to the desirable new estates: saltmaster:
money-changer: commissioner for oaths: martyrologist: the friend of
Charlemagne.

'I liked that,' said Offa, 'sing it again.'

VII

Gasholders, russet among fields. Milldams, marlpools that lay unstirring.
Eel-swarms. Coagulations of frogs: once, with branches and half-
bricks, he battered a ditchful; then sidled away from the stillness and
silence.

Ceolred was his friend and remained so, even after the day of the lost
fighter: a biplane, already obsolete and irreplaceable, two inches of
heavy snub silver. Ceolred let it spin through a hole in the classroom-
floorboards, softly, into the rat-droppings and coins.

After school he lured Ceolred, who was sniggering with fright, down to
the old quarries, and flayed him. Then, leaving Ceolred, he journeyed
for hours, calm and alone, in his private derelict sandlorry named
Albion.

XXV

Brooding on the eightieth letter of *Fors Clavigera,* I speak this in memory
of my grandmother, whose childhood and prime womanhood were
spent in the nailer's darg.

The nailshop stood back of the cottage, by the fold. It reeked stale mineral
sweat. Sparks had furred its low roof. In dawn-light the troughed
water floated a damson-bloom of dust –

not to be shaken by posthumous clamour. It is one thing to celebrate
the 'quick forge', another to cradle a face hare-lipped by the searing
wire.

Brooding on the eightieth letter of *Fors Clavigera*, I speak this in memory
of my grandmother, whose childhood and prime womanhood were
spent in the nailer's darg.

ADRIAN MITCHELL (b.1932)

*Adrian Mitchell was born in London in 1932, and worked as a journalist before becoming
a full-time writer in 1966. Well-known for public performances of his poetry, he has also
written for the stage and for television and radio. Adrian Mitchell's Greatest Hits was
published in 1991.*

Celia Celia

When I am sad and weary
When I think all hope has gone
When I walk along High Holborn
I think of you with nothing on

PETER REDGROVE (b.1932)

Peter Redgrove was born in 1932 in Kingston, Surrey, and lives in Falmouth, Cornwall.
He was conscripted into the army at eighteen, has worked as a journalist and copy-writer,
and has held posts in universities in Britain and abroad. His output includes novels, short
stories, dramatic work, and his selected poems from 1954 to 1987 are contained within
The Moon Disposes *(1987). In 1996 he received the Queen's Gold Medal for Poetry,*
and further collections include Assembling a Ghost *(1997).*

A Twelvemonth

In the month called Bride
there is pale spectral honey
and in-laws made of chain-mail and whiskers.

In the month called Hue-and-Cry
green blood falls with a patter
and the pilchard-shoal flinches.

The month called Houseboat
is for conversing by perfume
and raising beer-steins:
great stone-and-foam masks.

In the month called Treasurechest
snails open jalousies onto their vitals:
pinecones, pollen-packed.

In the month called Brickbat
the sea is gorgeous with carpets
of orange jelly-fish squads:
and the people ride.

The month called Meatforest
is for flowers in the abattoirs,
catafalques for the steers.

In the month known as William
we watch the deer grazing on seaweed;
police open the strongroom of Christ.

In the month called Clocks
the poets decide
whether they shall draw salary,

And in the month called Horsewhip
they pluck their secret insurance
from the rotting rafters.

In the Mollycoddle month
barbers put up bearded mirrors
and no-one is allowed to die.

In the month called Yellow Maze
all the teddy-bears
celebrate their thousandth birthday.

In the month called Sleep-with-your-wife
the sea makes a living
along this quiet shore, somehow.

The First Earthquake

The birds squabbled and fell silent
In their million trees like colleges of monks
With their mean little ways and their beautiful songs;

The yachts like moored forests,
The yachts rocked in their haven
Like women in long dresses

And invisible feet
Bowing to the earthquake.
The mist had rolled in

And developed all the spiderwebs,
The trees in the groves draped
Like pearl-sewn yachts,

The million spiders in them asleep,
The spiders in their white roofs,
The dew-lapping spiders,

They nodded their toolchest faces,
Beards wet with dew,
Dew brimming their webs and their claws;

Complex water shivered everywhere like a single ghost.
Lovers, smelling of almonds and new bread,
Roused from their beds, pointed

Rubbing their eyes at the copses of yachts
That tugged at the tremor and dipped,
Shivering rain from their tackles,

Lovers who shivered like silk
As the rafters groaned
Within their white ceilings,

This earthquake shoved up fifty new fountains!
After the first shock we are ravenous,
The little silvery fishes grizzling in the shiny pans.

from Six Odes

IV   Wardrobe-Lady

She wears the long series of wonder-awakening dresses.
She wears the fishskin cloak,
She wears the gown of pearl with the constellations slashed into its
    dark lining,

She undresses out of the night sky, each night of the year a different
  sky,
She wears altitude dresses and vertigo dresses,
She plucks open the long staircase at the neck with the big buttons of
  bird-skulls in the white dress of sow-thistle.
She has leather britches known to be chimp-skin,
She has combed star-rays into a shaggy night-dress,
She has a bodice of bone-flounces, a turbinal blouse through which
  the air pours.
There is a gown she has that shimmers without slit or seam like the
  wall of an aquarium:
A starfish moves slowly on its pumps across her bosom,
A shark glides, a turtle rows silently between her knees,
And she adopts in turn the long dress of sewn louse-skin,
The romper suit of purple jam packed with tiny oval seeds,
The foggy grey dress, and lapping between its folds
Echo bird-cries and meteor-noises and declarations of love,
The ballgown of ticker-tape,
The evening dress of flexible swirling clockwork running against time,
The cocktail dress of bloody smoke and bullet-torn bandages,
And the little black dress of grave-soil that rends and seals as she turns.
Often she sits up all night in the philosopher's library
Sewing strong patches from his wardrobes of thought
Into her wounded dresses.

PETER SCUPHAM (b.1933)

*Peter Scupham was born in 1933 in Liverpool and educated at Cambridge, and was co-
founder of the Mandeville Press. He published his first pamphlet,* The Small Containers,
*when he was thirty-nine, since when there have been several more full-length collections.
His* Selected Poems *was published in 1990.*

Going Out: Lancasters, 1944

'They're going out', she said.
  Together we watch them go,
The dark crossed on the dusk,
  The slow slide overhead

And the garden growing cold,
  Flowers bent into grey,
The fields of earth and sky
  Losing their strength to hold

The common lights of day
  Which warm our faces still.
Feet in the rustling grass
  We watch them pass away,

The heavy web of sound
  Catching at her throat.
We stand there hand-in-hand,
  Our steady, shifting ground

Spreading itself to sand,
  The crisp and shining sea.
Wave upon wave they go,
  And we stand hand-in-hand,

The slow slide overhead,
  Stitched on a roll of air,
As if they knew the way,
  As if they were not dead.

ANNE STEVENSON (b.1933)

Anne Stevenson was born in 1933 in England of American parents. She grew up and was educated in the US, and returned to Britain in 1954. Her prose books include a critical study of Elizabeth Bishop and the Sylvia Plath biography Bitter Fame *(1989). The* Collected Poems 1955–1995 *brings together work from ten previous books. She lives in Gwynedd, Wales, and in Grantchester, near Cambridge.*

The Marriage

They will fit, she thinks,
but only if her backbone
cuts exactly into his rib cage,
and only if his knees
dock exactly under her knees
and all four
agree on a common angle.

All would be well
if only
they could face each other.

Even as it is
there are compensations
for having to meet
nose to neck
chest to scapula
groin to rump
when they sleep.

They look, at least,
as if they were going
in the same direction.

The Fish are all Sick

The fish are all sick, the great whales dead,
the villages stranded in stone on the coast,
ornamental, like pearls on the fringe of a coat.
Sea men, who knew what the ocean did,
turned their low houses away from the surf.
But new men, who come to be rural and safe,
add big glass views and begonia beds.

Water keeps to itself.
White lip after lip
curls to a close on the littered beach.
Something is sicker and blacker than fish.
And closing its grip, and closing its grip.

Where the Animals Go

The Beasts in Eden
cradle the returning souls of earth's animals.

The horse, limp cargo, craned down to the terrible quay,
is butchered into the heaven of his own hoofed kind.

The retriever mangled on the motorway, the shot
Alsatian by the sheepfold, the mutilated black-faced sheep –
they rise like steam, like cumulus, crowding in together,
each into the haunches of its archetype.

The drowned vole, the pheasant brought down with his fires,
the kitten in the jacket of its panicking fleas,
flying souls, furred, feathered, scaled, shelled, streaming
upward, upward through the wide thoughtless rose empyrean.

God absorbs them neatly in his green teeming cells.
There, sexed as here, they're without hurt or fear.
Heaven is honeycombed with their arrivals and entries.

Two of each Butterfly. Two of each Beetle.
A great Cowness sways on her full uddered way.
All kinds of Cat watch over the hive like churches.
Their pricked ears, pinnacles. Their gold eyes, windows.

The Fiction-Makers

We were the wrecked elect,
the ruined few. Youth,
youth, the Café Iruña
and the bullfight set,
looped on Lepanto brandy
but talking 'truth' –
Hem, the 4 a.m. wisecrack,
the hard way in,
that story we were all at the end of
and couldn't begin –
we thought we were living now,
but we were living then.

Sanctified Pound, a knot
of nerves in his fist,
squeezing the Goddamn iamb
out of our verse,
making it new in his
archaeological plot –
to maintain 'the sublime'
in the factive? Couldn't be done.
Something went wrong
with 'new' in the Pisan pen.
He thought he was making now,
but he was making then.

Virginia, Vanessa,
a teapot, a Fitzroy fuss,
'Semen?' asks Lytton,

eyeing a smudge on a dress.
How to educate England
and keep a correct address
on the path to the river through
Auschwitz? Belsen?
Auden and Isherwood
stalking glad boys in Berlin –
they thought they were suffering now,
but they were suffering then.

Out of pink-cheeked Cwmdonkin,
Dylan with his Soho grin.
Planted in the fiercest of flames,
gold ash on a stem.
When Henry jumped out of his joke,
Mr Bones sat in.
Even you, with your breakable heart
in your ruined skin,
those poems all written
that have to be you, dear friend,
you guessed you were dying now,
but you were dying then.

Here is a table with glasses,
ribbed cages tipped back,
or turned on a hinge to each other
to talk, to talk,
mouths that are drinking or smiling
or quoting some book,
or laughing out laughter as candletongues
lick at the dark –
so bright in this fiction
forever becoming its end,
we think we are laughing now,
but we are laughing then.

FLEUR ADCOCK (b.1934)

Fleur Adcock was born in 1934 in New Zealand, where she was educated and where she worked in Dunedin and Wellington before settling in England in 1963. Her first collection, The Eye of the Hurricane, *was published in Wellington in 1964, and her* Selected Poems *(1983) includes poems from four further books, plus new work. She lives in London.*

A Surprise in The Peninsula

When I came in that night I found
the skin of a dog stretched flat and
nailed upon my wall between the
two windows. It seemed freshly killed –
there was blood at the edges. Not
my dog: I have never owned one,
I rather dislike them. (Perhaps
whoever did it knew that.) It
was a light brown dog, with smooth hair;
no head, but the tail still remained.
On the flat surface of the pelt
was branded the outline of the
peninsula, singed in thick black
strokes into the fur: a coarse map.
The position of the town was
marked by a bullet-hole; it went
right through the wall. I placed my eye
to it, and could see the dark trees
outside the house, flecked with moonlight.
I locked the door then, and sat up
all night, drinking small cups of the
bitter local coffee. A dog
would have been useful, I thought, for
protection. But perhaps the one
I had been given performed that

function; for no one came that night,
nor for three more. On the fourth day
it was time to leave. The dog-skin
still hung on the wall, stiff and dry
by now, the flies and the smell gone.
Could it, I wondered, have been meant
not as a warning, but a gift?
And, scarcely shuddering, I drew
the nails out and took it with me.

Country Station

First she made a little garden
of sorrel stalks wedged among
some yellowy-brown moss-cushions

and fenced it with ice-lolly sticks
(there were just enough); then she
set out biscuit-crumbs on a brick

for the ants; now she sits on a
deserted luggage-trolley
to watch them come for their dinner.

It's nice here – cloudy but quite warm.
Five trains have swooshed through, and one
stopped, but at the other platform.

Later, when no one is looking,
she may climb the roof of that
low shed. Her mother is making

another telephone call (she
isn't crying any more).
Perhaps they will stay here all day.

Against Coupling

I write in praise of the solitary act:
of not feeling a trespassing tongue
forced into one's mouth, one's breath
smothered, nipples crushed against the
ribcage, and that metallic tingling
in the chin set off by a certain odd nerve:

unpleasure. Just to avoid those eyes would help –
such eyes as a young girl draws life from,
listening to the vegetal
rustle within her, as his gaze
stirs polypal fronds in the obscure
sea-bed of her body, and her own eyes blur.

There is much to be said for abandoning
this no longer novel exercise –
for not 'participating in
a total experience' – when
one feels like the lady in Leeds who
had seen *The Sound of Music* eighty-six times;

or more, perhaps, like the school drama mistress
producing *A Midsummer Night's Dream*
for the seventh year running, with
yet another cast from 5B.
Pyramus and Thisbe are dead, but
the hole in the wall can still be troublesome.

I advise you, then, to embrace it without
encumbrance. No need to set the scene,
dress up (or undress), make speeches.
Five minutes of solitude are
enough – in the bath, or to fill
that gap between the Sunday papers and lunch.

The Ex-Queen among the Astronomers

They serve revolving saucer eyes,
dishes of stars; they wait upon
huge lenses hung aloft to frame
the slow procession of the skies.

They calculate, adjust, record,
watch transits, measure distances.
They carry pocket telescopes
to spy through when they walk abroad.

Spectra possess their eyes; they face
upwards, alert for meteorites,
cherishing little glassy worlds:
receptacles for outer space.

But she, exile, expelled, ex-queen,
swishes among the men of science
waiting for cloudy skies, for nights
when constellations can't be seen.

She wears the rings he let her keep;
she walks as she was taught to walk
for his approval, years ago.
His bitter features taunt her sleep.

And so when these have laid aside
their telescopes, when lids are closed
between machine and sky, she seeks
terrestrial bodies to bestride.

She plucks this one or that among
the astronomers, and is become
his canopy, his occultation;
she sucks at earlobe, penis, tongue

mouthing the tubes of flesh; her hair
crackles, her eyes are comet-sparks.
She brings the distant briefly close
above his dreamy abstract stare.

BRENDAN KENNELLY (b.1936)

Brendan Kennelly was born in 1936 in Ballylongford, County Kerry, and is Professor of Modern Literature at Trinity College, Dublin. A well-known public figure in Ireland, he has published over twenty books of poetry, edited several anthologies, written for the theatre and translated poems from the Irish. His best-known works are Cromwell *(first published in Ireland in 1983) and* The Book of Judas *(1991), which at one point topped the Irish bestseller list.* Poetry My Arse *(1995) is a more recent collection.*

A Holy War

'We suffered the little children to be cut out of women
"Their bellys were rippitt upp"
This was a holy war, a just rebellion
And little lords in the womb must not escape
Their due. Certain women not great with child
Were stripped and made to dig a hole
Big enough to contain them all.
We buried these women alive
And covered them with rubbish, earth and stones.
Some who were not properly smothered
Yet could not rise
(They tried hard) got for their pains
Our pykes in their breasts. People heard
(Or said they heard) the ground make women's cries.'

The Visit

To get the people's minds off disease and death
We organised a visit from the Queen.
She landed in Cork in the royal yacht
And continued by sea to Dublin.
There was a banquet at the Viceregal Lodge.
Her Majesty held a royal *levée* at which some
2000 people were presented, and a *Drawing Room*
At which 1700 ladies were accorded the same

Privilege. But the noblest scene of all was
The military spectacle in the Phoenix Park
In which 6000 troops took part.
'This is great' glowed Her Majesty, 'This is truly great.'
We considered the visit a resonant success
Though the poor went on dying at their usual rate.

GILLIAN CLARKE (b.1937)

Gillian Clarke was born in Cardiff in 1937 and has lived in Wales most of her life. She was for some time editor of the Anglo-Welsh Review, *and works as a broadcaster, writer and lecturer. Her books include* Letter from a Far Country *(1982),* Selected Poems *(1985),* Letting in the Rumour *(1989) and* The King of Britain's Daughter *(1993).*

Chalk Pebble

The heels of the foetus knead
the stone's roundness out of shape,
downtreading flesh, distorting
the ellipses of the sphere.

It is unexpectedly
salty to touch, its texture
warmer, rougher, weightier
in my hand than I had thought.

Boisterous in its bone
cradle, a stone-breaker,
thief in its mother's orchard,
it is apple-round.

Here the navel
knots it from its chalk down;
there the pressure as the embryo
kicks against ribcage and hip.

The cicatrice of a flower
is printed on one of its
curved surfaces. I carry it
as I walk Glamorgan beaches,

a warm, strange thing to worry
with my fingers. The fossil locked
in its belly stirs, a tender
fresh upheaval of the stone.

Overheard in County Sligo

I married a man from County Roscommon
and I live at the back of beyond
with a field of cows and a yard of hens
and six white geese on the pond.

At my door's a square of yellow corn
caught up by its corners and shaken,
and the road runs down through the open gate
and freedom's there for the taking.

I had thought to work on the Abbey stage
or have my name in a book,
to see my thought on the printed page,
or still the crowd with a look.

But I turn to fold the breakfast cloth
and to polish the lustre and brass,
to order and dust the tumbled rooms
and find my face in the glass.

I ought to feel I'm a happy woman
for I lie in the lap of the land,
and I married a man from County Roscommon
and I live in the back of beyond.

JOHN FULLER (b.1937)

John Fuller, son of the poet Roy Fuller, was born in Ashford, Kent, in 1937, and lives in Oxford. His first collection, Fairground Music, *was published in 1961, since when he has written over a dozen volumes of verse, four novels and a number of books for children. He teaches at Oxford, and his* Collected Poems *was published in 1997.*

The Cook's Lesson

When the King at last could not manage an erection,
The tables were wiped down and a banquet prepared.
The Cook was a renegade, a master of innuendo,
And was later hanged for some imaginary subversion,
Found laughing in the quarter of the filthy poor.
This, had we known it, was to be his last banquet,
And as such was fittingly dissident and experimental.
Often he had confided to us the tenets of his craft,
How a true artist is obsessed with the nature of his material,
And must make evident the process of creation in preference

To the predictable appearance of the finished product.
The charcoal-burners were lit, the porcelain laid
And the simple broths prepared in which the meal was enacted,
For this was a living meal, a biological history of food.
I cannot remember much. We sweated and fainted and were revived
With fragrant towels. We ate furiously and were rewarded
With knowledge of a kind we did not even recognise.
Spawn in the luke gruel divided, gilled and finned,
Swam down flowered channels to the brink of oil
And fell to the plate. Before our eyes
The litter spurted into the fire, picked out by tongs,
Eggs hatched into the soup, embryos bled,
Seeds sprouted in the spoon. As I said, we ate fast,
Far back into life, eating fast into life.
Now I understand that food is never really dead:
Frilled and forked, towered, dusted, sliced,
In mimic aspic or dispersed in sauces,
Food is something that will not willingly lie down.
The bland liquids slid over our tongues as
Heartbeats under crusts, mouthfuls of feathers.

Concerto for Double Bass

He is a drunk leaning companionably
Around a lamp post or doing up
With intermittent concentration
Another drunk's coat.

He is a polite but devoted Valentino,
Cheek to cheek, forgetting the next step.
He is feeling the pulse of the fat lady
Or cutting her in half.

But close your eyes and it is sunset
At the edge of the world. It is the language
Of dolphins, the growth of tree-roots,
The heart-beat slowing down.

TONY HARRISON (b.1937)

Tony Harrison was born in Leeds in 1937 and read Classics at Leeds University. He lived for four years in Nigeria and also in Prague, before returning to Britain where he held fellowships at the Universities of Newcastle-upon-Tyne and Durham. He has published several books of poetry and is perhaps best-known for the ongoing sequence The School of Eloquence, *included in* Selected Poems *(1984). He has also written extensively for the theatre, the stage and for other media such as television, and his long poem* V *caused much controversy when it was broadcast on national television in 1987. He lives in Northumberland.*

Them & [uz]

for Professors Richard Hoggart & Leon Cortez

I

αἰαῖ, ay, ay! . . . stutterer Demosthenes
gob full of pebbles outshouting seas –

4 words only of *mi 'art aches* and . . . 'Mine's broken,
you barbarian, T.W.!' *He* was nicely spoken.
'Can't have our glorious heritage done to death!'

I played the Drunken Porter in *Macbeth*.

'Poetry's the speech of kings. You're one of those
Shakespeare gives the comic bits to: prose!
All poetry (even Cockney Keats?) you see
's been dubbed by [Λs] into RP,
Received Pronunciation, please believe [Λs]
your speech is in the hands of the Receivers.'

'We say [Λs] not [ʊz], T. W.!' That shut my trap.
I doffed my flat a's (as in 'flat cap')
my mouth all stuffed with glottals, great
lumps to hawk up and spit out . . . *E-nun-ci-ate!*

II

So right, yer buggers, then! We'll occupy
your lousy leasehold Poetry.

I chewed up Littererchewer and spat the bones
into the lap of dozing Daniel Jones,
dropped the initials I'd been harried as
and used my *name* and own voice: [ʊz] [ʊz] [ʊz],
ended sentences with by, with, from,
and spoke the language that I spoke at home.
RIP RP, RIP T. W.
I'm *Tony* Harrison no longer you!

You can tell the Receivers where to go
(and not aspirate it) once you know
Wordsworth's *matter/water* are full rhymes,
[ʊz] can be loving as well as funny.

My first mention in the *Times*
automatically made Tony Anthony!

Book Ends

I

Baked the day she suddenly dropped dead
we chew it slowly that last apple pie.

Shocked into sleeplessness you're scared of bed.
We never could talk much, and now don't try.

You're like book ends, the pair of you, she'd say,
Hog that grate, say nothing, sit, sleep, stare . . .

The 'scholar' me, you, worn out on poor pay,
only our silence made us seem a pair.

Not as good for staring in, blue gas,
too regular each bud, each yellow spike.

A night you need my company to pass
and she not here to tell us we're alike!

Your life's all shattered into smithereens.

Back in our silences and sullen looks,
for all the Scotch we drink, what's still between 's
not the thirty or so years, but books, books, books.

II

The stone's too full. The wording must be terse.
There's scarcely room to carve the FLORENCE on it –

Come on, it's not as if we're wanting verse.
It's not as if we're wanting a whole sonnet!

After tumblers of neat *Johnny Walker*
(I think that both of us we're on our third)
you said you'd always been a clumsy talker

and couldn't find another, shorter word
for 'beloved' or for 'wife' in the inscription,
but not too clumsy that you can't still cut:

*You're supposed to be the bright boy at description
and you can't tell them what the fuck to put!*

I've got to find the right words on my own.

I've got the envelope that he'd been scrawling,
mis-spelt, mawkish, stylistically appalling
but I can't squeeze more love into their stone.

Continuous

James Cagney was the one up both our streets.
His was the only art we ever shared.
A gangster film and choc ice were the treats
that showed about as much love as he dared.

He'd be my own age now in '49!
The hand that glinted with the ring he wore,
his father's, tipped the cold bar into mine
just as the organist dropped through the floor.

He's on the platform lowered out of sight
to organ music, this time on looped tape,
into a furnace with a blinding light
where only his father's ring will keep its shape.

I wear it now to Cagneys on my own
and sense my father's hands cupped round my treat –

they feel as though they've been chilled to the bone
from holding my ice cream all through *White Heat*.

Marked With D.

When the chilled dough of his flesh went in an oven
not unlike those he fuelled all his life,
I thought of his cataracts ablaze with Heaven
and radiant with the sight of his dead wife,
light streaming from his mouth to shape her name,
'not Florence and not Flo but always Florrie'.
I thought how his cold tongue burst into flame
but only literally, which makes me sorry,
sorry for his sake there's no Heaven to reach.
I get it all from Earth my daily bread
but he hungered for release from mortal speech
that kept him down, the tongue that weighed like lead.

The baker's man that no one will see rise
and England made to feel like some dull oaf
is smoke, enough to sting one person's eyes
and ash (not unlike flour) for one small loaf.

Timer

Gold survives the fire that's hot enough
to make you ashes in a standard urn.
An envelope of coarse official buff
contains your wedding ring which wouldn't burn.

Dad told me I'd to tell them at St James's
that the ring should go in the incinerator.
That 'eternity' inscribed with both their names is
his surety that they'd be together, 'later'.

I signed for the parcelled clothing as the son,
the cardy, apron, pants, bra, dress –

the clerk phoned down: *6–8–8–3–1?*
Has she still her ring on? (Slight pause) *Yes!*

It's on my warm palm now, your burnished ring!

I feel your ashes, head, arms, breasts, womb, legs,
sift through its circle slowly, like that thing
you used to let me watch to time the eggs.

ROGER McGOUGH (b.1937)

Roger McGough was born in 1937, and came to prominence as one of the Liverpool Poets after the publication of The Mersey Sound *in 1967. He has written extensively for children as well as adults, and his two-volume selected poems* Blazing Fruit *and* You at the Back *were published in 1989 and 1991.*

Goodbat Nightman

God bless all policemen
and fighters of crime,
May thieves go to jail
for a very long time.

They've had a hard day
helping clean up the town,
Now they hang from the mantelpiece
both upside down.

A glass of warm blood
and then straight up the stairs,
Batman and Robin
are saying their prayers.

★   ★   ★

They've locked all the doors
and they've put out the bat,
Put on their batjamas
(They like doing that)

They've filled their batwater-bottles
made their batbeds,
With two springy battresses
for sleepy batheads.

They're closing red eyes
and they're counting black sheep,
Batman and Robin
are falling asleep.

KEN SMITH (b.1938)

Ken Smith was born in 1938 in Rudston, East Yorkshire, and has worked in Britain and the USA as a teacher, editor, barman and potato-picker. He has also held a number of fellowships and residencies, and was writer in residence in Wormwood Scrubs prison from 1985 to 1987. The Poet Reclining (1982) brings together work from over a dozen books and there have been several publications since then, plus a number of prose volumes. He lives in East London.

The road to Henrietta's house

Well there's a lot of ways to get there a lot of ways to go.
For a start you can stop off at the Rainbow Café and drink
drink yourself beyond yourself into silence through the jukebox
through all the chatter of the pinball machines till its *Time*.

That would be the end of it that would be the tale. But suppose.
Suppose you have the one drink leave set out across the city.
You take the bus you take the tram you take the train you walk.
You come to the river there you wake the sleepy boatman.

For sure for certain he's sure in a foul mood, and sore drunk.
And when he's rowed you over there's the marshes and the wild
   beasts.
There's the vipers and the soldier ants and the roaches and the flies.
You have to catch your own wild horse you have to tame it, ride it

at last at long last down the long road to Henrietta's house,
and just because all hell has broken broken loose broken loose
you're thinking someone something in the universe doesn't want
the two of you to meet, ever. Suppose you just keep going

to the end the road makes in the door that opens into light
water in the kettle wine in the dark red bottle and her beads.
And now she wants to dance she wants to click her fingers laugh
fling out her braids flying in the window in the candle's flame.

SEAMUS HEANEY (b.1939)

Seamus Heaney was born in 1939 in County Derry and lives in Dublin. He studied at Queen's University, Belfast, and taught for many years at different colleges and universities in Ireland and America, including Harvard. His first book, Death of a Naturalist, *was published in 1966, since when he has become one of the best-known and most widely regarded poets writing in the English language. His critical books include* The Government of the Tongue *(1988) and* The Redress of Poetry *(1995), a collection of lectures delivered during his term as Professor of Poetry at Oxford.* New Selected Poems 1966–1987 *draws from nine collections of poetry, and further publications include* The Spirit Level, *which won the 1996 Whitbread Book of the Year. In 1995 he was awarded the Nobel Prize for Literature.*

Digging

Between my finger and my thumb
The squat pen rests; snug as a gun.

Under my window, a clean rasping sound
When the spade sinks into gravelly ground:
My father, digging. I look down

Till his straining rump among the flowerbeds
Bends low, comes up twenty years away
Stooping in rhythm through potato drills
Where he was digging.

The coarse boot nestled on the lug, the shaft
Against the inside knee was levered firmly.
He rooted out tall tops, buried the bright edge deep
To scatter new potatoes that we picked
Loving their cool hardness in our hands.

By God, the old man could handle a spade.
Just like his old man.

My grandfather cut more turf in a day
Than any other man on Toner's bog.
Once I carried him milk in a bottle
Corked sloppily with paper. He straightened up
To drink it, then fell to right away
Nicking and slicing neatly, heaving sods
Over his shoulder, going down and down
For the good turf. Digging.

The cold smell of potato mould, the squelch and slap
Of soggy peat, the curt cuts of an edge
Through living roots awaken in my head.
But I've no spade to follow men like them.

Between my finger and my thumb
The squat pen rests.
I'll dig with it.

Punishment

I can feel the tug
of the halter at the nape
of her neck, the wind
on her naked front.

It blows her nipples
to amber beads,
it shakes the frail rigging
of her ribs.

I can see her drowned
body in the bog,
the weighing stone,
the floating rods and boughs.

Under which at first
she was a barked sapling
that is dug up
oak-bone, brain-firkin:

her shaved head
like a stubble of black corn,
her blindfold a soiled bandage,
her noose a ring

to store
the memories of love.
Little adulteress,
before they punished you

you were flaxen-haired,
undernourished, and your
tar-black face was beautiful.
My poor scapegoat,

I almost love you
but would have cast, I know,
the stones of silence.
I am the artful voyeur

of your brain's exposed
and darkened combs,
your muscles' webbing
and all your numbered bones:

I who have stood dumb
when your betraying sisters,
cauled in tar,
wept by the railings,

who would connive
in civilized outrage
yet understand the exact
and tribal, intimate revenge.

The Harvest Bow

As you plaited the harvest bow
You implicated the mellowed silence in you
In wheat that does not rust
But brightens as it tightens twist by twist
Into a knowable corona,
A throwaway love-knot of straw.

Hands that aged round ashplants and cane sticks
And lapped the spurs on a lifetime of game cocks
Harked to their gift and worked with fine intent

Until your fingers moved somnambulant:
I tell and finger it like braille,
Gleaning the unsaid off the palpable.

And if I spy into its golden loops
I see us walk between the railway slopes
Into an evening of long grass and midges,
Blue smoke straight up, old beds and ploughs in hedges,
An auction notice on an outhouse wall –
You with a harvest bow in your lapel,

Me with the fishing rod, already homesick
For the big lift of these evenings, as your stick
Whacking the tips off weeds and bushes
Beats out of time, and beats, but flushes
Nothing: that original townland
Still tongue-tied in the straw tied by your hand.

The end of art is peace
Could be the motto of this frail device
That I have pinned up on our deal dresser –
Like a drawn snare
Slipped lately by the spirit of the corn
Yet burnished by its passage, and still warm.

The Railway Children

When we climbed the slopes of the cutting
We were eye-level with the white cups
Of the telegraph poles and the sizzling wires.

Like lovely freehand they curved for miles
East and miles west beyond us, sagging
Under their burden of swallows.

We were small and thought we knew nothing
Worth knowing. We thought words travelled the wires
In the shiny pouches of raindrops,

Each one seeded full with the light
Of the sky, the gleam of the lines, and ourselves
So infinitesimally scaled

We could stream through the eye of a needle.

Seeing Things

I

Inishbofin on a Sunday morning.
Sunlight, turfsmoke, seagulls, boatslip, diesel.
One by one we were being handed down
Into a boat that dipped and shilly-shallied
Scaresomely every time. We sat tight
On short cross-benches, in nervous twos and threes,
Obedient, newly close, nobody speaking
Except the boatmen, as the gunwales sank
And seemed they might ship water any minute.
The sea was very calm but even so,
When the engine kicked and our ferryman
Swayed for balance, reaching for the tiller,
I panicked at the shiftiness and heft
Of the craft itself. What guaranteed us –
That quick response and buoyancy and swim –
Kept me in agony. All the time
As we went sailing evenly across
The deep, still, seeable-down-into water,
It was as if I looked from another boat
Sailing through air, far up, and could see
How riskily we fared into the morning,
And loved in vain our bare, bowed, numbered heads.

II

Claritas. The dry-eyed Latin word
Is perfect for the carved stone of the water
Where Jesus stands up to his unwet knees
And John the Baptist pours out more water
Over his head: all this in bright sunlight
On the façade of a cathedral. Lines
Hard and thin and sinuous represent
The flowing river. Down between the lines
Little antic fish are all go. Nothing else.
And yet in that utter visibility
The stone's alive with what's invisible:
Waterweed, stirred sand-grains hurrying off,
The shadowy, unshadowed stream itself.
All afternoon, heat wavered on the steps
And the air we stood up to our eyes in wavered
Like the zig-zag hieroglyph for life itself.

III

Once upon a time my undrowned father
Walked into our yard. He had gone to spray
Potatoes in a field on the riverbank
And wouldn't bring me with him. The horse-sprayer
Was too big and new-fangled, bluestone might
Burn me in the eyes, the horse was fresh, I
Might scare the horse, and so on. I threw stones
At a bird on the shed roof, as much for
The clatter of the stones as anything,
But when he came back, I was inside the house
And saw him out the window, scatter-eyed
And daunted, strange without his hat,
His step unguided, his ghosthood immanent.
When he was turning on the riverbank,
The horse had rusted and reared up and pitched
Cart and sprayer and everything off balance

So the whole rig went over into a deep
Whirlpool, hoofs, chains, shafts, cartwheels, barrel
And tackle, all tumbling off the world,
And the hat already merrily swept along
The quieter reaches. That afternoon
I saw him face to face, he came to me
With his damp footprints out of the river,
And there was nothing between us there
That might not still be happily ever after.

MICHAEL LONGLEY (b.1939)

Michael Longley was born in Belfast in 1939. He studied Classics at Trinity College, Dublin, and has worked as a teacher and for the Arts Council of Northern Ireland. He also edited and introduced Louis MacNeice's Selected Poems *(1988). His collections include* Poems 1963–1983, Gorse Fires *which won the 1991 Whitbread Poetry Award and* The Ghost Orchid *(1995). He is married to the critic Edna Longley and lives in Belfast.*

Wounds

Here are two pictures from my father's head –
I have kept them like secrets until now:
First, the Ulster Division at the Somme
Going over the top with 'Fuck the Pope!'
'No Surrender!': a boy about to die,
Screaming 'Give 'em one for the Shankill!'
'Wilder than Gurkhas' were my father's words
Of admiration and bewilderment.
Next comes the London-Scottish padre
Resettling kilts with his swagger-stick,
With a stylish backhand and a prayer.
Over a landscape of dead buttocks

My father followed him for fifty years.
At last, a belated casualty,
He said – lead traces flaring till they hurt –
'I am dying for King and Country, slowly.'
I touched his hand, his thin head I touched.

Now, with military honours of a kind,
With his badges, his medals like rainbows,
His spinning compass, I bury beside him
Three teenage soldiers, bellies full of
Bullets and Irish beer, their flies undone.
A packet of Woodbines I throw in,
A lucifer, the Sacred Heart of Jesus
Paralysed as heavy guns put out
The night-light in a nursery for ever;
Also a bus-conductor's uniform –
He collapsed beside his carpet-slippers
Without a murmur, shot through the head
By a shivering boy who wandered in
Before they could turn the television down
Or tidy away the supper dishes.
To the children, to a bewildered wife,
I think 'Sorry Missus' was what he said.

The Linen Industry

Pulling up flax after the blue flowers have fallen
And laying our handfuls in the peaty water
To rot those grasses to the bone, or building stooks
That recall the skirts of an invisible dancer,

We become a part of the linen industry
And follow its processes to the grubby town
Where fields are compacted into window-boxes
And there is little room among the big machines.

But even in our attic under the skylight
We make love on a bleach green, the whole meadow
Draped with material turning white in the sun
As though snow reluctant to melt were our attire.

What's passion but a battering of stubborn stalks,
Then a gentle combing out of fibres like hair
And a weaving of these into christening robes,
Into garments for a marriage or funeral?

Since it's like a bereavement once the labour's done
To find ourselves last workers in a dying trade,
Let flax be our matchmaker, our undertaker,
The provider of sheets for whatever the bed –

And be shy of your breasts in the presence of death,
Say that you look more beautiful in linen
Wearing white petticoats, the bow on your bodice
A butterfly attending the embroidered flowers.

Detour

I want my funeral to include this detour
Down the single street of a small market town,
On either side of the procession such names
As Philbin, O'Malley, MacNamara, Keane.
A reverent pause to let a herd of milkers pass
Will bring me face to face with grubby parsnips,
Cauliflowers that glitter after a sunshower,
Then hay rakes, broom handles, gas cylinders.
Reflected in the slow sequence of shop windows
I shall be part of the action when his wife
Draining the potatoes into a steamy sink
Calls to the butcher to get ready for dinner
And the publican descends to change a barrel.
From behind the one locked door for miles around

I shall prolong a detailed conversation
With the man in the concrete telephone kiosk
About where my funeral might be going next.

An Amish Rug

As if a one-room schoolhouse were all we knew
And our clothes were black, our underclothes black,
Marriage a horse and buggy going to church
And the children silhouettes in a snowy field,

I bring you this patchwork like a smallholding
Where I served as the hired boy behind the harrow,
Its threads the colour of cantaloupe and cherry
Securing hay bales, corn cobs, tobacco leaves.

You may hang it on the wall, a cathedral window,
Or lay it out on the floor beside our bed
So that whenever we undress for sleep or love
We shall step over it as over a flowerbed.

Ceasefire

I

Put in mind of his own father and moved to tears
Achilles took him by the hand and pushed the old king
Gently away, but Priam curled up at his feet and
Wept with him until their sadness filled the building.

II

Taking Hector's corpse into his own hands Achilles
Made sure it was washed and, for the old king's sake,
Laid out in uniform, ready for Priam to carry
Wrapped like a present home to Troy at daybreak.

III

When they had eaten together, it pleased them both
To stare at each other's beauty as lovers might,
Achilles built like a god, Priam good-looking still
And full of conversation, who earlier had sighed:

IV

'I get down on my knees and do what must be done
And kiss Achilles' hand, the killer of my son.'

PAULINE STAINER (b.1941)

Pauline Stainer was born in Essex in 1941, was educated at Oxford and has worked in a
mental hospital, a pub and a library. She was one of the New Generation Poets in 1994,
and her collections include The Ice Pilot Speaks *(1994) and* The Wound-dresser's
Dream *(1996).*

Sighting the Slave Ship

We came to unexpected latitudes –
sighted the slave ship
during divine service
on deck.

In earlier dog-days
we had made landfall
between forests of sandalwood,
taken on salt, falcons and sulphur.

What haunted us later
was not the cool dispensing
of sacrament
in the burnished doldrums

but something more exotic –
that sense
of a slight shift of cargo
while becalmed.

DEREK MAHON (b.1941)

Derek Mahon was born in Belfast in 1941 and educated at Trinity College, Dublin. For some years he worked in London as a journalist, theatre critic, screenwriter, features and poetry editor. He has published several books of poetry and a number of verse translations, including Molière's The School for Wives *(1986) and* Selected Poems of Philippe Jaccottet *(1988). His* Selected Poems, *containing poems from almost thirty years, was published in 1992.*

As It Should Be

We hunted the mad bastard
Through bog, moorland, rock, to the star-lit west
And gunned him down in a blind yard
Between ten sleeping lorries
And an electricity generator.

Let us hear no idle talk
Of the moon in the Yellow River.
The air blows softer since his departure.

Since his tide burial during school hours
Our kiddies have known no bad dreams.
Their cries echo lightly along the coast.

This is as it should be.
They will thank us for it when they grow up
To a world with method in it.

The Last of the Fire Kings

I want to be
Like the man who descends
At two milk churns

With a bulging
String bag and vanishes
Where the lane turns,

Or the man
Who drops at night
From a moving train

And strikes out over the fields
Where fireflies glow
Not knowing a word of the language.

Either way, I am
Through with history –
Who lives by the sword

Dies by the sword.
Last of the fire kings, I shall
Break with tradition and

Die by my own hand
Rather than perpetuate
The barbarous cycle.

Five years I have reigned
During which time
I have lain awake each night

And prowled by day
In the sacred grove
For fear of the usurper,

Perfecting my cold dream
Of a place out of time,
A palace of porcelain

Where the frugivorous
Inheritors recline
In their rich fabrics
Far from the sea.

But the fire-loving
People, rightly perhaps,
Will not countenance this.

Demanding that I inhabit,
Like them, a world of
Sirens, bin-lids
And bricked-up windows –

Not to release them
From the ancient curse
But to die their creature and be thankful.

Matthew V. 29–30

Lord, mine eye offended, so I plucked it out.
　　Imagine my chagrin
when the offence continued.
　　So I plucked out
the other; but the offence continued.

In the dark now, and working by touch,
　　I shaved my head.
(The offence continued.)
　　Removed an ear,
another, dispatched the nose.
　　The offence continued.
Imagine my chagrin.

Next, in long strips, the skin –
   razored the tongue, the toes,
the personal nitty-gritty.
    The offence continued.

But now, the thing finding its own momentum,
   the more so since
     the offence continued,
I entered upon a prolonged course
   of lobotomy and vivisection,
    reducing the self
to a rubble of organs, a wreckage of bones
   in the midst of which, somewhere,
    the offence continued.

Quicklime, then, for the calcium, paraquat
   for the unregenerate offal;
a spreading of topsoil
   a ploughing of this
    and a sowing of it with barley.

Paraffin for the records of birth, flu
   and abortive scholarship,
for the whimsical postcards, the cheques
   dancing like hail,
the surviving copies of poems published
   and unpublished; a scalpel
for the casual turns of phrase engraved
   on the minds of others;
an aerosol for the stray thoughts
   hanging in air,
for the people who breathed them in.

Sadly, therefore, deletion of the many people
   from their desks, beds, breakfasts,
    buses and catamarans;
deletion of their machinery and architecture,

all evidence whatever
of civility and reflection,
of laughter and tears.

Destruction of all things on which
that reflection fed,
of vegetable and bird;
erosion of all rocks
from the holiest mountain
to the least stone;
evaporation of all seas,
the extinction of heavenly bodies –
until, at last, offence
was not to be found
in that silence without bound.

Only then was I fit for human society.

A Disused Shed in Co. Wexford

Let them not forget us, the weak souls among
the asphodels –
Seferis, *Mythistorema*

for J. G. Farrell

Even now there are places where a thought might grow –
Peruvian mines, worked out and abandoned
To a slow clock of condensation,
An echo trapped for ever, and a flutter
Of wildflowers in the lift-shaft,
Indian compounds where the wind dances
And a door bangs with diminished confidence,
Lime crevices behind rippling rainbarrels,
Dog corners for bone burials;
And in a disused shed in Co. Wexford,

Deep in the grounds of a burnt-out hotel,
Among the bathtubs and the washbasins
A thousand mushrooms crowd to a keyhole.
This is the one star in their firmament
Or frames a star within a star.
What should they do there but desire?
So many days beyond the rhododendrons
With the world waltzing in its bowl of cloud,
They have learnt patience and silence
Listening to the rooks querulous in the high wood.

They have been waiting for us in a foetor
Of vegetable sweat since civil war days,
Since the gravel-crunching, interminable departure
Of the expropriated mycologist.
He never came back, and light since then
Is a keyhole rusting gently after rain.
Spiders have spun, flies dusted to mildew
And once a day, perhaps, they have heard something –
A trickle of masonry, a shout from the blue
Or a lorry changing gear at the end of the lane.

There have been deaths, the pale flesh flaking
Into the earth that nourished it;
And nightmares, born of these and the grim
Dominion of stale air and rank moisture.
Those nearest the door grow strong –
'Elbow room! Elbow room!'
The rest, dim in a twilight of crumbling
Utensils and broken flower-pots, groaning
For their deliverance, have been so long
Expectant that there is left only the posture.

A half century, without visitors, in the dark –
Poor preparation for the cracking lock
And creak of hinges. Magi, moonmen,
Powdery prisoners of the old regime,

Web-throated, stalked like triffids, racked by drought
And insomnia, only the ghost of a scream
At the flash-bulb firing squad we wake them with
Shows there is life yet in their feverish forms.
Grown beyond nature now, soft food for worms,
They lift frail heads in gravity and good faith.

They are begging us, you see, in their wordless way,
To do something, to speak on their behalf
Or at least not to close the door again.
Lost people of Treblinka and Pompeii!
'Save us, save us,' they seem to say,
'Let the god not abandon us
Who have come so far in darkness and in pain.
We too had our lives to live.
You with your light meter and relaxed itinerary,
Let not our naive labours have been in vain!'

EILÉAN NÍ CHUILLEANÁIN (b.1942)

Eiléan Ní Chuilleanáin was born in Cork in 1942 and lives in Dublin, where she teaches at Trinity College. She is co-editor of the magazine Cyphers. *Her books include* The Second Voyage *(1986) and* The Magdalene Sermon *(1989).*

Deaths and Engines

We came down above the houses
In a stiff curve, and
At the edge of Paris airport
Saw an empty tunnel
– The back half of a plane, black
On the snow, nobody near it,
Tubular, burnt-out and frozen.

When we faced again
The snow-white runways in the dark
No sound came over
The loudspeakers, except the sighs
Of the lonely pilot.

The cold of metal wings is contagious:
Soon you will need wings of your own,
Cornered in the angle where
Time and life like a knife and fork
Cross, and the lifeline in your palm
Breaks, and the curve of an aeroplane's track
Meets the straight skyline.

The images of relief:
Hospital pyjamas, screens round a bed
A man with a bloody face
Sitting up in bed, conversing cheerfully
Through cut lips:
These will fail you some time.

You will find yourself alone
Accelerating down a blind
Alley, too late to stop
And know how light your death is;
You will be scattered like wreckage,
The pieces every one a different shape
Will spin and lodge in the hearts
Of all who love you.

DOUGLAS DUNN (b.1942)

Douglas Dunn was born in 1942 in Inchinnan and grew up in Renfrewshire. He worked as a librarian at the University of Hull, and his first book, Terry Street *(1969), drew on his experiences and observations of that city. He has won numerous awards for his work, including the Whitbread Book of the Year in 1985 for his collection* Elegies. *He has also published drama, short stories and edited* The Faber Book of Twentieth Century Scottish Poetry *(1992). He is a professor in the School of English at the University of St Andrews and lives in North Fife.*

On Roofs of Terry Street

Television aerials, Chinese characters
In the lower sky, wave gently in the smoke.

Nest-building sparrows peck at moss,
Urban flora and fauna, soft, unscrupulous.

Rain drying on the slates shines sometimes.
A builder is repairing someone's leaking roof.

He kneels upright to rest his back.
His trowel catches the light and becomes precious.

The Come-on

'. . . the guardian, the king's son, who kept watch over the gates of the garden in which I wanted to live.'
Albert Camus

To have watched the soul of my people
   Fingered by the callous
Enlivens the bitter ooze from my grudge.
   Mere seepage from 'background'
Takes over, blacking out what intellect
   Was nursed by school or book

Or had accrued by questioning the world.
    Enchanting, beloved texts
Searched in for a generous mandate for
    Believing who I am,
What I have lived and felt, might just as well
    Not exist when the vile
Come on with their 'coals in the bath' stories
    Or mock at your accent.
Even now I am an embarrassment
    To myself, my candour.
Listen now to the 'professional classes'
    Renewing claims to 'rights',
Possession of land, ownership of work,
    Decency of 'standards'.
In the bleep-bleep of versicles, leisure-novels,
    Black traffic of Oxbridge –
Books and bicycles, the bile of success –
    Men dressed in prunella
Utter credentials and their culture rules us,
    A culture of connivance,
Of 'authority', arts of bland recoveries.
    Where, then, is 'poetry'?
Brothers, they say that we have no culture.
    We are of the wrong world,
Our level is the popular, the media,
    The sensational columns,
Unless we enter through a narrow gate
    In a wall they have built
To join them in the 'disinterested tradition'
    Of tea, of couplets dipped
In sherry and the decanted, portentous remark.
    Therefore, we'll deafen them
With the dull staccato of our typewriters.
    But do not misbehave –
Threats and thrashings won't work: we're outnumbered.
    Drink ale if you must still,

But learn to tell one good wine from another –
    Our honesty is cunning.
We will beat them with decorum, with manners,
    As sly as language is.
Take tea with the king's son at the seminars –
    He won't know what's happening.
Carry your learning as does the mimic his face.
    Know one knife from another.
You will lose heart: don't show it. Be patient;
    And sit on that high wall
In its obstacle glass chips, its barbed wire,
    Watching the gardeners.
One day we will leap down, into the garden,
    And open the gate – *wide, wide.*
We too shall be kings' sons and guardians,
    And then there will be no wall:
Our grudges will look quaint and terrible.

St Kilda's Parliament: 1879–1979

The photographer revisits his picture

On either side of a rock-paved lane,
Two files of men are standing barefooted,
Bearded, waistcoated, each with a tam-o'-shanter
On his head, and most with a set half-smile
That comes from their companionship with rock,
With soft mists, with rain, with roaring gales,
And from a diet of solan goose and eggs,
A diet of dulse and sloke and sea-tangle,
And ignorance of what a pig, a bee, a rat,
Or rabbit look like, although they remember
The three apples brought here by a traveller
Five years ago, and have discussed them since.
And there are several dogs doing nothing

Who seem contemptuous of my camera,
And a woman who might not believe it
If she were told of the populous mainland.
A man sits on a bank by the door of his house,
Staring out to sea and at a small craft
Bobbing there, the little boat that brought me here,
Whose carpentry was slowly shaped by waves,
By a history of these northern waters.
Wise men or simpletons – it is hard to tell –
But in that way they almost look alike
You also see how each is individual,
Proud of his shyness and of his small life
On this outcast of the Hebrides
With his eyes full of weather and seabirds,
Fish, and whatever morsel he grows here.
Clear, too, is manhood, and how each man looks
Secure in the love of a woman who
Also knows the wisdom of the sun rising,
Of weather in the eyes like landmarks.
Fifty years before depopulation –
Before the boats came at their own request
To ease them from their dying babies –
It was easy, even then, to imagine
St Kilda return to its naked self,
Its archaeology of hazelraw
And footprints stratified beneath the lichen.
See, how simple it all is, these toes
Playfully clutching the edge of a boulder.
It is a remote democracy, where men,
In manacles of place, outstare a sea
That rattes back its manacles of salt,
The moody jailer of the wild Atlantic.
      Traveller, tourist with your mind set on
Romantic Staffas and materials for
Winter conversations, if you should go there,
Landing at sunrise on its difficult shores,

On St Kilda you will surely hear Gaelic
Spoken softly like a poetry of ghosts
By those who never were contorted by
Hierarchies of cuisine and literacy.
You need only look at the faces of these men
Standing there like everybody's ancestors,
This flick of time I shuttered on a face.
Look at their sly, assuring mockery.
They are aware of what we are up to
With our internal explorations, our
Designs of affluence and education.
They know us so well, and are not jealous,
Whose be-all and end-all was an eternal
Casual husbandry upon a toehold
Of Europe, which, when failing, was not their fault.
You can see they have already prophesied
A day when survivors look across the stern
Of a departing vessel for the last time
At their gannet-shrouded cliffs, and the farewells
Of the St Kilda mouse and St Kilda wren
As they fall into the texts of specialists,
Ornithological visitors at the prow
Of a sullenly managed boat from the future.
They pose for ever outside their parliament,
Looking at me, as if they have grown from
Affection scattered across my own eyes.
And it is because of this that I, who took
This photograph in a year of many events –
The Zulu massacres, Tchaikovsky's opera –
Return to tell you this, and that after
My many photographs of distressed cities,
My portraits of successive elegants,
Of the emaciated dead, the lost empires,
Exploded fleets, and of the writhing flesh
Of dead civilians and commercial copulations,
That after so much of that larger franchise

It is to this island that I return.
Here I whittle time, like a dry stick,
From sunrise to sunset, among the groans
And sighings of a tongue I cannot speak,
Outside a parliament, looking at them,
As they, too, must always look at me
Looking through my apparatus at them
Looking. Benevolent, or malign? But who,
At this late stage, could tell, or think it worth it?
For I was there, and am, and I forget.

Reading Pascal in the Lowlands

His aunt has gone astray in her concern
And the boy's mum leans across his wheelchair
To talk to him. She points to the river.
An aged angler and a boy they know
Cast lazily into the rippled sun.
They go there, into the dappled grass, shadows
Bickering and falling from the shaken leaves.

His father keeps apart from them, walking
On the beautiful grass that is bright green
In the sunlight of July at 7 p.m.
He sits on the bench beside me, saying
It is a lovely evening, and I rise
From my sorrows, agreeing with him.
His large hand picks tobacco from a tin;

His smile falls at my feet, on the baked earth
Shoes have shuffled over and ungrassed.
It is discourteous to ask about
Accidents, or of the sick, the unfortunate.
I do not need to, for he says 'Leukaemia'.
We look at the river, his son holding a rod,
The line going downstream in a cloud of flies.

I close my book, the *Pensées* of Pascal.
I am light with meditation, religiose
And mystic with a day of solitude.
I do not tell him of my own sorrows.
He is bored with misery and premonition.
He has seen the limits of time, asking 'Why?'
Nature is silent on that question.

A swing squeaks in the distance. Runners jog
Round the perimeter. He is indiscreet.
His son is eight years old, with months to live.
His right hand trembles on his cigarette.
He sees my book, and then he looks at me,
Knowing me for a stranger. I have said
I am sorry. What more is there to say?

He is called over to the riverbank.
I go away, leaving the Park, walking through
The Golf Course, and then a wood, climbing,
And then bracken and gorse, sheep pasturage.
From a panoptic hill I look down on
A little town, its estuary, its bridge,
Its houses, churches, its undramatic streets.

Land Love

We stood here in the coupledom of us.
I showed her this – a pool with leaping trout,
Split-second saints drawn in a rippled nimbus.

We heard the night-boys in the fir trees shout.
Dusk was an insect-hovered dark water,
The calling of lost children, stars coming out.

With all the feelings of a widower
Who does not live there now, I dream my place.
I go by the soft paths, alone with her.

Dusk is a listening, a whispered grace
Voiced on a bank, a time that is all ears
For the snapped twig, the strange wind on your face.

She waits at the door of the hemisphere
In her harvest dress, in the remote
Local August that is everywhere and here.

What rustles in the leaves, if it is not
What I asked for, an opening of doors
To a half-heard religious anecdote?

Monogamous swans on the darkened mirrors
Picture the private grace of man and wife
In its white poise, its sleepy portraitures.

Night is its Dog Star, its eyelet of grief
A high, lit echo of the starry sheaves.
A puff of hedge-dust loosens in the leaves.
Such love that lingers on the fields of life!

HUGO WILLIAMS (b.1942)

Hugo Williams was born in Windsor in 1942 and grew up in Sussex. He has worked as a journalist, editor, theatre and television critic, and is currently the film critic for Harper's & Queen *and a columnist for the* Times Literary Supplement. *His prose works include the travel book,* No Particular Place To Go *(1980), and a collection of essays,* Freelancing – Adventures of a Poet *(1995). His volumes of poetry include* Selected Poems *(1989) and more recently* Dock Leaves *(1994).*

A Picture of a Girl in a Bikini

I look over the bannisters and see, far down,
Miss Pyke taking Callover. I push my feet
into a pair of Cambridge house shoes

half my size and shuffle downstairs.
When I answer my name there is a long silence,
then Miss Pyke asks me where I've been.
I tell her I was reading a book
and didn't notice the time.

I see I have a smaller desk this term
as a punishment for being late.
I have to sit sideways, facing Armitage,
who eats little pieces of blotting paper
dipped in ink. When the bell goes
I barge off down Lower Corridor
with my head down and my elbows out,
knocking everyone flying.

Hurrah! There's a letter for me today.
I'd rather have a parcel, but I'm always happy
when I see the familiar blue envelope
propped on the mantelpiece
on the other side of School Hall.
I don't open it straight away, of course.
I shove it in my pocket
and read it later, like a man.

I'm standing outside the Headmaster's Study
waiting for the green light to come on.
Either I've failed Common Entrance
or my parents have died. When I go in
he's sitting at his desk, staring out the window.
For a long time we watch Sgt Burrows
pushing his marker round Long Field,
Mr Harvey taking fielding practice.

The Headmaster pulls his writing case towards him
and opens it with his paper knife.
Inside is the worst news in the world,
my copy of Man Junior with a picture of a girl
in a bikini playing with a beach ball.

I must have left it under my mattress.
The Headmaster looks at me in disbelief
and asks, 'What is the meaning of this?'

Standstill

*A last visit to the long-abandoned 'Gosses' on Harold Macmillan's
Birch Grove estate, soon to be levelled as part of a new golf course.*

I apologize to the driver
for the branches closing in,
almost bringing us to a standstill.
He doesn't seem to mind.
'I'm like you,' he tells me, as we move aside
a tree blown across the drive by the storm.
'I had to come back home
to see my own particular corner of the UK
before I died. Our daughter wanted to stay out there
in New Zealand and get married.
Don't ask me why.
She's a karate champion.'

We have turned a corner in the drive, past the swing,
past the gibbet, past the tree
where we buried the screaming idol's head
of Elsie Byers, the American agent.
Flowering creepers and bushes
crowd round the old house,
as if some great party were being given there
long ago, the party of the season.
Look, the same door! The same knocker!
The same doorhandle I held
when I came back from going round the world!
The same footscraper!

The driver seems to share my astonishment
that everything is the same yet different
when you look through a window
into your old room
and see your head lying there on the pillow,
innocent of your life, but dreaming your dreams.
'Where is it you say old Supermac used to live?
I want to see the field
where President Kennedy landed in his helicopter.
I was cheering and waving the American flag.
Our daughter had just been born. We were on our way
to start a new life in New Zealand.'

Old Boy

Our lesson is really idiotic today,
as if Mr Ray has forgotten
everything he ever knew
about the Reformation
and is making it up as he goes along.

I feel like pointing out
where he's going astray,
but I'm frightened he'll hold up
some of my grey hair
and accuse me of cheating.

How embarrassing
if I turned out to be wrong after all
and Mr Ray was right. Luckily,
I'm in the top class
and come top easily, without trying,
the way it should be.

I could do better
in the written answer questions,
but everyone looks up to me
because I've been round the world.
and have my own wife and motorbike.

I'm wearing my old school scarf
that I thought was lost forever.
Brown and magenta quarters,
the smartest colours in the world.
It was round my neck all the time.

VICKI FEAVER (b.1943)

Vicki Feaver was born in 1943 in Nottingham, read music at university and teaches English and creative writing at the West Sussex Institute. Her collections include Close Relatives *(1981) and* The Handless Maiden *(1994).*

Rope

I gripped with my feet, climbed
until I could see through the hoops
of the netball posts; slid back –
burning the skin off my fingers.
Under the mound of coarse new hair,
curved bone, secretly-folded flesh,
where the rope pressed, I'd roused
a live nest: a wriggling litter
like the baby voles I'd found
in a squeaking hole in the grass –
hearts palpitating in furless,
pastry-thin sides; or featherless
chicks – all claws and beaks

and black-veined wings –
that dropped from gutters.
I had to squeeze my thighs
to stop them breaking out –
squealing and squawking
into the gym's blue steel rafters,
or scrabbling down the inside
of my legs, over whitened plimsolls,
making the games mistress shriek.

TOM LEONARD (b.1944)

Tom Leonard was born in Glasgow in 1944 and studied at Glasgow University. Much of his work extends from the speaking voice associated with that city, being written in phonetically spelt Glasgow dialect, and his reputation was established in 1970 with the publication of Six Glasgow Poems *and* A Priest Came on at Merkland Street. *In 1984 he published* Intimate Voices: Selected Work 1965–1983.

The Voyeur

what's your favourite word dearie
is it wee
I hope it's wee
wee's such a nice wee word
like a wee hairy dog
with two wee eyes
such a nice wee word to play with dearie
you can say it quickly
with a wee smile
and a wee glance to the side
or you can say it slowly dearie
with your mouth a wee bit open
and a wee sigh dearie

a wee sigh
put your wee head on my shoulder dearie
oh my
a great wee word
and Scottish
it makes you proud

from Unrelated Incidents

(3)
this is thi
six a clock
news thi
man said n
thi reason
a talk wia
BBC accent
iz coz yi
widny wahnt
mi ti talk
aboot thi
trooth wia
voice lik
wanna yoo
scruff. if
a toktaboot
thi trooth
lik wanna yoo
scruff yi
widny thingk
it wuz troo.
jist wanna yoo
scruff tokn.
thirza right
way ti spell

ana right way
ti tok it. this
is me tokn yir
right way a
spellin. this
is ma trooth.
yooz doant no
thi trooth
yirsellz cawz
yi canny talk
right. this is
the six a clock
nyooz. belt up.

hangup

aye bit naw

naw bit
aye bit

away
away yi go
whut

mini whut
minimalism

aw minimalism
minimalism aye

aye right
aye right inuff
aye right inuff definitely

aye bit
naw bit

a stull think yi huvty say sumhm

CRAIG RAINE (b.1944)

Craig Raine was born in Shildon, Co. Durham, in 1944, and was educated at Oxford, where he is now Fellow in English at New College. His book A Martian Sends a Postcard Home *(1979) gave rise to the so-called 'Martian school' of poetry, and more recent collections include the book-length poem-novel* History: The Home Movie, *published in 1994. He has also written theatre work, a libretto, a book of essays and has edited selections of Kipling's poetry and prose. His other collections of poetry include* The Onion, Memory *(1978),* Rich *(1984) and* Clay. Whereabouts Unknown *(1996).*

The Onion, Memory

Divorced, but friends again at last,
we walk old ground together
in bright blue uncomplicated weather.
We laugh and pause
to hack to bits these tiny dinosaurs,
prehistoric, crenellated, cast
between the tractor ruts in mud.

On the green, a junior Douglas Fairbanks,
swinging on the chestnut's unlit chandelier,
defies the corporation spears –
a single rank around the bole,
rusty with blood.
Green, tacky phalluses curve up, romance.
A gust – the old flag blazes on its pole.

In the village bakery
the pasty babies pass
from milky slump to crusty cadaver,
from crib to coffin – without palaver.
All's over in a flash,
too silently . . .

Tonight the arum lilies fold
back napkins monogrammed in gold,
crisp and laundered fresh.
Those crustaceous gladioli, on the sly,
reveal the crimson flower-flesh
inside their emerald armour plate.
The uncooked herrings blink a tearful eye.
The candles palpitate.
The Oistrakhs bow and scrape
in evening dress, on Emi-tape.

Outside the trees are bending over backwards
to please the wind: the shining sword
grass flattens on its belly.
The white-thorn's frillies offer no resistance.
In the fridge, a heart-shaped jelly
strives to keep a sense of balance.

I slice up the onions. You sew up a dress.
This is the quiet echo – flesh –
white muscle on white muscle,
intimately folded skin,
finished with a satin rustle.
One button only to undo, sewn up with shabby thread.
It is the onion, memory,
that makes me cry.

Because there's everything and nothing to be said,
the clock with hands held up before its face,
stammers softly on, trying to complete a phrase –
while we, together and apart,
repeat unfinished gestures got by heart.

And afterwards, I blunder with the washing on the line –
headless torsos, faceless lovers, friends of mine.

A Martian Sends a Postcard Home

Caxtons are mechanical birds with many wings
and some are treasured for their markings –

they cause the eyes to melt
or the body to shriek without pain.

I have never seen one fly, but
sometimes they perch on the hand.

Mist is when the sky is tired of flight
and rests its soft machine on ground:

then the world is dim and bookish
like engravings under tissue paper.

Rain is when the earth is television.
It has the property of making colours darker.

Model T is a room with the lock inside –
a key is turned to free the world

for movement, so quick there is a film
to watch for anything missed.

But time is tied to the wrist
or kept in a box, ticking with impatience.

In homes, a haunted apparatus sleeps,
that snores when you pick it up.

If the ghost cries, they carry it
to their lips and soothe it to sleep

with sounds. And yet, they wake it up
deliberately, by tickling with a finger.

Only the young are allowed to suffer
openly. Adults go to a punishment room

with water but nothing to eat.
They lock the door and suffer the noises

alone. No one is exempt
and everyone's pain has a different smell.

At night, when all the colours die,
they hide in pairs

and read about themselves –
in colour, with their eyelids shut.

The Man Who Invented Pain

He lifted the wicker lid
and pigeons poured
past his hands,

a ravel of light
like oxygen
escaping underwater.

Loss of privileges
in peacetime; in war,
a capital offence.

He offered no defence,
simply composed
a non-existent life

in letters home,
enough for a year,
to be posted in order,

of which the last began:
Dear Mother, Dear Dad,
Thanks for yours.

Today, a Tuesday,
we shot a man
at 0800 hours.

Try to imagine,
if you can,
the subdued feel

of a Sunday morning
and the quiet clash
of a dixie lid,

lifting and lapsing
like a censer
at mass.

Imagine held hats,
blown about hair
and the firing squad

down on one knee,
close enough to see
his Adam's apple

genuflect
just once
before they fired.

And then imagine
the rest of the day:
the decent interval

before the men
began to form a queue
with mess tins,

the way in which
the day remained
a Sunday until dark.

Things were touched
with reverence.
Even the sergeant,

feeling for fags
in his battle dress,
patted his pockets

uncertainly,
in turn, and again,
as if he'd forgotten

the sign of the cross,
and the captain
on a canvas stool

sat like a priest,
with praying eyes
and inclined head,

while his batman cut
and curls fell
all over his surplice.

Imagine the sun
waking the flies
to a confessional buzz

in the camp latrines,
and each latrine
a taut box kite

waiting for wind
on the kind of day
a man might read

the Sunday paper
by his pigeon cree,
or nervously

walk out to bat
and notice the green
on a fielder's knee.

JEFFREY WAINWRIGHT (b.1944)

Jeffrey Wainwright was born in Stoke-on-Trent in 1944. He has taught in Wales and America, and is currently a lecturer at the Metropolitan University of Manchester, in the city where he lives. His work includes a translation of Charles Peguy's play The Mystery of the Charity of Joan of Arc, *and his* Selected Poems *was published in 1985.*

As He Found Her

She lay a long time as he found her,
Half on her side, askew, her cheek pressed to the floor.
He sat at the table there and watched,
His mind sometimes all over the place,
And then asking over and over
If she were dead: 'Are you dead, Poll, are you dead?'

For these hours, each one dressed in its figure
On the mantelpiece, love sits with him.
Habit, mutuality, sweetheartedness,
Drop through his body,
And he is not able now to touch her –
A bar of daylight, no more than
Across a table, flows between them.

KIT WRIGHT (b.1944)

Kit Wright was born in Kent in 1944 and has worked as a lecturer in Britain and abroad. He is well-known for his books of children's poetry as well as his adult work, and his collections include Poems 1974–1983 *(1988) and* Short Afternoons *(1989).*

I Found South African Breweries Most Hospitable

Meat smell of blood in locked rooms I cannot smell it,
Screams of the brave in torture loges I never heard nor heard of
Apartheid I wouldn't know how to spell it,
None of these things am I paid to believe a word of
For I am a stranger to cant and contumely.
I am a professional cricketer.
My only consideration is my family.

I get my head down nothing to me or mine
Blood is geysering now from ear, from mouth, from eye,
How they take a fresh guard after breaking the spine,
I must play wherever I like or die
So spare me your news your views spare me your homily.
I am a professional cricketer.
My only consideration is my family.

Electrodes wired to their brains they should have had helmets,
Balls wired up they should have been wearing a box,
The danger was the game would turn into a stalemate,
Skin of their feet burnt off I like thick woollen socks
With buckskin boots that accommodate them roomily
For I am a professional cricketer.
My only consideration is my family.

They keep falling out of the window they must be clumsy
And unprofessional not that anyone told me,
Spare me your wittering spare me your whimsy,
Sixty thousand pounds is what they sold me

And I have no brain. I am an anomaly.
I am a professional cricketer.
My only consideration is my family.

DAVID CONSTANTINE (b.1944)

David Constantine was born in Salford in 1944, has lectured in German at Durham University and is Fellow in German at Queen's College, Oxford. He has published novels and short stories, as well as academic work, including a critical introduction to and translations of Friedrich Hölderlin. His Selected Poems *(1991) was followed in 1994 by the book-length poem* Casper Hauser. *He lives in Oxford.*

The Door

Yes, that is the door and behind it they live,
But not grossly as we do. Through a fine sieve
Their people pass the incoming air. They are said
To circulate thoughtfully in walled gardens, the aged –
And they live long – wheeling in chairs. They exchange
Nothing but traditional courtesies. Most strange
However is their manner of dying, for they know the hour,
When it comes, as old elephants do. They devour
Their usual breakfast of plovers' eggs and rise
Then or are lifted by the janitors and without goodbyes
They step or are borne aloft through that door there –
And thus they end. For of course meeting the air,
The air we breathe, they perish instantly,
They go all into dust, into dead dust, and Stanley,
The Sweeper, comes with his brush and shovel and little cart
And sweeps them up and shovels them not apart

But into one black plastic bag with dimps, dog-shit
And all our common dirt. But this they intend and it
Signals their gracious willingness to reside
In the poor heart of life, once they have died.

Watching for Dolphins

In the summer months on every crossing to Piraeus
One noticed that certain passengers soon rose
From seats in the packed saloon and with serious
Looks and no acknowledgement of a common purpose
Passed forward through the small door into the bows
To watch for dolphins. One saw them lose

Every other wish. Even the lovers
Turned their desires on the sea, and a fat man
Hung with equipment to photograph the occasion
Stared like a saint, through sad bi-focals; others,
Hopeless themselves, looked to the children for they
Would see dolphins if anyone would. Day after day

Or on their last opportunity all gazed
Undecided whether a flat calm were favourable
Or a sea the sun and the wind between them raised
To a likeness of dolphins. Were gulls a sign, that fell
Screeching from the sky or over an unremarkable place
Sat in a silent school? Every face

After its character implored the sea.
All, unaccustomed, wanted epiphany,
Praying the sky would clang and the abused Aegean
Reverberate with cymbal, gong and drum.
We could not imagine more prayer, and had they then
On the waves, on the climax of our longing come

Smiling, snub-nosed, domed like satyrs, oh
We should have laughed and lifted the children up
Stranger to stranger, pointing how with a leap
They left their element, three or four times, centred
On grace, and heavily and warm re-entered,
Looping the keel. We should have felt them go

Further and further into the deep parts. But soon
We were among the great tankers, under their chains
In black water. We had not seen the dolphins
But woke, blinking. Eyes cast down
With no admission of disappointment the company
Dispersed and prepared to land in the city.

EAVAN BOLAND (b.1944)

Eavan Boland was born in Dublin in 1944 and educated in Ireland, London and New York. She lectured at Trinity College, Dublin, until 1968, and continues to teach, most recently in the United States. Her prose book, Object Lessons, *appeared in 1995, the same year as the publication of her* Collected Poems, *consisting of seven collections published over twenty years.*

Mountain Time

Time is shadowless there: mornings re-occur
only as enchantments, only as time for her

to watch berries ripen by on the mountain ash;
for him, at a short distance from her, to catch fish.

Afterwards, darkness will be only what is left of
a mouth after kissing or a hand laced in a hand;

a branch; a river; will be what is lost of words
as they turn to silences and then to sleep. Yet

when they leave the mountain what he will remember is
the rowan trees: that blemish, that scarlet. She will think of

the arc of the salmon after sudden capture –
its glitter a larceny of daylight on slate.

The Black Lace Fan my Mother Gave Me

It was the first gift he ever gave her,
buying it for five francs in the Galeries
in pre-war Paris. It was stifling.
A starless drought made the nights stormy.

They stayed in the city for the summer.
They met in cafés. She was always early.
He was late. That evening he was later.
They wrapped the fan. He looked at his watch.

She looked down the Boulevard des Capucines.
She ordered more coffee. She stood up.
The streets were emptying. The heat was killing.
She thought the distance smelled of rain and lightning.

These are wild roses, appliqued on silk by hand,
darkly picked, stitched boldly, quickly.
The rest is tortoiseshell and has the reticent,
clear patience of its element. It is

a worn-out, underwater bullion and it keeps,
even now, an inference of its violation.
The lace is overcast as if the weather
it opened for and offset had entered it.

The past is an empty café terrace.
An airless dusk before thunder. A man running.
And no way now to know what happened then –
none at all – unless, of course, you improvise:

The blackbird on this first sultry morning,
in summer, finding buds, worms, fruit,
feels the heat. Suddenly she puts out her wing –
the whole, full, flirtatious span of it.

The Dolls Museum in Dublin

The wounds are terrible. The paint is old.
The cracks along the lips and on the cheeks
cannot be fixed. The cotton lawn is soiled.
The arms are ivory dissolved to wax.

Recall the Quadrille. Hum the waltz.
Promenade on the yacht-club terraces.
Put back the lamps in their copper holders,
the carriage wheels on the cobbled quays.

And recreate Easter in Dublin.
Booted officers. Their mistresses.
Sunlight criss-crossing College Green.
Steam hissing from the flanks of horses.

Here they are. Cradled and cleaned,
held close in the arms of their owners.
Their cold hands clasped by warm hands,
their faces memorized like perfect manners.

The altars are mannerly with linen.
The lilies are whiter than surplices.
The candles are burning and warning:
Rejoice, they whisper. After sacrifice.

Horse-chestnuts hold up their candles.
The Green is vivid with parasols.
Sunlight is pastel and windless.
The bar of the Shelbourne is full.

Laughter and gossip on the terraces.
Rumour and alarm at the barracks.
The Empire is summoning its officers.
The carriages are turning: they are turning back.

Past children walking with governesses,
Looking down, cossetting their dolls,
then looking up as the carriage passes,
the shadow chilling them. Twilight falls.

It is twilight in the dolls' museum. Shadows
remain on the parchment-coloured waists,
are bruises on the stitched cotton clothes,
are hidden in the dimples on the wrists.

The eyes are wide. They cannot address
the helplessness which has lingered in
the airless peace of each glass case:
to have survived. To have been stronger than

a moment. To be the hostages ignorance
takes from time and ornament from destiny. Both.
To be the present of the past. To infer the difference
with a terrible stare. But not feel it. And not know it.

from Writing in a Time of Violence: A Sequence

1:   *That the Science of Cartography is Limited*

– and not simply by the fact that this shading of
forest cannot show the fragrance of balsam,
the gloom of cypresses
is what I wish to prove.

When you and I were first in love we drove
to the borders of Connacht
and entered a wood there.

Look down you said: this was once a famine road.

I looked down at ivy and the scutch grass
rough-cast stone had
disappeared into as you told me
in the second winter of their ordeal, in

1847, when the crop had failed twice,
Relief Committees gave
the starving Irish such roads to build.

Where they died, there the road ended

and ends still and when I take down
the map of this island, it is never so
I can say here is
the masterful, the apt rendering of

the spherical as flat, nor
an ingenious design which persuades a curve
into a plane,
but to tell myself again that

the line which says woodland and cries hunger
and gives out among sweet pine and cypress,
and finds no horizon

will not be there.

PAUL DURCAN (b.1944)

Paul Durcan was born in Dublin in 1944 and studied archaeology and medieval history at University College Cork. He published his first book in 1967, since when there have been fourteen further collections, including Daddy, Daddy *which won the 1990 Whitbread Poetry Prize, and* A Snail in My Prime: New and Selected Poems *(1993). He has given public readings in many countries of the world, and written two books inspired and accompanied by pictures from the National Gallery, London, and the National Gallery of Ireland. He lives in Dublin.*

The Hay-Carrier

After Veronica Bolay

Have you ever saved hay in Mayo in the rain?
Have you ever made hay in Mayo in the sun?
Have you ever carried above your head a haycock on a pitchfork?
Have you ever slept in a haybarn on the road from Mayo into Egypt?
I am a hay-carrier.
My father was a hay-carrier.
My mother was a hay-carrier.
My brothers were hay-carriers.
My sisters were hay-carriers.
My wife is a hay-carrier.
My son is a hay-carrier.
His sons are hay-carriers.
His daughters are hay-carriers.
We were always all hay-carriers.
We will always be hay-carriers.
For the great gate of night stands painted red
And all of heaven lies waiting to be fed.

In Memory of Those Murdered
in the Dublin Massacre, May 1974

In the grime-ridden sunlight in the downtown Wimpy bar
I think of all the crucial aeons – and of the labels
That freedom fighters stick onto the lost destinies of unborn children;
The early morning sunlight carries in the whole street from outside;
The whole wide street from outside through the plate-glass windows;
Wholly, sparklingly, surgingly, carried in from outside;
And the waitresses cannot help but be happy and gay
As they swipe at the tabletops with their dishcloths –
Such a moment as would provide the heroic freedom fighter
With his perfect meat.
And I think of those heroes – heroes? – heroes.

And as I stand up to walk out –
The aproned old woman who's been sweeping the floor
Has mop stuck in bucket, leaning on it;
And she's trembling all over, like a flower in the breeze.
She'd make a mighty fine explosion now, if you were to blow her up:
An explosion of petals, of aeons, and the waitresses too, flying breasts
   and limbs,
For a free Ireland.

Ulysses

I am hiding from my father
On the roof of Joyce's Tower
In Sandycove.
He is downstairs in the gloom
Of the Joyce Museum
Exchanging euphemisms with the curator,
The poet Michael Hartnett,
Meteorological euphemisms,
Wet and cold for June.

I am standing at the battlements.
I am eighteen years old.
The battle is whether or not
He will buy a copy of *Ulysses*.
It is a battle about money
But it is a battle also about morality
Or 'morals' as it is called.
It began this morning at the breakfast table
When I asked him for twenty-one shillings
To buy a copy of *Ulysses*.
He refused on the grounds that on top
Of it being an outrageous sum of money
Which a poorly paid judge could ill afford,
It was a notoriously immoral book.

Even the most liberal-minded Jesuits
Had condemned *Ulysses*
As being blasphemous as well as pornographic.
My mother jumped around from the kitchen sink:
'Give him the money for the wretched book
And let the pair of you stop this nonsense
For pity's sake.
Will we ever see peace and sense in this house?'
My father stormed out of the kitchen,
The *Irish Independent* under his arm:
'I'll not be party to subsidising that blackguard
Bringing works of blasphemy into this house.
In the year of Our Lord nineteen hundred and sixty-three
I will not be an accessory to blasphemy.'

I caught the 46A bus out to Joyce's Tower,
Newly opened as a museum.
The curator offered to share with me
A carafe of vodka left over
From a literary soirée of the night before.
It was the day after Bloomsday.
Monday, 17 June 1963.
We sat in a compatible silence,
Contemplatively, affably,
Until upheaval of gravel
Eradicated reverie.
I rushed to the door and glimpsed
My father at the foot of the iron steps.
I climbed up to the roof, hoping to hide
From him up there in the marine fog,
Foghorns bleating in the bay.

I hear footsteps behind me, I know it is he.
He declares: 'I suppose we will have to buy that book.
What did you say the name of it is?'
I tell him that the name of it is *Ulysses*.
I follow him down the staircase and he submits:

'Mr Hartnett, I understand
You stock copies of a book entitled *Ulysses*.
I would like to purchase one copy of same.'
'Certainly, Your Lordship, certainly,'
Replies the ever-courteous, Chinese-eyed curator.
When from his wingbacked chair behind his desk
He takes from a drawer
A copy of the jade-jacketed *Ulysses*,
The Bodley Head edition,
My father asks him if he would have brown paper
With which to wrap the green, satanic novel,
Make a parcel out of it.
The curator peers into a wastepaper basket
'Made by the Blind',
As if peering down into a bottomless lift shaft,
Casts a funicular, questing second glance at my father
Before fishing out crumpled bags of brown paper
Which the night before had ferried bottles of vodka.
He lays them out on the desk top
And smoothes them, taking pains
To be obsequiously
Extra punctilious, extra fastidious.
Formally, he hands it over to my father,
As if delivering to some abstract and intractable potentate
A peace gift of a pair of old shoes.
My father pronounces: 'Thank you, Mr Hartnett.'
The curator, at his most extravagantly unctuous, replies:
'Very glad to be able to oblige you, Your Lordship.'

My father departed Joyce's Tower with the book.
The next day when I asked my mother if she'd seen it
She said it was in their bedroom beside my father's bed.
Her bed was beside the window and his bed
Was between her bed and the wall.
There it was, on his bedside table,
Ulysses,

With a bookmarker in it – a fruitgum wrapper –
At the close of the opening episode.
When a few weeks later
I got to reading *Ulysses* myself
I found it as strange as my father
And as discordant.
It was not until four years later
When a musical friend
Gave me my first lessons
That *Ulysses* began to sing for me
And I began to sing for my father:
Daddy, Daddy,
My little man, I adore you.

CAROL RUMENS (b.1944)

Carol Rumens was born in London in 1944, and has held several writing fellowships,
most recently at Queen's University, Belfast. She has written plays, short stories, a novel
and has translated poetry from Russian. Her collections of poetry include Thinking
of Skins: New and Selected Poems *(1993) and* Best China Sky *(1995). She is the*
editor of New Women Poets *(1990).*

Stealing the Genre

It was the shortest night of the year. I'd been drinking
But I was quite lucid and calm. So, having seen her
The other side of the bar, shedding her light
On no one who specially deserved it, I got to my feet
And simply went over and asked her, in a low voice,
If she'd come to my bed. She raised her eyebrows strangely
But didn't say 'no'. I went out. I felt her follow.

My mind was a storm as we silently crossed the courtyard
In the moist white chill of the dawn. Dear God, I loved her.
I'd loved her in books, I'd adored her at the first sighting.
But no, I'm a woman, English, not young. How could I?
She'd vanished for years. And now she was walking beside me.
Oh what am I going to do, what are *we* going to do?
Perhaps she'll know. She's probably an old hand
– But this sudden thought was the most disturbing of all.

As soon as we reached my room, though, it was plain
She hadn't a clue. We stood like window-displays
In our dawn-damp suits with the short, straight, hip-hugging skirts
(Our styles are strangely alike, I suppose it's because
Even she has to fight her corner in a man's world)
And discussed the rain, which was coming down, and the view,
Which was nothing much, a fuchsia hedge and some trees,
And we watched each other, as women do watch each other,
And tried not to yawn. Why don't you lie down for a bit?
I whispered, inspired. She gratefully kicked off her shoes.

She was onto the bed in no time, and lay as if dumped
On the furthest edge, her face – dear God – to the wall.
I watched for a while, and, thinking she might be in tears,
Caressed the foam-padded viscose that passed for her shoulder,
And begged her not to feel guilty. Then I discovered
That all she was doing was breathing, dead to the world.

It wasn't an insult, exactly, but it was a let-down
– And yet I admired her. Sleep. If only I could.
I rested my hand at an uncontroversial location
South of her breasts, maybe North, I don't remember,
And ached with desire and regret and rationalisation.
I'd asked her to bed. And she'd come to bed. End of story.
Only it wasn't the story I'd wanted to tell.
Roll on, tomorrow, I urged, but tomorrow retorted:
I'm here already, and nothing ever gets better.

But then, unexpectedly, I began to feel pleased.
To think she was here, at my side, so condensed, so weighty!
In my humble position (a woman, English, not young,
Et cetera) what more could I ask of an Irish dawn
Than this vision, alive, though dead to the world, on my duvet?
What have I done to deserve her? Oh, never mind,
Don't think about words like 'deserve'. So we lay in grace.
The light. Her hair. My hand. Her breath. And the fuchsias.
I thought of the poem I'd write, and fell asleep, smiling.

I woke in a daze of sublime self-congratulation
And saw she was gone. My meadow, my cloud, my aisling!
I could hardly believe my own memory. I wanted to scream
All over the courtyard, come back, come to bed, but how could I?
She might be anywhere, people were thick in the day
Already, and things were normal. Why are things normal?

I keened her name to the walls, I swam bitterest rivers,
I buried my face in the cloth where her blushes had slipped
And left a miraculous print that would baffle the laundry:
Oh let me die now. And the dark was all flame as I drank
The heart-breaking odour of Muguets des Bois and red wine
– Hers, though I have to admit, it could have been mine.

SELIMA HILL (b.1945)

*Selima Hill was born in London in 1945, read Moral Sciences at Cambridge,
and lives in Dorset. In 1988 she won the Arvon/Observer International Poetry
Competition. Her collections include* Saying Hello at the Station *(1985),*
My Darling Camel *(1988),* The Accumulation of Small Acts of Kindness
(1989), A Little Book of Meat *(1993),* Trembling Hearts in the Bodies
of Dogs *(1994) and* Violet *(1997).*

The Significance of Significance

She was worried he couldn't be happy
just loafing about by the river,
like she liked doing.
Plans, and plans about plans, and sex,
was *his* idea of happiness.
He wore a floppy hat.
She felt so lonely!

Another thing, she couldn't spell.
Laborinth. Itiniry. Elann.
She cooked him cockles
in a thick orange sauce,
and bought him a suit-case –
'for the Great Man'.

They sat on a rocky mountain
dressed in leather.
Sardines and beer.
Parois vertigineuses.

Their children were his books.
She understood that.
O Significado De Significado,
lecture notes.

'The blissfully well-run nursing-home'
is now public knowledge –
her little lump, like longing,
prized from her oesophagus;
her crawling from the hut
on her knees.

A tortoise-shell comb,
embroidery,
The Crack.
A lovely moth.

'The nurse is a crashing bore'
. . . poking about among her mysteries.
God bless you, Patty.

The Unsuccessful Wedding-Night

It's all because of Buster.
Of course, it's unreasonable,
he couldn't possibly have come –
his barking, his midnight walk,
the way he scratches at the blankets –

but as she presses her face
into the pillow of the small hotel,
she can't help missing him
terribly. She imagines the two of them
hiking in bright sunshine

over the Western Ghats; and soon
she begins to whimper to herself,
her runny nose trailing
over the foam pillows
like the Vasco da Gama of snails.

Cow

I want to be a cow
and not my mother's daughter.
I want to be a cow
and not in love with you.
I want to feel free to feel calm.
I want to be a cow who never knows
the kind of love you 'fall in love with' with;
a queenly cow, with hips as big and sound
as a department store,

a cow the farmer milks on bended knee,
who when she dies will feel dawn
bending over her like lawn to wet her lips.

I want to be a cow,
nothing fancy –
a cargo of grass,
a hammock of soupy milk
whose floating and rocking and dribbling's undisturbed
by the echo of hooves to the city;
of crunching boots;
of suspicious-looking trailers parked on verges;
of unscrupulous restaurant-owners
who stumble, pink-eyed, from stale beds
into a world of lobsters and warm telephones;
of streamlined Japanese freighters
ironing the night,
heavy with sweet desire like bowls of jam.

The Tibetans have 85 words for states of consciousness.
This dozy cow I want to be has none.
She doesn't speak.
She doesn't do housework or worry about her appearance.
She doesn't roam.
Safe in her fleet
of shorn-white-bowl-like friends,
she needs, and loves, and's loved by,
only this –
the farm I want to be a cow on too.

Don't come looking for me.
Don't come walking out into the bright sunlight
looking for me,
black in your gloves and stockings and sleeves
and large hat.
Don't call the tractorman.
Don't call the neighbours.

Don't make a special fruit-cake for when I come home:
I'm not coming home.
I'm going to be a cowman's counted cow.
I'm going to be a cow
and you won't know me.

Don't Let's Talk About Being In Love

Don't let's talk about being in love, OK?
– about *me* being in love, in fact, OK?
about your bloated face, like a magnolia;
about marsupials,
whose little blunted pouches
I'd like to crawl inside, lips first;
about the crashing of a million waterfalls
– as if LOVE were a dome of glass beneath a lake
entered through a maze of dripping tunnels
I hoped and prayed I'd never be found inside.

At night I dream that your bedroom's crammed with ducks.
You smell of mashed-up meal and scrambled egg.
Some of the ducks are broody, and won't stand up.
And I dream of the fingers of your various wives
reaching into your private parts like beaks.
And you're lying across the bed like a man shouldn't be.
And I'm startled awake by the sound of creaking glass
as if the whole affair's about to collapse
and water come pouring in with a rush of fishes
going *slurpetty-slurpetty-slurp* with their low-slung mouths.

BERNARD O'DONOGHUE (b.1945)

Bernard O'Donoghue was born in Cullen, County Cork, in 1945. He teaches medieval literature at Oxford University and has published books on that subject. His collections include The Weakness *(1991) and* Gunpowder *which was the winner of the 1995 Whitbread Award for Poetry.*

O'Regan the Amateur Anatomist

The gander clapped out its flat despair
While O'Regan sawed at its legs with his penknife.
He looked at me with a friendly smile as blood
Dripped in huge, dark drips. I didn't protest
Or flail out at him, but smiled in return,
Knowing what grown-ups do, whatever breeds
About their hearts, is always for the best.
Worms are cold-blooded; babies learn in the night
By being left to cry. Another time (a man
So generous, they said, he'd give you the sweet
From his mouth) he halved a robin with that knife.
Finally, racing his brother back from a funeral
Down a darkening road he drove his car
Under a lightless lorry, cutting his head off.
I wonder what he thought he was up to then?

WENDY COPE (b.1945)

Wendy Cope was born in Erith, Kent, in 1945. She studied history at Oxford, and worked for fifteen years as a primary school teacher in London. She is one of the most popular poets in Britain – both Making Cocoa for Kingsley Amis *(1986) and* Serious Concerns *(1992) are poetry best-sellers. She has also written for children.*

Waste Land Limericks

I

In April one seldom feels cheerful;
Dry stones, sun and dust make me fearful;
Clairvoyantes distress me,
Commuters depress me –
Met Stetson and gave him an earful.

II

She sat on a mighty fine chair,
Sparks flew as she tidied her hair;
She asks many questions,
I make few suggestions –
Bad as Albert and Lil – what a pair!

III

The Thames runs, bones rattle, rats creep;
Tiresias fancies a peep –
A typist is laid,
A record is played –
Wei la la. After this it gets deep.

IV

A Phoenician called Phlebas forgot
About birds and his business – the lot,
Which is no surprise,
Since he'd met his demise
And been left in the ocean to rot.

V

No water. Dry rocks and dry throats,
Then thunder, a shower of quotes
From the Sanskrit and Dante.
Da. Damyata. Shantih.
I hope you'll make sense of the notes.

Two Cures for Love

1   Don't see him. Don't phone or write a letter.
2   The easy way: get to know him better.

PETER DIDSBURY (b.1946)

Peter Didsbury was born in 1946 in Fleetwood, Lancashire, and lives in Hull. He read English and Hebrew at university, and now works as an archaeologist for Hull County Council. His collections include The Butchers of Hull *(1982),* The Classical Farm *(1987) and* That Old-Time Religion *(1994).*

The Guitar

And what if all of animated nature
Be but organic Harps diversely framed,
That tremble into thought . . .
Coleridge

Aerial songs, estuarial poetry.
An electric guitar is being played.
Its neck is five miles long,
and forms a margin of the River Humber,
where the thin soils are.

Aeolus swoops down, and begins to bounce on it.
He has serpents in his eyes.
He plucks the strings
with his Nebuchadnezzar toenails.
He's composing a piece called Early Memorials.
A train comes. His pinions take him
half a mile high in a lift.
The train courses over
the frets of the guitar,
but it is going backwards,
towards the hole in the middle.
Coleridge is sitting at a window
with his back towards the engine.
He must have been lunching in Goole,
but now he's fallen asleep.
'Dutch River,' he murmurs, 'Dutch River.'
He's dreaming of the advent of the railways
but will not remember, because I intend to
keep it from him.
It's a mercy that is available to me.
The train steams through fields of bright chives,
then it reverses and comes back as a diesel.
A madman steps out of a cabin and salutes it.
He stands by the flagpole outside his summer *kraal*.
The engine-driver waves.
The engine-driver and the madman
both went to the same school as me.
They sport the red blazer and the nose.
They chat for a bit while the engine grazes
on the chives that spring up through the ballast.
'Nice bit of road,' one says. 'Aye, nice road,' says the other.
The sky is like an entry in The Oxford English Dictionary.
The earliest reference for it is 1764,
in Randall's *Semi-Virgilian Husbandry*.
The loco swings its head from side to side
with the movements of an old-fashioned camera,

or a caterpillar. The mythic god of the winds, however,
who is still aloft, is getting tired of attending.
He flies up the line and starts twisting on the pegs.
Lunatic, driver, and diesel all look up.
Their faces assume an almost communal rictus.
They all jump in the carriage with Coleridge,
as the mighty lexicon twangs. They wish they were asleep.
The god puts his face right up to the window
and shakes his horrid locks at them.
They stare at the cattle grazing in his fields.
They note the herbaceous stubble
which makes frightful his visage of mud.

The Shore

A minute past noon,
and deeply cold on the shore.
The sun with its rare but un-marvellous halo
starts climbing back down the sky.
The air stills. Wind lies over field
like a razor held above a leather strop.
The beach is locked and hard.
Its uncut gems, and small round leaves
like patinated coins,
it keeps beneath plate glass.
How empty things are.
The cliff behind us acts from some notion of presence,
but very faintly, like a host of spirits
crowding to sip at a pool.
The world of phenomena gathers at the surface
of a system of unity powered by emptiness.
Hills. River. Line of winter farms.
A barge coming down the navigable channel
from somewhere inland, with nothing in its hold.

An Expedition

Down to the end of the garden in the night.
With cigarette and glass of ice-cold milk.
I pick my way over heaps of builders' rubble.
Light from the new kitchen window comes along too.

PETER READING (b.1946)

Peter Reading was born in 1946 in Liverpool, and has worked as a teacher, a lecturer in art history, a writer in residence and as a weighbridge operator. His work has received many honours, including the Cholmondeley Award for Poetry, the Dylan Thomas Award and the Whitbread Poetry Prize. One of the most prolific and individual of all contemporary poets, he published his Collected Poems *in two volumes:* Poems 1970–1984 *(1995) and* Poems 1985–1996 *(1996). They take in a total of seventeen previous books, and further publications include* Work in Regress *(1997). He lives in Shropshire.*

Midnight,

          a hotel bedroom, open window,
sibilant tyres on rain-washed asphalt streets
whispering a repetitious *finish, finish.*
You stroke your lover comprehensively,
who purrs contentment, clings to your neck and sobs.
Sibilant tyres on rain-washed asphalt streets
whispering a repetitious *finish, finish.*

from Ukulele Music

Dear sir,

I come in this morning instead of tomorrow as I have to take ~~Budige bugdie~~ Bird to the Vets, as he got out of cage door for the first time, By <u>accident</u>. As I was putting seed in. & taking out sand sheet. He went mad. & banged himself against THE wall. & fell down on to the Magic coal fire. got jammed in the back of coal effect. Broken leg and side of his body awfull state. he is in. good job fire was not on.

faithly Viv

p.S. could you oblige the next weeks money this wk. be in tomorrow Morning, Only the Capting which I chars for tuesdays has let me off this Tues but has PAID yrs Viv

> *Few atrocities*
> *of which* H. sap. *can conceive*
> *remain unfulfilled*

'They must have been about 17/18, possibly 19:
one, tattooed on his hand MAM; one, tattooed on his arm LOVE.

One of them grabbed at my handbag but I just belted him with it,
caught him one under the ear, then I yelled "Somebody, help!"

Even although it was lunchtime and several people were watching
nobody wanted to know. Two women just walked right past.'

She had been pushing her 8-month-old, Sharen-Jayne, in the buggy.
Now the kid started to scrawk; one of our heroes smirked, spat,

fondled the empty pint bottle he had in his hand and then smashed it
on an adjacent brick wall, held the bits to the child's throat.

'I said "Hurt me if you like but don't injure the innocent baby –
it can't defend itself, see? Don't do it don't do it *please*!"

He said "If I do the baby I'll get what I want, so I'll cut it."
He shoved the glass in her cheek; twisted the jagged edge in.

He told me "This is how we earn our living, this and the dole like."
Then he just wiggled the sharp, smashed slivers into her eye.'

Promptly the mother gave over her golden wedding-ring, also
three pounds in cash and a watch (silver, engraved 'My True Love'),
but the attackers slashed Sharen twice more – in the mouth, and a
   deep cut
neatly round one chubby knee. Then they strolled leisurely off.

'Sharon was screaming and bleeding a lot and I thought they had
   killed her.'
CID officers say 'This is a callous assault . . .'

Dear Sir,

*will finish of your hoovering and such tomorrow as my hand is still bad, my right
one. As last wk. there is a lady two doors off me has a bitch and a little boy over the
road had been playing with it. and since then where all the dogs came from I do not
know. But one of them had pinned the boy against the wall. I ran out with a hand
full of pepper to throw at the dogs face. I throw it. but it had bit me in the hand.
just above my right thumb where the bone is. I ran after the dog. with a whitening
brush also and I fell also over the fence. bruised my knee's. But my knee is alright.
My hand I have sufferd. The dog got put down to sleep. I have been to Hospitle
But I heard later. that another dog had pinned the same boy he is only four yrs old.
and MARLD him in the face and eyes he has had 5 stitches across his left eye. The
other dog also had to be put down to sleep I tell you it has been awfull over there
with the dogs. The woman who the bitch belongs to, had forgotten she had left her
kitchen window open One of the dogs had jump in through the window. her Husband
had delt with the dog. But slammed the kitchen window and all of the glass had
fallen out in pieces. (It is awfull. when the little girls are about.) There mothers have
to keep them in. or take them with them. the pain is going all the way up my arm.
I have had a TECNAS. you know, a little RED CARD.*

YRS Viv.

Someone has left a whole crateful of empty lemonade bottles
on the pedestrian bridge. Here come three ten-year-old boys.

Queuing for buses, the off-peak shoppers are gathered together
under the cast concrete span (aerosolled WANKERS and TREV).

Each of the children has picked up an empty and, quite nonchalantly,
hurls it down onto the grans, young mums and spinsters and babes.

No one evinces surprise or alarm or even vexation,
fox-trotting through the smashed bits, Terpsichorean and deft.

Each boy throws four bottles, spits from the parapet into our faces,
shouts 'Fucking bastards' and yelps. Glass crunches under a bus.

Blood smears the calf of an elderly lady silently weeping.
'Kids' our conductor observes 'should be done something about.'

Grans are bewildered by post-Coronation disintegration;
offspring of offspring of *their* offspring infest and despoil.

('You think you're doing a fine job of work don't you, oh yes, but you're
not. Stop it stop it, it's dirty dirty dirty in the streets like that' an old woman
shopper informs two boys of ten or eleven who slouch against a butcher's
window in busy Northcote Rd, SW11. Moist beige tripes gleam. Around
the Chopper bikes blobs of bubbly saliva streaked green and yellow describe
a semi-circle on the greasy pavement. The boys giggle and one of them
remarks sotto voce 'Fuck off old cow'. 'What did you say?' They giggle
and do not answer. One boy spits afresh at his colleague's cycle. A glycerite
sac depends from the canary-coloured spokes, elongates gradually. 'Dirty
little devils. Look at them look at them!' she appeals to those of us nearby.
We evince neither surprise nor concern. She turns begrudgingly. Silver
streaks jet concurrently from gaps between the front teeth of each boy. She
continues upon her way unaware that her pink leatherette mac is sullied by
twin viscid drools.)

Stubbornly, Taffs, at their damn-fool anachronistic eisteddfods,
still, with this breach in the hull, twang (ineffectual lyres).

Mercury falls, it's no go, and the pink geraniums shrivel:
ceilidh and Old Viennese drone as the packet goes down.

When all the cities were felled by the pongoid subspecies in them
(Belfast, Jerusalem, Brum., Liverpool, Beirut) and when

blood-swilling (Allah is wonderful) Middle-East Yahoos had purchased
nuclear hardware, he found distich the only form apt.

Too Many Of Us and Dwindled Resources and War had undone us.
Matter impartially throve (quark, strangeness, charm) not as *us*.

Sing in Your Bath if You Want to Seem Sexy and Blood–Bath in Jordan
vie for front page in the tabs. Doh ray me fah soh lah te

well, Sir

Only, the Capting has said I was not really wanted so I have gone to you instead.
only. You are not here as you know. So have let myself in with spare key but he
has PAY me just the same as he is kind old man with heart of gold etc. and has
told me how underneath. and he has seen it with OWN eyes so knows it is true.
where I thought it was just Underground Car Park ect. under ~~Civic~~ Civet Centre
is not just Car Park but bunk for FALL if there is trouble, that sometimes seems
likely with uSA and russiens with there bomb warfair. but what can you do? nothing
and he say there are SARDINES stored in there for after siren. with DRINK.
so we are all prepared thank God. But what I want to know is when you vote the
different Goverments do NOT do what you ask do they? Because I want NO
TROUBLE but it seems no difference what you want the Rulers just do a
DIFFERENT THING. So you can only keep CHEERFUL and keep trying
your best. sir. for Exsample I have done the floors but their is one of Yr writings
there that ALAS is swept in the Hoover bag, and I got it out all right but is VERY
twisted with the thing that BEATS as SWEEPS as CLEANS the one about a
Piano and Man AND woman that I think is DIRTY but it takes all sorts and
did you REALLY work at such a club in uSA? I never knew you had been there
but I would not want sardines ALL THE TIME who would? noone. but it would
be emergency like in the last one where it was tin sheeting. But now they are on the
streets the ARMY against thugs and Mugers as that is where the REAL war is on

NOW, cities in 2 halfs with police and army and nice folks against dirty animals, so may HAVE to go DOWN soon for THAT war. But I have throw it away, the poetry writing on the Piano at top of kitchin bin VERY TOP if you want it back.

and Oblige Viv.

Beetrooty colonels explain to the Lounge Bar how, in the 'Last Show', they had a marvellous time, and how we need a new war

if we are going to get this Great Country back on its feet, sir
(also all beards should be shaved: also the Dole should be stopped).

Life still goes on and *It isn't the end of the world* (the child-soothing platitudes weaken now Cruise proves them potentially false).

Lieder's no art against these sorry times (anguished Paramour likens mountainy crags and a crow to the flint heart of his Frau).

Dear sir,

have done some hoover of the front room. but am going now be back tomorrow morning if you can oblige with next week money same as last time. Only my sister. not the one in Australia the other one here. was standing at the bus station when boys threw bottles and ones broken glass flew up and cut leg BAD CUT. only about ten also, she says so must go and help as she is lost a husband recently too. I tell you no one knows how bad it is here with these children ALL OVER. They will be the death of us no mistake. also the world situton no better, America Russia jews and Arabians irish and such. what can you do as it gets worse like one of yr poetry Works that I saw when cleaning desk with wax which I need more of soon as possible please. The same as in the empty tin. but well what can you do only get on with it. as you can't sort it all out can you? we are like the man in music Hall song that goes he plays his ~~Uku uker~~ Youkalaylee while the ship went down. only we all have problems like my sister and Goverments so can only carry on best we can, the next weeks money this week please as am short due to various things and the new wax pollish Viv.

PS. doctor said it is not SO bad but has had 6 stitch.

Glossy black slices of smooth slab are all laid facing towards due
East – in the twerpish conceit sunrise might pleasure them *now*!

Glittery gilt lists the names and the dates and the bullshit about them
– 'Fell Asleep', 'Gone to Rest' (tcha!), 'Resting in Jesus' Arms' (pah!).

'Gone Where We'll All Join Again on the Happy Shore Everafter'
(spew, vomit, puke, throw-up, retch), 'Went Without Saying
   Goodbye'.

Inside a shed with the Council's coat-of-arms blazoned on it
there is a Flymo and spades. Here comes a gent with a pick:

'Wouldn't it make you want to dip your bread in the piss-pot
– some of the bilge they write there? Fuckin daft sods' (he opines).

Sweet peas are cunningly wrought in a huge pink crucifix resting
fresh on damp just-replaced turf. Wet clay outlines a new slot.

Biro-smudged sympathy-cards blow about and one is signed 'Viv, The
Depest Regrett Always Felt' (it shows a wren on a wreath).

On a diminutive gravy-hued sandstone wafer is chiselled
that which, despite mawkishness, prompts a sharp intake of breath.

Aged 10.
Little Boy,
We Would Not
Wake You To
Suffer Again.

Oh sir,

*only I havnt known. which way to TURN since the Funeral. It was the sisters
youngest such a good lad too and only ten it seems wrong. somehow, and they would
play in the streets though they was told often enough GOD only knows. So it was
a bus when they was playing football and the poor little mite had gone when they
got him. to the Hospitle so that is why I didn't come for 3 days but was in this
morning and hope you find this note behind the tea pot and with thanks for the new
Polish which have done the desk and chairs with. My oldest Trevor has been
TOWER OF strenth since tragdy but will get those tatoos just like his DAD in*

*that way just last week got MAM done on his hand which is nice he is a good lad
to his Mother and a Tower. So can I have last weeks moneys though I did not come
and not have money next week instead. Only the flowers which was a cross of pink
flowers. very nicely done. do cost such a lot not that you bigrudge it do you when its
your own Sisters youngest? So if you could leave it buy the dusters and furnature
wax it will be fine tomorrow.*

Obliged, Viv.

*PS we take her to the zoo next weekend to take her out of herself. the sister. as it
will be a nice change our Trevor says.*

'Them animals is disgusting.'

In London Zoo is a large flat painted Disneyesque lion
sporting a circular hole cut where the face ought to be.

On its reverse is a step upon which the visitor stands and
puts his own face through the hole – so that he may be thus snapped.

So, the resultant photograph shows the face of a friend or
relative grinning like mad out of a leonine frame.

This seems to be a very popular piece of equipment –
Arabs in nightshirts and Japs queue with Jews. Polaroids click.

Tabloids blown underfoot headline a couple of global débâcles.
Gran, from the lion's mouth, leers: toothless, cadaverous, blithe.

Oh it is very funny to put your head through the facial
orifice of a joke lion – races and creeds are agreed.

Down the old Monkey House there is a *Cercopithecus* wanking
and a baboon (with its thumb stuck up its arse) to revile.

PENELOPE SHUTTLE (b.1947)

Penelope Shuttle was born in 1947 in Staines, Middlesex, and lives in Cornwall. She began publishing poetry in her twenties, and has also written drama, fiction and non-fiction, as well as books in collaboration with her husband, the poet Peter Redgrove. Her recent volumes include Adventures with my Horse *(1986) and* Taxing the Rain *(1992).*

Taxing the Rain

When I wake the rain's falling
and I think, as always, it's for the best,

I remember how much I love rain,
the weakest and strongest of us all;

as I listen to its yesses and no's,
I think how many men and women

would, if they could,
against all sense and nature,

tax the rain for its privileges;

make it pay for soaking our earth
and splashing all over our leaves;

pay for muddying our grass
and amusing itself with our roots.

Let rain be taxed, they say,
for riding on our rivers
and drenching our sleeves;

for loitering in our lakes
and reservoirs. Make rain pay its way.

Make it pay for lying full length
in the long straight sedate green waters

of our city canals,
and for working its way through processes

of dreamy complexity
until this too-long untaxed rain comes indoors

and touches our lips,
bringing assuagement – for rain comes

to slake all our thirsts, spurting
brusque and thrilling in hot needles,

showering on to anyone naked;
or balming our skins in the shape of scented baths.

Yes, there are many who'd like to tax the rain;
even now they whisper, it can be done, it must be done.

LIZ LOCHHEAD (b.1947)

Liz Lochhead was born in Motherwell, Lanarkshire, in 1947, and attended Glasgow School of Art. Her first collection was published in 1972 and she works as a dramatist, broadcaster and performing poet. Dreaming Frankenstein and Collected Poems *was published in 1984 and* Bagpipe Muzak *in 1991. She lives in Glasgow.*

My Mother's Suitors

have come to court me
have come to call oh
yes with their wonderful world
war two moustaches their long
stem roses their cultivated
accents (they're English aren't they
at very least they're
educated-Scots).

They are absolutely
au fait with menu-French
they know the language of flowers
& oh they'd die
rather than send a dozen yellow
they always get them right & red.
Their handwriting on the florist's card
slants neither too much to the left or right.

They are good sorts.
They have the profile for it – note
the not too much nose
the plenty chin. The
stockings they bring have no strings
& their square
capable hands are forever
lifting your hair and gently
pushing your head away from them
to fumble endearingly at your nape
with the clasp of the pretty heirloom
little necklace they know their
grandmother would have wanted
you to have.
(never opals – they know
that pearls mean tears).

They have come to call & we'll all
go walking under the black sky's
droning big bombers
among the ratatat of ack-ack.
We'll go dancing & tonight
shall I wear the lilac, or the
scarlet, or the white?

What The Pool Said,
On Midsummer's Day

I've led you by my garrulous banks, babbling
on and on till – drunk on air
and sure it's only water talking –
you come at last to my silence.
Listen, I'm dark
and still and deep enough.
Even this hottest gonging sun
on this longest day
can't white me out.
What are you waiting for?
I lie here, inviting, winking you in.

The woman was easy.
Like to like, I called her, she came.
In no time I had her
out of herself, slipping on my water-stockings,
leaning into, being cupped and clasped
in my green glass bra.
But it's you I want, and you know it, man.
I watch you, stripped, knee-deep
in my shallows, telling yourself
that what makes you gasp
and balls your gut
is not my coldness but your own fear.

– Your reasonable fear,
what's true in me admits it.
(Though deeper, oh
older than any reason).
Yes, I could
drown you, you
could foul my depths, it's not
unheard of. What's fish
in me could make flesh of you,

my wet weeds against your thigh, it
could turn nasty.
I could have you
gulping fistfuls fighting yourself
back from me.

I get darker and darker, suck harder.
On-the-brink man, you
wish I'd flash and dazzle again.
You'd make a fetish of zazzing dragonflies?
You want I should zip myself up
with the kingfisher's flightpath, be beautiful?
I say no tricks. I say just trust,
I'll soak through your skin and
slake your thirst.

I watch. You clench,
clench and come into me.

JOHN ASH (b.1948)

John Ash was born in Manchester in 1948, studied English at the University of Birmingham, taught for a year in Cyprus and lives in New York. His books include The Goodbyes *(1982),* The Branching Stairs *(1984),* Disbelief *(1987) and* The Burnt Pages *(1991).*

Unwilling Suspension

The cab should take off at this point
climbing straight over the river like a gull.
You can get so far but no nearer.
The island may be mirage or projection:
its towers remain on the horizon, –

the work of an ambitious child with scissors.
The bridges haven't been built, or they are
pitifully few. The roadway moans.

This is not The Good Place
and it assuredly is. In the evening
the sun makes it a glory
and deep in fissures, under fire-escapes,
are people who go hungry
and they seem to complain so little
they might be saints who had chosen
this way. Why have you come here?
It will not bring comfort, –
if you want that look somewhere else,
in the pages of an album or the far reaches of a park.

With oaths and hand gestures
the route changes: we shift north
passing between subsiding warehouses,
under obscure constructions of rusted girders,
discovering isolated houses with floral balconies,
carved doorframes. For some time we watch
elevators rising and falling in a distant building.

There needs to be a new religion of the city, –
a bible only of long-lined psalms
for long-lined buildings and their lights.

People sleep on the vents.
At night fireflies buzz the towers.
But we aren't getting any nearer
and how can I tell you how it feels
to spend an hour advancing by inches toward
something resembling a faded, theatrical curtain?

How can I tell you? The legends accumulate
like wealth or grain at the edge of a famine.
You will never be bored and you will never

conclude your investigations since the crime
has no culprit, or too many to fill the old courthouse.

The cab stalls on the far bank, its headlights ablaze.
I couldn't photograph any of this for you.
I couldn't show its reflection in a windshield.
I could tell you about the rain: it is not raining.

Party Damage

The invitations were returned
or people arrived on the wrong evening,
so your worst fears were fulfilled
and you sent the singers home, still in costume.
The weather changed and changed again.
The hospital was a kind of inverted cake
with white, glazed icing dripping from its eaves.

It is as natural that confusion
and anxiety should be our companions
as it is that old women should complain
in pharmacies; yet some things should be clear
as summer's red sail turning in the bay.

'Please understand I mean exactly what I say,
no more.' A word is spoken, an ordinary word,
and it becomes an entire landscape, –
an open and illustrated city: you might be
alone in a desert at noon with nothing
but the mirage of a Pepsi Cola sign to guide
your feet, or penniless on Fifth Avenue
without even a scarf to sell as Christmas approaches, –
or else you are the young prince in his walled paradise
idly shooting song birds with a jeweled arrow.

Please return the arrow: I think I put that jewel there.
Don't harm the animals or birds. Leave
heaven or hell out of consideration.
Certain things are, in the end, unforgivable
though it may take years for this to be noticed,
like a red stain pressing through a wall.

'The other day I was walking up an avenue, –
I forget its number, – when I saw the word SAVE
written in skywriting far above the city.
I am not making this up: it happened.'

Early Views of Manchester and Paris: First View

It makes us uncomfortable: the pillars
and shadowed arches of these monuments
to commerce are a furniture we can't
or daren't throw out. Hard not to admire
such a total dedication to redundancy, –

as if the whole city were a railway station
and the line diverted. In the photographs
of that age the only people to be visible
were those who stood for long periods
without moving. Only when it began
to die did the running mob appear
as dim smudges on a bridge in Paris.

And now are they visible?
Do they move freely?

DENISE RILEY (b.1948)

Denise Riley was born in Carlisle in 1948. She has been writer in residence at the Tate Gallery, and teaches at Goldsmith's College. She has published a number of prose books as author and editor. Her poetry collections include Mop Mop Georgette, New and Selected Poems 1986–1993. *She lives in London.*

Shantung

It's true that anyone can fall
in love with anyone at all.
Later, they can't. Ouf, ouf.

How much mascara washes away each day
and internationally, making the blue one black.
Come on everybody. Especially you girls.

Each day I think of something about dying.
Does everybody? do they think too, I mean.
My friends! some answers. Gently
unstrap my wristwatch. Lay it face down.

CIARAN CARSON (b.1948)

Ciaran Carson was born in Belfast in 1948 and works there as an arts officer. A writer and musician, his Pocket Guide to Irish Traditional Music *was published in 1986. A winner of many prizes in Britain and Ireland, his books include* The Irish for No *(1988),* Belfast Confetti *(1990),* First Language *(1993) and* Opera Et Cetera *(1996).*

Dresden

Horse Boyle was called Horse Boyle because of his brother Mule;
Though why Mule was called Mule is anybody's guess. I stayed there
    once,
Or rather, I nearly stayed there once. But that's another story.
At any rate they lived in this decrepit caravan, not two miles out of
    Carrick,
Encroached upon by baroque pyramids of empty baked bean tins, rusts
And ochres, hints of autumn merging into twilight. Horse believed
They were as good as a watchdog, and to tell you the truth
You couldn't go near the place without something falling over:
A minor avalanche would ensue – more like a shop bell, really,

The old-fashioned ones on string, connected to the latch, I think,
And as you entered in, the bell would tinkle in the empty shop, a
    musk
Of soap and turf and sweets would hit you from the gloom. Tobacco.
Baling wire. Twine. And, of course, shelves and pyramids of tins.
An old woman would appear from the back – there was a sizzling pan
    in there,
Somewhere, a whiff of eggs and bacon – and ask you what you
    wanted;
Or rather, she wouldn't ask; she would talk about the weather. It had
    rained
That day, but it was looking better. They had just put in the spuds.
I had only come to pass the time of day, so I bought a token packet of
    Gold Leaf.

All this time the fry was frying away. Maybe she'd a daughter in there
Somewhere, though I hadn't heard the neighbours talk of it; if
    anybody knew,
It would be Horse. Horse kept his ears to the ground.
And he was a great man for current affairs; he owned the only TV in
    the place.
Come dusk he'd set off on his rounds, to tell the whole townland the
    latest

Situation in the Middle East, a mortar bomb attack in Mullaghbawn –
The damn things never worked, of course – and so he'd tell the story
How in his young day it was very different. Take young Flynn, for
  instance,
Who was ordered to take this bus and smuggle some sticks of gelignite

Across the border, into Derry, when the RUC – or was it the RIC? –
Got wind of it. The bus was stopped, the peeler stepped on. Young
  Flynn
Took it like a man, of course: he owned up right away. He opened
  the bag
And produced the bomb, his rank and serial number. For all the world
Like a pound of sausages. Of course, the thing was, the peeler's bike
Had got a puncture, and he didn't know young Flynn from Adam. All
  he wanted
Was to get home for his tea. Flynn was in for seven years and learned
  to speak
The best of Irish. He had thirteen words for a cow in heat;
A word for the third thwart in a boat, the wake of a boat on the ebb
  tide.

He knew the extinct names of insects, flowers, why this place was
  called
Whatever: *Carrick*, for example, was *a rock*. He was damn right there –
As the man said, *When you buy meat you buy bones, when you buy land
  you buy stones.*
You'd be hard put to find a square foot in the whole bloody parish
That wasn't thick with flints and pebbles. To this day he could hear
  the grate
And scrape as the spade struck home, for it reminded him of broken
  bones:
Digging a graveyard, maybe – or better still, trying to dig a reclaimed
  tip
Of broken delph and crockery ware – you know that sound that sets
  your teeth on edge
When the chalk squeaks on the blackboard, or you shovel ashes from
  the stove?

Master McGinty – he'd be on about McGinty then, and discipline, the
  capitals
Of South America, Moore's *Melodies*, the Battle of Clontarf, and
Tell me this, an educated man like you: What goes on four legs when it's
  young,
Two legs when it's grown up, and three legs when it's old? I'd pretend
I didn't know. McGinty's leather strap would come up then, stuffed
With threepenny bits to give it weight and sting. Of course, it never
  did him
Any harm: *You could take a horse to water but you couldn't make him drink.*
He himself was nearly going on to be a priest.
And many's the young cub left the school, as wise as when he came.

Carrowkeel was where McGinty came from – *Narrow Quarter*, Flynn
  explained –
Back before the Troubles, a place that was so mean and crabbed,
Horse would have it, men were known to eat their dinner from a
  drawer.
Which they'd slide shut the minute you'd walk in.
He'd demonstrate this at the kitchen table, hunched and furtive,
  squinting
Out the window – past the teetering minarets of rust, down the
  hedge-dark aisle –
To where a stranger might appear, a passer-by, or what was maybe
  worse,
Someone he knew. Someone who wanted something. Someone who
  was hungry.
Of course who should come tottering up the lane that instant but his
  brother

Mule. I forgot to mention they were twins. They were as like two –
No, not peas in a pod, for this is not the time nor the place to go into
Comparisons, and this is really Horse's story, Horse who – now I'm
  getting
Round to it – flew over Dresden in the war. He'd emigrated first, to
Manchester. Something to do with scrap – redundant mill machinery,

Giant flywheels, broken looms that would, eventually, be ships, or
    aeroplanes.
He said he wore his fingers to the bone.
And so, on impulse, he had joined the RAF. He became a rear
    gunner.
Of all the missions, Dresden broke his heart. It reminded him of
    china.

As he remembered it, long afterwards, he could hear, or almost hear
Between the rapid desultory thunderclaps, a thousand tinkling
    echoes –
All across the map of Dresden, store-rooms full of china shivered,
    teetered
And collapsed, an avalanche of porcelain, slushing and cascading:
    cherubs,
Shepherdesses, figurines of Hope and Peace and Victory, delicate bone
    fragments.
He recalled in particular a figure from his childhood, a milkmaid
Standing on the mantelpiece. Each night as they knelt down for the
    rosary,
His eyes would wander up to where she seemed to beckon to him,
    smiling,
Offering him, eternally, her pitcher of milk, her mouth of rose and
    cream.

One day, reaching up to hold her yet again, his fingers stumbled, and
    she fell.
He lifted down a biscuit tin, and opened it.
It breathed an antique incense: things like pencils, snuff, tobacco.
His war medals. A broken rosary. And there, the milkmaid's creamy
    hand, the outstretched
Pitcher of milk, all that survived. Outside, there was a scraping
And a tittering; I knew Mule's step by now, his careful drunken
    weaving
Through the tin-stacks. I might have stayed the night, but there's no
    time

To go back to that now; I could hardly, at any rate, pick up the
    thread.
I wandered out through the steeples of rust, the gate that was a broken
    bed.

Belfast Confetti

Suddenly as the riot squad moved in, it was raining exclamation
    marks,
Nuts, bolts, nails, car-keys. A fount of broken type. And the explosion
Itself – an asterisk on the map. This hyphenated line, a burst of rapid
    fire . . .
I was trying to complete a sentence in my head, but it kept stuttering,
All the alleyways and side-streets blocked with stops and colons.

I know this labyrinth so well – Balaclava, Raglan, Inkerman, Odessa
    Street –
Why can't I escape? Every move is punctuated. Crimea Street. Dead
    end again.
A Saracen, Kremlin-2 mesh. Makrolon face-shields. Walkie-talkies.
    What is
My name? Where am I coming from? Where am I going? A fusillade
    of question-marks.

Bloody Hand

Your man, says the Man, *will walk into the bar like this* – here his fingers
Mimic a pair of legs, one stiff at the knee – *so you'll know exactly*
What to do. He sticks a finger to his head. Pretend it's child's play –
The hand might be a horse's mouth, a rabbit or a dog. Five handclaps.
Walls have ears: the shadows you throw are the shadows you try to
    throw off.

I snuffed out the candle between finger and thumb. Was it the left
    hand
Hacked off at the wrist and thrown to the shores of Ulster? Did Ulster
Exist? Or the Right Hand of God, saying *Stop* to this and *No* to that?
My thumb is the hammer of a gun. The thumb goes up. The thumb
    goes down.

The Brain of Edward Carson

They cracked the skull and watched its two halves creak apart, like the
    decks
Of some Byzantine trireme. The herringboned, zipped oars, the chains
    and shackles.
The bronze circuitry. The locks. The Titanic, legal depositions of the
    cells.
The hammered rivets. The rivetted, internal gaze. The screws. The
    nails.
The caulked bulwarks. The slaves, embalmed in honeycomb prismatic.

Barbaric instruments inserted there, like hook and razor, iron picks
By which they will extrapolate its history: the bronze, eternal static
Of his right, uplifted hand. The left hand like a shield. The bolted-on,
    external
Eyes. The seraphic frown. The borders and the chains contained
    therein. The fraternal
Gaze of the Exclusive Brethren: orange and bruised purple, cataleptic.

The map of Ulster opened up, hexagonal and intricate, tectonic:
Its shifting plates were clunked and welded into place by laws
    Masonic.
The ladder and the rope. The codicils. The compasses by which they
    sail
Uncharted futures. The outstretched hand. The crown. The sash. The
    secret nail.
And then disintegration intervened, the brain eluded them:
    Sphinxlike, catatonic.

TOM PAULIN (b.1949)

Tom Paulin was born in Leeds in 1949 and grew up in Belfast. He studied at the universities of Hull and Oxford, and teaches at Oxford. He is a regular reviewer of the arts, particularly on television, and has written several books of criticism as well as dramatic adaptations and a play. He is the editor of The Faber Book of Political Verse *(1986)* and The Faber Book of Vernacular Verse *(1990). Poems from his first four collections were contained in* Selected Poems 1972–1990, *and in 1994 he published* Walking a Line. *He lives in Oxford.*

Settlers

They cross from Glasgow to a black city
   Of gantries, mills and steeples. They begin to belong.
He manages the Iceworks, is an elder of the Kirk;
   She becomes, briefly, a nurse in Carson's Army.
Some mornings, walking through the company gate,
   He touches the bonnet of a brown lorry.
It is warm. The men watch and say nothing.
   'Queer, how it runs off in the night,'
He says to McCullough, then climbs to his office.
   He stores a warm knowledge on his palm.

   Nightlandings on the Antrim coast, the movement of guns
Now snug in their oiled paper below the floors
   Of sundry kirks and tabernacles in that county.

A Lyric Afterwards

There was a taut dryness all that summer
and you sat each day in the hot garden
until those uniformed comedians
filled the street with their big white ambulance,
fetching you and bringing you back to me.

Far from the sea of ourselves we waited
and prayed for the tight blue silence to give.
In your absence I climbed to a square room
where there were dried flowers, folders of sonnets
and crossword puzzles: call them musical

snuffboxes or mannered anachronisms,
they were all too uselessly intricate,
caskets of the dead spirit. Their bitter
constraints and formal pleasures were a style
of being perfect in despair; they spoke

with the vicious trapped crying of a wren.
But that is changed now, and when I see you
walking by the river, a step from me,
there is this great kindness everywhere:
now in the grace of the world and always.

Peacetime

We moved house
in '63.

My brother cried
quietly in his room.

Stuff in the loft,
my dad said burn it.

I cut the brass buttons
from his khaki tunic,

sploshed petrol,
felt in the back pocket

of the heavy trousers –
no wallet,

only four sheets
of folded bog-roll

(he'd been an officer
and planned ahead).

I chucked a match.
Whap!

GILLIAN ALLNUTT (b.1949)

Gillian Allnutt was born in London in 1949, and now lives in County Durham where she works as a freelance writer and tutor. She is the co-editor of Berthing: A Poetry Workbook *(1991), and her collections include* Beginning the Avocado *(1987) and* Nantucket and the Angel *(1997).*

Convent

a fistful of notes
my heart

a thin must
covers the keyboard of ivory soldiers

girls are expected
to wear gloves

and a labour of love is lost
in plain sewing

each finger stitched
to the palm

the loose hem of the street
catches me

the tune
of a barrel organ

the monkey
playing alone

streetheart
no penny can buy it

I ought
to give my pocket

money for a poor child
going begging in the east

while the bell rings for angelus
here are gloves of silk a purse

on a string
worn over the shoulder

and nothing
in it

after prayers
there will be bread and butter soldiers

a measure of milk
plainsong

CHRISTOPHER REID (b.1949)

Christopher Reid was born in Hong Kong in 1949 and lives in London. His books include Katerina Brac *(1985) and* Expanded Universes *(1996). He has received the Somerset Maugham Award, the Hawthornden Prize and the Cholmondeley Award for his work, and is poetry editor at Faber & Faber.*

Stones and Bones

Second Genesis

> 'inde genus durum sumus'
> Ovid: *Metamorphoses*, Book I

Two survived the flood.
We are not of their blood,
springing instead from the bones
of the Great Mother – stones,
what have you, rocks, boulders –
hurled over their shoulders
by that pious pair
and becoming people, where
and as they hit the ground.
Since when, we have always found
something hard, ungracious,
obdurate in our natures,
a strain of the very earth
that gave us our abrupt birth;
but a pang, too, at the back
of the mind: a loss . . . a lack . . .

Skull Garden

> Ewen Henderson's

For a brief while, you must stand
in this dour patch of land
and draw a deep breath.
Fragrance of life, death
and something more: the sense
of a dark intelligence
determined to conjure the whole
from a pitiless rigmarole

of making and unmaking.
To feel, within you, waking
the same idea that powers
the occasional, upstart flowers,
or drives that twisted tree
through its slow dance, is easy.
But what ancient seed was sown
to yield this crop of stone?
And why all these skulls blooming?
To know that would be something.

JAMES FENTON (b.1949)

James Fenton was born in Lincoln in 1949. He has worked as a drama critic, journalist and war correspondent, and has published prose pieces on the Far East, as well as essays and travel writing. His poetry collections include The Memory of War and Children in Exile *(1983) and* Out of Danger *(1994). He was elected Oxford Professor of Poetry in 1994.*

A German Requiem

It is not what they built. It is what they knocked down.
It is not the houses. It is the spaces between the houses.
It is not the streets that exist. It is the streets that no longer exist.
It is not your memories which haunt you.
It is not what you have written down.
It is what you have forgotten, what you must forget.
What you must go on forgetting all your life.

And with any luck oblivion should discover a ritual.
You will find out that you are not alone in the enterprise.
Yesterday the very furniture seemed to reproach you.
Today you take your place in the Widow's Shuttle.

¶

The bus is waiting at the southern gate
To take you to the city of your ancestors
Which stands on the hill opposite, with gleaming pediments,
As vivid as this charming square, your home.
Are you shy? You should be. It is almost like a wedding,
The way you clasp your flowers and give a little tug at your veil. Oh,
The hideous bridesmaids, it is natural that you should resent them
Just a little, on this first day.
But that will pass, and the cemetery is not far.
Here comes the driver, flicking a toothpick into the gutter,
His tongue still searching between his teeth.
See, he has not noticed you. No one has noticed you.
It will pass, young lady, it will pass.

¶

How comforting it is, once or twice a year,
To get together and forget the old times.
As on those special days, ladies and gentlemen,
When the boiled shirts gather at the graveside
And a leering waistcoat approaches the rostrum.
It is like a solemn pact between the survivors.
The mayor has signed it on behalf of the freemasonry.
The priest has sealed it on behalf of all the rest.
Nothing more need be said, and it is better that way –

¶

The better for the widow, that she should not live in fear of surprise,
The better for the young man, that he should move at liberty between
    the armchairs,
The better that these bent figures who flutter among the graves
Tending the nightlights and replacing the chrysanthemums
Are not ghosts,
That they shall go home.
The bus is waiting, and on the upper terraces
The workmen are dismantling the houses of the dead.

¶

But when so many had died, so many and at such speed,
There were no cities waiting for the victims.
They unscrewed the name-plates from the shattered doorways
And carried them away with the coffins.
So the squares and parks were filled with the eloquence of young
    cemeteries:
The smell of fresh earth, the improvised crosses
And all the impossible directions in brass and enamel.

¶

'Doctor Gliedschirm, skin specialist, surgeries 14−16 hours or by
    appointment.'
Professor Sargnagel was buried with four degrees, two associate
    memberships
And instructions to tradesmen to use the back entrance.
Your uncle's grave informed you that he lived on the third floor, left.
You were asked please to ring, and he would come down in the lift
To which one needed a key . . .

¶

Would come down, would ever come down
With a smile like thin gruel, and never too much to say.
How he shrank through the years.
How you towered over him in the narrow cage.
How he shrinks now . . .

¶

But come. Grief must have its term? Guilt too, then.
And it seems there is no limit to the resourcefulness of recollection.
So that a man might say and think:
When the world was at its darkest,
When the black wings passed over the rooftops
(And who can divine His purposes?) even then
There was always, always a fire in this hearth.
You see this cupboard? A priest-hole!
And in that lumber-room whole generations have been housed and
    fed.
Oh, if I were to begin, if I were to begin to tell you
The half, the quarter, a mere smattering of what we went through!

¶

His wife nods, and a secret smile,
Like a breeze with enough strength to carry one dry leaf
Over two pavingstones, passes from chair to chair.
Even the enquirer is charmed.
He forgets to pursue the point.
It is not what he wants to know.
It is what he wants not to know.
It is not what they say.
It is what they do not say.

A Staffordshire Murderer

Every fear is a desire. Every desire is fear.
The cigarettes are burning under the trees
Where the Staffordshire murderers wait for their accomplices
And victims. Every victim is an accomplice.

It takes a lifetime to stroll to the carpark
Stopping at the footbridge for reassurance,
Looking down at the stream, observing
(With one eye) the mallard's diagonal progress backwards.

You could cut and run, now. It is not too late.
But your fear is like a long-case clock
In the last whirring second before the hour,
The hammer drawn back, the heart ready to chime.

Fear turns the ignition. The van is unlocked.
You may learn now what you ought to know:
That every journey begins with a death,
That the suicide travels alone, that the murderer needs company.

And the Staffordshire murderers, nervous though they are,
Are masters of the conciliatory smile.
A cigarette? A tablet in a tin?
Would you care for a boiled sweet from the famous poisoner

Of Rugeley? These are his own brand.
He has never had any complaints.
He speaks of his victims as a sexual braggart
With a tradesman's emphasis on the word 'satisfaction'.

You are flattered as never before. He appreciates
So much, the little things – your willingness for instance
To bequeath your body at once to his experiments.
He sees the point of you as no one else does.

Large parts of Staffordshire have been undermined.
The trees are in it up to their necks. Fish
Nest in their branches. In one of the Five Towns
An ornamental pond disappeared overnight

Dragging the ducks down with it, down to the old seams
With a sound as of a gigantic bath running out,
Which is in turn the sound of ducks in distress.
Thus History murders mallards, while we hear nothing

Or what we hear we do not understand.
It is heard as the tramp's rage in the crowded precinct:
'Woe to the bloody city of Lichfield.'
It is lost in the enthusiasm of the windows

From which we are offered on the easiest terms
Five times over in colour and once in monochrome
The first reprisals after the drill-sergeant's coup.
How speedily the murder detail makes its way

Along the green beach, past the pink breakers,
And binds the whole cabinet to the oil-drums,
Where death is a preoccupied tossing of the head,
Where no decorative cloud lingers at the gun's mouth.

At the Dame's School dust gathers on the highwayman,
On Sankey and Moody, Wesley and Fox,
On the snoring churchwarden, on Palmer the Poisoner
And Palmer's house and Stanfield Hall.

The brilliant moss has been chipped from the Red Barn.
They say that Cromwell played ping-pong with the cathedral.
We train roses over the arches. In the Minster Pool
Crayfish live under carved stones. Every spring

The rats pick off the young mallards and
The good weather brings out the murderers
By the Floral Clock, by the footbridge,
The pottery murderers in jackets of prussian blue.

'Alack, George, where are thy shoes?'
He lifted up his head and espied the three
Steeple-house spires, and they struck at his life.
And he went by his eye over hedge and ditch

And no one laid hands on him, and he went
Thus crying through the streets, where there seemed
To be a channel of blood running through the streets,
And the market-place appeared like a pool of blood.

For this field of corpses was Lichfield
Where a thousand Christian Britons fell
In Diocletian's day, and 'much could I write
Of the sense that I had of the blood –'

That winter Friday. Today it is hot.
The cowparsley is so high that the van cannot be seen
From the road. The bubbles rise in the warm canal.
Below the lock-gates you can hear mallards.

A coot hurries along the tow-path, like a Queen's Messenger.
On the heli-pad, an arrival in blue livery
Sends the water-boatmen off on urgent business.
News of a defeat. Keep calm. The cathedral chimes.

The house by the bridge is the house in your dream.
It stares through new frames, unwonted spectacles,
And the paint, you can tell, has been weeping.
In the yard, five striped oildrums. Flowers in a tyre.

This is where the murderer works. But it is Sunday.
Tomorrow's bank holiday will allow the bricks to set.
You see? he has thought of everything. He shows you
The snug little cavity he calls 'your future home'.

And 'Do you know,' he remarks, 'I have been counting my victims.
Nine hundred and ninety nine, the Number of the Beast!
That makes you . . .' But he sees he has overstepped the mark:
'I'm sorry, but you cannot seriously have thought you were the first?'

A thousand preachers, a thousand poisoners,
A thousand martyrs, a thousand murderers –
Surely these preachers are poisoners, these martyrs murderers?
Surely this is all a gigantic mistake?

But there has been no mistake. God and the weather are glorious.
You have come as an anchorite to kneel at your funeral.
Kneel then and pray. The blade flashes a smile.
This is your new life. This murder is yours.

The Ballad of the Imam and the Shah

An Old Persian Legend

To C. E. H.

It started with a stabbing at a well
Below the minarets of Isfahan.
The widow took her son to see them kill
The officer who'd murdered her old man.
The child looked up and saw the hangman's work –
The man who'd killed his father swinging high.
The mother said: 'My child, now be at peace.
The wolf has had the fruits of all his crime.'

From felony to felony to crime
From robbery to robbery to loss
From calumny to calumny to spite
From rivalry to rivalry to zeal

All this was many centuries ago –
The kind of thing that couldn't happen now –
When Persia was the empire of the Shah
And many were the furrows on his brow.
The peacock the symbol of his throne
And many were its jewels and its eyes

And many were the prisons in the land
And many were the torturers and spies.

From tyranny to tyranny to war
From dynasty to dynasty to hate
From villainy to villainy to death
From policy to policy to grave

The child grew up a clever sort of chap
And he became a mullah, like his dad –
Spent many years in exile and disgrace
Because he told the world the Shah was bad.
'Believe in God,' he said, 'believe in me.
Believe me when I tell you who I am.
Now chop the arm of wickedness away.
Hear what I say. I am the great Imam.'

From heresy to heresy to fire
From clerisy to clerisy to fear
From litany to litany to sword
From fallacy to fallacy to wrong

And so the Shah was forced to flee abroad.
The Imam was the ruler in his place.
He started killing everyone he could
To make up for the years of his disgrace.
And when there were no enemies at home
He sent his men to Babylon to fight.
And when he'd lost an army in that way
He knew what God was telling him was right.

From poverty to poverty to wrath
From agony to agony to doubt
From malady to malady to shame
From misery to misery to fight

He sent the little children out to war.
They went out with his portrait in their hands.
The desert and the marshes filled with blood.
The mothers heard the news in Isfahan.
Now Babylon is buried under dirt.
Persepolis is peeping through the sand.
The child who saw his father's killer killed
Has slaughtered half the children in the land.

From felony
to robbery
to calumny
to rivalry
to tyranny
to dynasty
to villainy
to policy
to heresy
to clerisy
to litany
to fallacy
to poverty
to agony
to malady
to misery —

The song is yours. Arrange it as you will.
Remember where each word fits in the line
And every combination will be true
And every permutation will be fine:

From policy to felony to fear
From litany to heresy to fire
From villainy to tyranny to war
From tyranny to dynasty to shame

From poverty to malady to grave
From malady to agony to spite
From agony to misery to hate
From misery to policy to fight!

JOHN AGARD (b.1949)

John Agard was born in British Guyana (Guyana) in 1949 and came to England in 1977.
His work incorporates dub poetry, native dialect performance-based texts and poems using
musical accompaniment. Mangoes and Bullets: Selected and New Poems 1972−1984
contains much of his early work, and there have been further collections since that date, as
well as books of children's writing. He lives in Sussex.

Listen Mr Oxford don

Me not no Oxford don
me a simple immigrant
from Clapham Common
I didn't graduate
I immigrate

But listen Mr Oxford don
I'm a man on de run
and a man on de run
is a dangerous one

I ent have no gun
I ent have no knife
but mugging de Queen's English
is the story of my life

I dont need no axe
to split/ up yu syntax
I dont need no hammer
to mash/ up yu grammar

I warning you Mr Oxford don
I'm a wanted man
and a wanted man
is a dangerous one

Dem accuse me of assault
on de Oxford dictionary/
imagine a concise peaceful man like me/
dem want me serve time
for inciting rhyme to riot
but I tekking it quiet
down here in Clapham Common

I'm not a violent man Mr Oxford don
I only armed wit mih human breath
but human breath
is a dangerous weapon

So mek dem send one big word after me
I ent serving no jail sentence
I slashing suffix in self-defence
I bashing future wit present tense
and if necessary

I making de Queen's English accessory/to my offence

GRACE NICHOLS (b.1950)

Grace Nichols was born in British Guyana (Guyana) in 1950, and came to England in 1977 after working as a teacher and a journalist. Her books include i is a long memoried woman *which won the 1983 Commonwealth Poetry Prize and most recently* Sunris *(1996). She has also written for children and lives in Sussex.*

Thoughts drifting through the fat black woman's head while having a full bubble bath

Steatopygous sky
Steatopygous sea
Steatopygous waves
Steatopygous me

O how I long to place my foot
on the head of anthropology

to swig my breasts
in the face of history

to scrub my back
with the dogma of theology

to put my soap
in the slimming industry's
profitsome spoke

Steatopygous sky
Steatopygous sea
Steatopygous waves
Steatopygous me

Mystery

Mystery, it was a mystery to me
dih way Miss Sheila
chocolate queen of dih rundown
tumbledown tenement yard
come back cool-cool from Uncle Sam
to live with her ruin-face
one-time criminal man

Hardly going any place
only showing smiling window face

Rumour had it in dih yard
dat she was dih one
to dash dih acid pon dih man
then up and leave for Uncle Sam

Rumour had it in dih yard
how she come back of she own accord
typee-love bring she back
without a word, yes Lord

Rumour had it in dih yard
dat he must work some obeah pon her

Mystery, it was a mystery to me
dih way Miss Sheila
chocolate queen of dih rundown
tumbledown tenement yard
just come back cool-cool from Uncle Sam
to live with her ruin-face
one-time criminal man.

BLAKE MORRISON (b.1950)

Blake Morrison was born in Skipton, Yorkshire, in 1950. He has worked as a journalist, and written a number of critical studies as well as the autobiography And When Did You Last See Your Father. *He co-edited* The Penguin Book of Contemporary British Poetry *(1982), and his poetry collections include* The Ballad of the Yorkshire Ripper *(1987). He lives in London.*

from The Ballad of the Yorkshire Ripper

The 'Red Death' had long devastated the country. No pestilence had ever been so fatal, or so hideous. Blood was its Avatar and its seal . . .
Edgar Allan Poe, 'The Masque of the Red Death'

I were just cleaning up streets our kid. Just cleaning up streets.
Peter Sutcliffe to his brother Carl:
Somebody's Husband, Somebody's Son by Gordon Burn

Ower t'ills o Bingley
stormclouds clap an drain,
like opened blood-black blisters
leakin pus an pain.

Ail teems down like stair-rods,
an swells canals an becks,
an fills up studmarked goalmouths,
an bursts on mind like sex.

Cos sex is like a stormclap,
a swellin in thi cells,
when lightnin arrers through thi
an tha knows there in't owt else.

Ah've felt it in misen, like,
ikin ome part-fresh
ower limestone outcrops
like knuckles white through flesh:

ow men clap down on women
t'old em there for good
an soak up all their softness
an lounder em wi blood.

It's then I think on t'Ripper
an what e did an why,
an ow mi mates ate women,
an ow Pete med em die.

I love em for misen, like,
their skimmerin lips an eyes,
their ankles light as jinnyspins,
their seggy whisps an sighs,

their braided locks like catkins,
an t'curlies glashy black,
the peepin o their linnet tongues,
their way o cheekin back.

An ah look on em as equals.
But mates all say they're not,
that men must have t'owerance
or world will go to rot.

Lad-loupin molls an gadabouts,
fellow-fond an sly,
flappy-skets an drabbletails
oo'll bleed a bloke bone-dry:

that's ow I ear em spoke of
when lads are on their tod,
an ow tha's got to leather em
to stop em gi'in t'nod.

An some o t'same in Bible
where Paul screams fit to bust
ow men are fallen creatures
but womenfolk are t'wust.

Now I reckon this fired Peter,
an men-talk were is goad,
an culprit were our belderin God
an is ancient, bullyin road.

No, Pete weren't drove by vengeance,
rountwistedness or ale,
but to show isen a baufy man –
but let me tell thi tale.

MEDBH McGUCKIAN (b.1950)

Medbh McGuckian was born in Belfast in 1950, studied at Queen's University in that city and has since taught there, as well as at the University of California, Berkeley. She was the winner of the National Poetry Competition in 1979 and has received many prizes and awards for her work, including the Bass Ireland Award for Literature in 1991. Her recent publications include Marconi's Cottage, *published in Britain in 1992, and* Captain Lavender, *published in 1994.*

Slips

The studied poverty of a moon roof,
The earthenware of dairies cooled by apple trees,
The apple tree that makes the whitest wash . . .

But I forget names, remembering them wrongly
Where they touch upon another name,
A town in France like a woman's Christian name.

My childhood is preserved as a nation's history,
My favourite fairytales the shells
Leased by the hermit crab.

I see my grandmother's death as a piece of ice,
My mother's slimness restored to her,
My own key slotted in your door –

Tricks you might guess from this unfastened button,
A pen mislaid, a word misread,
My hair coming down in the middle of a conversation.

Venus and the Rain

White on white, I can never be viewed
Against a heavy sky – my gibbous voice
Passes from leaf to leaf, retelling the story
Of its own provocative fractures, till
Their facing coasts might almost fill each other
And they ask me in reply if I've
Decided to stop trying to make diamonds.

On one occasion, I rang like a bell
For a whole month, promising their torn edges
The birth of a new ocean (as all of us
Who have hollow bodies tend to do at times):
What clues to distance could they have,
So self-excited by my sagging sea,
Widening ten times faster than it really did?

Whatever rivers sawed their present lairs
Through my lightest, still-warm rocks,
I told them they were only giving up
A sun for sun, that cruising moonships find
Those icy domes relaxing, when they take her
Rind to pieces, and a waterfall
Unstitching itself down the front stairs.

Yeastlight

You speak like the rain, as if you were the weather.
I can almost see the passage of wine through your throat
As you swallow, its colour seems to be standing
Behind you, in the designer-blue air. When I found
In the very cup of the town those poems sewn
Into cushions, or pushed into saucepans or shoes,
I took the arm of someone I didn't know
Who turned over all my mattresses
And shook out every book.

I could not have imagined pearls had such warmth,
My house planned to catch the sun in all
Its rooms, in the shape of a fan, seemed no better
Than other houses; its clear note had gone out
And fallen in with the wind which sometimes
Sounds so much like rain, the passing
Of wise hands over shoulders, the frisking
Of clothing that remoulds you and restrains you,
Back into the narrow bed of a girl.

Still my dining-room with its gold oak-leaf
Paper, has three long windows looking west
Upon a ligulate forest, and famille rose,
Famille verte, china for an up-with-the-kettle,
Round-with-the-car, man, if you could not bear
To have it going on one moment longer,
Doors with their fertile roar, their desert
Glances, closing from the inside, not the out,
Or to have it ever stopped.

JOHN COOPER CLARKE (b.1950)

John Cooper Clarke was born in Salford in 1950 and after leaving school at fifteen worked as a mechanic, fire-watcher, dishwasher, mortuary attendant, bingo caller and stand-up comic. He came to prominence during the punk rock era, performing his work at music festivals and concerts, and has recorded and released records as well as publishing his poetry. Collections include The Cooper Clarke Directory *(1979) and* Ten Years in an Open-Necked Shirt *(1982).*

beezley street

far flung crazy pavements crack
the sound of empty rooms
a clinical arrangement
a dirty afternoon
where the fecal germs of mr freud
are rendered obsolete
the legal term is null and void
in the case of beezley street

in the cheap seats where murder breeds
somebody is out of breath
sleep is a luxury they don't need
a sneak preview of death
deadly nightshade is your flower
manslaughter your meat
spend a year in a couple of hours
on the edge of beezley street

where the action isn't
that's where it is
state your position
vacancies exist
in an x certificate exercise

ex servicemen explete
keith joseph smiles and a baby dies
in a box on beezley street

from the boarding houses and the bedsits
full of accidents and fleas
somebody gets it
where the missing persons freeze
wearing dead men's overcoats
you can't see their feet
a riff joint shuts and opens up
right down on beezley street

cars collide colours clash
disaster movie stuff
for the man with the fu manchu moustache
revenge is not enough
there's a dead canary on a swivel seat
there's a rainbow in the road
meanwhile on beezley street
silence is the mode

it's hot beneath the collar
an inspector calls
where the perishing stink of squalor
impregnates the walls
the rats have all got rickets
they spit through broken teeth
a blood stain is your ticket
one way down beezley street

the gangster and his hired hat
drive a borrowed car
he looks like the duke of edinburgh
but not so lah-di-dah
OAP mother-to-be

watch that three-piece suite
when shitstopper drains
and crocodile skis
are seen on beezley street

in the kingdom of the blind
where the one-eyed man is king
beauty problems are redefined
the doorbells do not ring
light bulbs pop like blisters
the only form of heat
where a fellow sells his sister
down the river on beezley street

the boys are on the wagon
the girls are on the shelf
their common problem
is that they're not someone else
the dirt blows out
the dust blows in
you can't keep it neat
it's a fully furnished dustbin
16 beezley street

vince the ageing savage
betrays no kind of life
but the smell of yesterday's cabbage
and the ghost of last year's wife
through a constant haze
of deodorant sprays
he says retreat
alsatians dog the dirty days
down the middle of beezley street

eyes dead as viscous fish
look around for laughs
if i could have just one wish

i would be a photograph
on this permanent monday morning
get lost or fall asleep
when the yellow cats are yawning
round the back of beezley street

people turn to poison quick
as lager turns to piss
sweethearts are physically sick
every time they kiss
it's a sociologist's paradise
each day repeats
uneasy cheesy greasy queasy beastly beezley street

FRANK KUPPNER (b.1951)

Frank Kuppner was born in Glasgow in 1951 and studied English and German at Glasgow University before leaving to train as an engineer. His books of poetry include A Bad Day for the Sung Dynasty *(1984),* The Intelligent Observations of Naked Women *(1987) and* Ridiculous! Absurd! Disgusting! *(1989). He has also published several novels.*

from A Bad Day for the Sung Dynasty

187.
The ridge reminiscent of a human hip-skeleton,
And the soft mountain an oddly nippled protrusion;
The drunkards in the riverside pavilion
Gaze away from the dancing girl, then back to her.

188.
A thick crowd is filling the busy shopping street;
The shopkeepers sit benignantly beneath their shutters;
No one whatever shops in the adjacent street;
But a crowd is racing either towards it or away from it, across a bridge.

189.
The photograph of the wall of the tomb includes some of the muddy
    ground;
There seem to be some footsteps at its very base;
A painted sheep stands above, its hooves eroded away;
Obviously the photographer did not go near enough to it.

190.
An elegant cart whirrs along the wide street;
Automatically the pedestrians adapt to it;
Neither of the men on board it in fact possesses a face;
But most are too intent on their own business to notice this.

191.
Plates spin juggle and twist, balls fly in clusters;
The king indulgently observes their trained antics;
When the panda plummets from the high pole,
The courtiers relax at the glimpse of regal amusement.

192.
Plates spin juggle and twist, balls fly in clusters;
The king indulgently observes their trained antics;
When the panda plummets from the high pole,
He stretches out a leisurely hand and catches it.

MENNA ELFYN (b.1951)

Menna Elfyn was born in 1951, brought up in the Swansea Valley and read Welsh at University College, Swansea. Since 1976 she has published several Welsh language collections. Her two collections with parallel translations include Eucalyptus *(1995) and* Cell Angel *(1996). She has twice been imprisoned for language campaigns, and works as a writer and in television. She lives in Llandysul.*

Dyn Eira

Mor syml yw'r sawl a godwn,
ei eni mewn orig. O'r bru gwyn
â dwylo brwd. Un solet,
a'i lygad uwch ysgwydd,
ef yw'n dyhead i'w ddal
yn ddiarfau,

a'i ddiffyg parhad.

Pelawdau o eira i ffwrdd,
ucheldiroedd a'i lethrau'n tynnu dyn
i weu simne o lwch glân,
yr eira'n benisel erlid –
pawennau'n dynesu at bydew –
am lechu. Am loches.

Uwchben, hofrenyddion digwsg
sy'n dwrdio'r ddaear a'i lliain,
nes daw'r nos hindrus
aeldremu'i guwch, uwch y lluwch;
                         a'r wlad

mor gegoer lonydd. Yna, dieithrio'r oriau
a wna. Rhifo'n rheibus y felltith
a'i blitha'n bla. Yna, daw'r achub,
cam dynion ar drywydd a'i faglodd,

a'i gario uwch yr olion
yn draed newydd atalnodus,
pob asgwrn a migwrn yn rhan o'r gredo.

Cyrraedd arall yw copa dynoliaeth,
y dyhead am glymiad. Am ildiad,
i ddoethineb arall. Yng nghysgod tafod lân,
daw'r eira yn rhwystr-iaith
er mwyn i ddynion ddod o hyd i allgaredd

sy'n uwch nag Everest,
yn isel megis crud.

Snowman*

*How simple the one we build
born in an hour. From a white embryo
with quick hands. Solid,
looking over his shoulder
he is the longing we keep
disarmed*

without future.

*Many snowballs away
are the high peaks that make a man
build a chimney from white dust
where low flying snow drives
paws to the lair. Cornered.*

*Above, the sleepless helicopters
scold the earth's linen
till hindering night comes
frowning over the drifts
                    and the land*

* Trans. by Gillian Clarke.

so dumb with cold, so still. The hours
turn strange, counting the cruel curse
that pours down plague. Then rescue comes,
men's footprints on the path which tripped him
and they bear him above their own tracks
freshly punctuating the snow
each bone, each knuckle part of the faith

in human summits,
the yearning to connect. To concede
to experience. So the clean language of snow
is stumble-tongued
so men may carry generosity

higher then Everest,
low as a crib.

PAUL MULDOON (b.1951)

Paul Muldoon was born in County Armagh in 1951, read English at Queen's University and published his first book, New Weather, *at the age of twenty-one. He has written a libretto and poetry for children, and is editor of* The Faber Book of Contemporary Irish Verse *(1988) and* The Faber Book of Beasts *(1997).* New Selected Poems 1968–1994 *contained poems from nine previous volumes, including* The Annals of Chile *which received the 1994 T. S. Eliot Prize. In 1986 he moved to the United States and is a professor at Princeton University, New Jersey.*

Incantata

In memory of Mary Farl Powers

I thought of you tonight, *a leanbh*, lying there in your long barrow
colder and dumber than a fish by Francisco de Herrera,
as I X-Actoed from a spud the Inca
glyph for a mouth: thought of that first time I saw your pink

spotted torso, distant-near as a nautilus,
when you undid your portfolio, yes indeedy,
and held the print of what looked like a cankered potato
at arm's length – your arms being longer, it seemed, than Lugh's.

Even Lugh of the Long (sometimes the Silver) Arm
would have wanted some distance between himself and the army-
    worms
that so clouded the sky over St Cloud you'd have to seal
the doors and windows and steel
yourself against their nightmarish *déjeuner sur l'herbe*:
try as you might to run a foil
across their tracks, it was to no avail;
the army-worms shinnied down the stove-pipe on an army-worm
    rope.

I can hardly believe that, when we met, my idea of 'R and R'
was to get smashed, almost every night, on sickly-sweet Demarara
rum and Coke: as well as leaving you a grass widow
(remember how Krapp looks up 'viduity'?),
after eight or ten or twelve of those dark rums
it might be eight or ten or twelve o'clock before I'd land
back home in Landseer Street, deaf and blind
to the fact that not only was I all at sea, but in the doldrums.

Again and again you'd hold forth on your own version of Thomism,
your own *Summa*
Theologiae that in everything there is an order,
that the things of the world sing out in a great oratorio:
it was Thomism, though, tempered by *La Nausée*,
by His Nibs Sam Bethicket,
and by that Dublin thing, that an artist must walk down Baggott
Street wearing a hair-shirt under the shirt of Nessus.

'*D'éirigh me ar maidin,*' I sang, '*a tharraingt chun aoinigh mhóir*':
our first night, you just had to let slip that your secret amour
for a friend of mine was such
that you'd ended up lying with him in a ditch

under a bit of whin, or gorse, or furze,
somewhere on the border of Leitrim, perhaps, or Roscommon:
'gamine,' I wanted to say, 'kimono';
even then it was clear I'd never be at the centre of your universe.

Nor should I have been, since you were there already, your own
   Ding
an sich, no less likely to take wing
than the Christ you drew for a Christmas card as a pupa
in swaddling clothes: and how resolutely you would pooh pooh
the idea I shared with Vladimir and Estragon,
with whom I'd been having a couple of jars,
that this image of the Christ-child swaddled and laid in the manger
could be traced directly to those army-worm dragoons.

I thought of the night Vladimir was explaining to all and sundry
the difference between *geantrai* and *suantrai*
and you remarked on how you used to have a crush
on Burt Lancaster as Elmer Gantry, and Vladimir went to brush
the ash off his sleeve with a legerdemain
that meant only one thing – 'Why does he put up with this crap?' –
and you weighed in with 'To live in a dustbin, eating scrap,
seemed to Nagg and Nell a most eminent domain.'

How little you were exercised by those tiresome literary intrigues,
how you urged me to have no more truck
than the Thane of Calder
with a fourth estate that professes itself to be '*égalitaire*'
but wants only blood on the sand: yet, irony of ironies,
you were the one who, in the end,
got yourself up as a *retiarius* and, armed with net and trident,
marched from Mount Street to the Merrion Square arena.

In the end, you were the one who went forth to beard the lion,
you who took the DART line
every day from Jane's flat in Dun Laoghaire, or Dalkey,
dreaming your dream that the subterranean Dodder and Tolka

might again be heard above the *hoi polloi*
for whom Irish 'art' means a High Cross at Carndonagh or Corofin
and *The Book of Kells*: not until the lion cried craven
would the poor Tolka and the poor Dodder again sing out for joy.

I saw you again tonight, in your jump-suit, thin as a rake,
your hand moving in such a deliberate arc
as you ground a lithographic stone
that your hand and the stone blurred to one
and your face blurred into the face of your mother, Betty Wahl,
who took your failing, ink-stained hand
in her failing, ink-stained hand
and together you ground down that stone by sheer force of will.

I remember your pooh poohing, as we sat there on the 'Enterprise',
my theory that if your name is Powers
you grow into it or, at least,
are less inclined to tremble before the likes of this bomb-blast
further up the track: I myself was shaking like a leaf
as we wondered whether the IRA or the Red
Hand Commandos or even the Red
Brigades had brought us to a standstill worthy of Hamm and Clov.

Hamm and Clov; Nagg and Nell; Watt and Knott;
the fact is that we'd been at a standstill long before the night
things came to a head,
long before we'd sat for half the day in the sweltering heat
somewhere just south of Killnasaggart
and I let slip a name – her name – off my tongue
and you turned away (I see it now) the better to deliver the sting
in your own tail, to let slip your own little secret.

I thought of you again tonight, thin as a rake, as you bent
over the copper plate of 'Emblements',
its tidal wave of army-worms into which you all but disappeared:
I wanted to catch something of its spirit
and yours, to body out your disembodied *vox*

clamantis in deserto, to let this all-too-cumbersome device
of a potato-mouth in a potato-face
speak out, unencumbered, from its long, low, mould-filled box.

I wanted it to speak to what seems always true of the truly great,
that you had a winningly inaccurate
sense of your own worth, that you would second-guess
yourself too readily by far, that you would rally to any cause
before your own, mine even,
though you detected in me a tendency to put
on too much artificiality, both as man and poet,
which is why you called me 'Polyester' or 'Polyurethane'.

That last time in Dublin, I copied with a quill dipped in oak-gall
onto a sheet of vellum, or maybe a human caul,
a poem for *The Great Book of Ireland*: as I watched the low
swoop over the lawn today of a swallow
I thought of your animated talk of Camille Pissarro
and André Derain's *The Turning Road, L'Estaque*:
when I saw in that swallow's nest a face in a mud-pack
from that muddy road I was filled again with a profound sorrow.

You must have known already, as we moved from the 'Hurly Burly'
to McDaid's or Riley's,
that something was amiss: I think you even mentioned a
     homeopath
as you showed off the great new acid-bath
in the Graphic Studio, and again undid your portfolio
to lay out your latest works; I try to imagine the strain
you must have been under, pretending to be as right as rain
while hearing the bells of a church from some long-flooded valley.

From the Quabbin reservoir, maybe, where the banks and bakeries
of a dozen little submerged Pompeii reliquaries
still do a roaring trade: as clearly as I saw your death-mask
in that swallow's nest, you must have heard the music

rise from the muddy ground between
your breasts as a nocturne, maybe, by John Field;
to think that you thought yourself so invulnerable, so inviolate,
that a little cancer could be beaten.

You must have known, as we walked through the ankle-deep
   clabber
with Katherine and Jean and the long-winded Quintus Calaber,
that cancer had already made such a breach
that you would almost surely perish:
you must have thought, as we walked through the woods
along the edge of the Quabbin,
that rather than let some doctor cut you open
you'd rely on infusions of hardock, hemlock, all the idle weeds.

I thought again of how art may be made, as it was by André Derain,
of nothing more than a turn
in the road where a swallow dips into the mire
or plucks a strand of bloody wool from a strand of barbed wire
in the aftermath of Chickamauga or Culloden
and builds from pain, from misery, from a deep-seated hurt,
a monument to the human heart
that shines like a golden dome among roofs rain-glazed and leaden.

I wanted the mouth in this potato-cut
to be heard far beyond the leaden, rain-glazed roofs of Quito,
to be heard all the way from the southern hemisphere
to Clontarf or Clondalkin, to wherever your sweet-severe
spirit might still find a toe-hold
in this world: it struck me then how you would be aghast
at the thought of my thinking you were some kind of ghost
who might still roam the earth in search of an earthly delight.

You'd be aghast at the idea of your spirit hanging over this vale
of tears like a jump-suited jump-jet whose vapour-trail
unravels a sky: for there's nothing, you'd say, nothing over
and above the sky itself, nothing but cloud-cover

reflected in a thousand lakes; it seems that Minne-
sota itself means 'sky-tinted water', that the sky is a great slab
of granite or iron ore that might at any moment slip
back into the worked-out sky-quarry, into the worked-out sky-
   mines.

To use the word 'might' is to betray you once too often, to betray
your notion that nothing's random, nothing arbitrary:
the gelignite weeps, the hands fly by on the alarm clock,
the 'Enterprise' goes clackety-clack
as they all must; even the car hijacked that morning in the Cross,
that was preordained, its owner spread on the bonnet
before being gagged and bound or bound
and gagged, that was fixed like the stars in the Southern Cross.

That fact that you were determined to cut yourself off in your prime
because it was *pre*-determined has my eyes abrim:
I crouch with Belacqua
and Lucky and Pozzo in the Acacacac-
ademy of Anthropopopometry, trying to make sense of the '*quaquaqua*'
of that potato-mouth; that mouth as prim
and proper as it's full of self-opprobrium,
with its '*quaquaqua*', with its 'Quoiquoiquoiquoiquoiquoiquoiq'.

That's all that's left of the voice of Enrico Caruso
from all that's left of an opera-house somewhere in Matto Grosso,
all that's left of the hogweed and horehound and cuckoo-pint,
of the eighteen soldiers dead at Warrenpoint,
of the Black Church clique and the Graphic Studio claque,
of the many moons of glasses on a tray,
of the brewery-carts drawn by moon-booted drays,
of those jump-suits worn under your bottle-green worsted cloak.

Of the great big dishes of chicken lo mein and beef chow mein,
of what's mine is yours and what's yours mine,
of the oxlips and cowslips
on the banks of the Liffey at Leixlip

where the salmon breaks through the either/or neither/nor nether
reaches despite the temple-veil
of itself being rent and the penny left out overnight on the rail
is a sheet of copper when the mail-train has passed over.

Of the bride carried over the threshold, hey, only to alight
on the limestone slab of another threshold,
of the swarm, the cast,
the colt, the spew of bees hanging like a bottle of Lucozade
from a branch the groom must sever,
of Emily Post's ruling, in *Etiquette*,
on how best to deal with the butler being in cahoots
with the cook when they're both in cahoots with the chauffeur.

Of that poplar-flanked stretch of road between Leiden
and The Hague, of the road between Rathmullen and Ramelton,
where we looked so long and hard
for some trace of Spinoza or Amelia Earhart,
both of them going down with their engines on fire:
of the stretch of road somewhere near Urney
where Orpheus was again overwhelmed by that urge to turn
back and lost not only Eurydice but his steel-strung lyre.

Of the sparrows and finches in their bell of suet,
of the bitter-sweet
bottle of Calvados we felt obliged to open
somewhere near Falaise, so as to toast our new-found *copains*,
of the priest of the parish
who came enquiring about our 'status', of the hedge-clippers
I somehow had to hand, of him running like the clappers
up Landseer Street, of my subsequent self-reproach.

Of the remnants of Airey Neave, of the remnants of Mountbatten,
of the famous *andouilles*, of the famous *boudins*
noirs et blancs, of the barrel-vault
of the Cathedral at Rouen, of the flashlight, fat and roll of felt
on each of their sledges, of the music

of Joseph Beuys's pack of huskies, of that baldy little bugger
mushing them all the way from Berncastel through Bacarrat
to Belfast, his head stuck with honey and gold-leaf like a mosque.

Of Benjamin Britten's *Lachrymae*, with its gut-wrenching viola,
of Vivaldi's *Four Seasons*, of Frankie Valli's,
of Braque's great painting *The Shower of Rain*,
of the fizzy, lemon or sherbet-green *Ranus ranus*
plonked down in Trinity like a little Naugahyde pouffe,
of eighteen soldiers dead in Oriel,
of the weakness for a little fol-de-rol-de-rolly
suggested by the gap between the front teeth of the Wife of Bath.

Of *A Sunday Afternoon on the Island of La Grande Jatte*, of Seurat's
piling of tesserae upon tesserae
to give us a monkey arching its back
and the smoke arching out from a smoke-stack,
of Sunday afternoons in the Botanic Gardens, going with the flow
of the burghers of Sandy Row and Donegal
Pass and Andersonstown and Rathcoole,
of the army Landrover flaunt-flouncing by with its heavy furbelow.

Of Marlborough Park, of Notting Hill, of the Fitzroy Avenue
immortalized by Van 'His real name's Ivan'
Morrison, 'and him the dead spit
of Padraic Fiacc', of John Hewitt, the famous expat,
in whose memory they offer every year six of their best milch cows,
of the Bard of Ballymacarrett,
of every ungodly poet in his or her godly garret,
of Medhbh and Michael and Frank and Ciaran and 'wee' John
    Qughes.

Of the Belfast school, so called, of the school of hard knocks,
of your fervent eschewal of stockings and socks
as you set out to hunt down your foes
as implacably as the *tóraidheacht* through the Fews
of Redmond O'Hanlon, of how that 'd' and that 'c' aspirate

in *tóraidheacht* make it sound like a last gasp in an oxygen-tent,
of your refusal to open a vent
but to breathe in spirit of salt, the mordant salt-spirit.

Of how mordantly hydrochloric acid must have scored and scarred,
of the claim that boiled skirrets
can cure the spitting of blood, of that dank
flat somewhere off Morehampton Road, of the unbelievable stink
of valerian or feverfew simmering over a low heat,
of your sitting there, pale and gaunt,
with that great prescriber of boiled skirrets, Dr John Arbuthnot,
your face in a bowl of feverfew, a towel over your head.

Of the great roll of paper like a bolt of cloth
running out again and again like a road at the edge of a cliff,
of how you called a Red Admiral a Red
Admirable, of how you were never in the red
on either the first or the last
of the month, of your habit of loosing the drawstring of your
     purse
and finding one scrunched-up, obstreperous
note and smoothing it out and holding it up, pristine and pellucid.

Of how you spent your whole life with your back to the wall,
of your generosity when all the while
you yourself lived from hand
to mouth, of Joseph Beuys's pack of hounds
crying out from their felt and fat 'Atone, atone, atone',
of Watt remembering the '*Krak! Krek! Krik!*'
of those three frogs' karaoke
like the still, sad, *basso continuo* of the great quotidian.

Of a ground bass of sadness, yes, but also a sennet of hautboys
as the fat and felt hounds of Beuys O'Beuys
bayed at the moon over a caravan
in Dunmore East, I'm pretty sure it was, or Dungarvan:
of my guest appearance in your self-portrait not as a hidalgo

from a long line
of hidalgos but a hound-dog, a *leanbh*,
a dog that skulks in the background, a dog that skulks and stalks.

Of that self-portrait, of the self-portraits by Rembrandt van Rijn,
of all that's revelation, all that's rune,
of all that's composed, all composed of odds and ends,
of that daft urge to make amends
when it's far too late, too late even to make sense of the clutter
of false trails and reversed horseshoe tracks
and the aniseed we took it in turn to drag
across each other's scents, when only a fish is dumber and colder.

Of your avoidance of canned goods, in the main,
on account of the exceeeeeeeeeeeeeeeedingly high risk of
    ptomaine,
of corned beef in particular being full of crap,
of your delight, so, in eating a banana as ceremoniously as Krapp
but flinging the skin over your shoulder like a thrush
flinging off a shell from which it's only just managed to disinter
a snail, like a stone-faced, twelfth-century
FitzKrapp eating his banana by the mellow, yellow light of a rush.

Of the 'Yes, let's go' spoken by Monsieur Tarragon,
of the early-ripening jardonelle, the tumorous jardon, the jargon
of jays, the jars
of tomato relish and the jars
of Victoria plums, absolutely *de rigueur* for a passable plum baba,
of the drawers full of balls of twine and butcher's string,
of Dire Straits playing 'The Sultans of Swing',
of the horse's hock suddenly erupting in those boils and buboes.

Of the Greek figurine of a pig, of the pig on a terracotta frieze,
of the sow dropping dead from some mysterious virus,
of your predilection for gammon
served with a sauce of coriander or cumin,

of the slippery elm, of the hornbeam or witch-, or even wych-,
hazel that's good for stopping a haemor-
rhage in mid-flow, of the merest of mere
hints of elderberry curing everything from sciatica to a stitch.

Of the decree *condemnator*, the decree *absolvitor*, the decree *nisi*,
of *Aosdána*, of *an chraobh cnuais*,
of the fields of buckwheat
taken over by garget, inkberry, scoke – all names for pokeweed –
of *Mother Courage*, of *Arturo Ui*,
of those Sunday mornings spent picking at sesame
noodles and all sorts and conditions of dim sum,
of tea and ham sandwiches in the Nesbitt Arms hotel in Ardara.

Of the day your father came to call, of your leaving your sick-room
in what can only have been a state of delirium,
of how you simply wouldn't relent
from your vision of a blind
watch-maker, of your fatal belief that fate
governs everything from the honey-rust of your father's terrier's
eyebrows to the horse that rusts and rears
in the furrow, of the furrows from which we can no more deviate

than they can from themselves, no more than the map of Europe
can be redrawn, than that Hermes might make a harp from his *harpe*,
than that we must live in a vale
of tears on the banks of the Lagan or the Foyle,
than that what we have is a done deal,
than that the Irish Hermes,
Lugh, might have leafed through his vast herbarium
for the leaf that had it within it, Mary, to anoint and anneal,

than that Lugh of the Long Arm might have found in the midst of *lus
na leac* or *lus na treatha* or *Frannc-lus*,
in the midst of eyebright, or speedwell, or tansy, an antidote,
than that this *Incantata*

might have you look up from your plate of copper or zinc
on which you've etched the row upon row
of army-worms, than that you might reach out, arrah,
and take in your ink-stained hands my own hands stained with ink.

NUALA NÍ DHOMHNAILL (b.1952)

Nuala Ní Dhomhnaill was born in Lancashire in 1952, grew up in West Kerry and lives in Dublin. Her books in Irish include Feis *(1991), and collections with English translations include* Rogha Danta/Selected Poems *(translated by Michael Hartnett, 1986),* Pharaoh's Daughter *(various translators, 1990) and* The Astrakhan Cloak *(translated by Paul Muldoon, 1992).*

Geasa

Má chuirim aon lámh ar an dtearmann beannaithe,
má thógaim droichead thar an abhainn,
gach a mbíonn tógtha isló ages na ceardaithe
bíonn sé leagtha ar maidin romham.

Tagann aníos an abhainn istoíche bád
is bean ina seasamh inti.
Tá coinneal ar lasadh ina súil is ina lámha.
Tá dhá mhaide rámha aici.

Tairrigíonn sí amach paca cártaí,
'An imréofá breith?' a deireann sí.
Imrímid is buann sí orm de shíor
is cuireann sí de cheist, de bhreith is de mhórualach orm

Gan an tarna béile a ithe in aon tigh,
ná an tarna oíche a chaitheamh faoi aon díon,
gan dhá shraic chodlata a dhéanamh ar aon leaba
go bhfaighead í. Nuair a fhiafraím di cá mbíonn sí,

'Dá mba siar é soir,' a deireann sí, 'dá mba soir é siar.'
Imíonn sí léi agus splancacha tintrí léi
is fágtar ansan mé ar an bport.
Tá an dá choinneal fós ar lasadh le mo thaobh.

D'fhág sí na maidí rámha agam.

The Bond*

If I use my forbidden hand
To raise a bridge across the river,
All the work of the builders
Has been blown up by sunrise.

A boat comes up the river by night
With a woman standing in it,
Twin candles lit in her eyes
And two oars in her hands.

She unsheathes a pack of cards,
'Will you play forfeits?' she says.
We play and she beats me hands down,
And she puts three banns upon me:

Not to have two meals in one house,
Not to pass two nights under one roof,
Not to sleep twice with the same man
Until I find her. When I ask her address,

'If it were north I'd tell you south,
If it were east, west.' She hooks
Off in a flash of lightning, leaving me
Stranded on the bank,

My eyes full of candles,
And the two dead oars.

* Trans. by Medbh McGuckian.

An tSeanbhean Bhocht

Féachann an tseanbhean orm le neamhshuim is uabhar
as a súile tréigthe atá ar dhath na mbugha
ag cuimhneamh siar ar laethanta geala a hóige,
gur thrua go raibh gach ní chomh buacach san aimsir ollfhoirfe.
Canathaobh an uair úd nuair a chan éan
gurbh í an neachtingeal a bhí i gcónaí ann?
Canathaobh fadó nuair a thug leannáin chúichi
fleascanna bláth gurb iad na cinn 'orchidé en fleur'
ab fhearr a fuaireadar? Nó b'fhéidir ar laethanta fuara
sailchuacha cumhra. I gcónaí bhíodh buidéal seaimpéin
ar an gclár i mbuicéad ard leac oighre, bhíodh lása Charraig
   Mhachaire Rois
ar chaola a láimhe is bhíodh diamaintí ar sileadh óna cluasa,
muince péarlaí casta seacht n-uaire thart faoina bráid,
is ar a méireanta bhíodh fáinní luachmhara, go háirithe
ceann gur chuimhin léi a bheith an-speisialta – ceann
ar a raibh smeargaidí chomh mór le húll do phíopáin.

Féachann sí orm anois leis an dtruamhéil fhuar
a chífeá go minic i súile a bhí tráth óg is breá,
ag meabhrú di féin im' fhianaise, leath os íseal
is leath os ard, gur mhéanar don té a fuair amharc
ar an gcéad lá a shiúil sí go mómharach síos an phromanáid
mar ríon faoina parasól; ar na céadta céadta gaiscíoch
is fear breá a chuaigh le saighdiúireacht in arm na Breataine
nó a theith leo ar bord loinge go dtí na tíortha teo,
aon ní ach éaló ós na saigheada éagóra
a theilgeadh sí orthu de shíor faoina fabhraí tiubha.

Caoineann sí, ag monabhar faoina hanáil go bog,
an tréimhse fhada, achar bliana is lae,
ar thug sí an svae léithi mar bhanríon na bplainéad:
na leanaí a bheirtí nuair a théadh sí faoi loch
i ndaigh uisce i lár na cistineach,
múchadh nó bá an chríoch bháis a bhíodh orthu

is dob é an chroch a bhí i ndán do gach n-aon.
a raibh de mhí-ádh air teacht ar an saol
nuair a bhí lúb na téide tarraingthe ar a muinéal.
Is iad siúd a chéadchonaic solas an lae
nuair a léimeadh sí sa tine gurbh é a ndeireadh
a bheith dóite is loiscithe le teann grá di féin,
chun gur thit na céadta ina sraithibh deas is clé
ní le grá bán nó breac ná grá pósta, mo léir
ach an grá dubh is an manglam dicé a leanann é.

Anois tá sí cancarach, ag tabhairt amach dom
ar dalladh. Tá sí bréan bodhar badráilte
ó bheith suite ina cathaoir rotha. Gan faic
na ngrást le déanamh aici ach a bheith ag féachaint
ar na ceithre fallaí. Rud eile,
níl na cailíní aimsire faoi mar a bhídís
cheana. Fágann siad rianta smeartha
ar an *antimacassar* lena méireanta salacha.
Fuair sí an píosa bróidnéireachta sin ó bhean
ambasadóra is bheadh an-dochma uirthi é a scaoileadh
chun siúil nó tré dhearmhad ligint dóibh siúd
é a mhilleadh.

Tugaim faoi ndeara nach nguíonn sí
sonuachar maith chúchu nuair a thagann siad
isteach leis an dtrádaire líonta síos go talamh
le gréithre póirseiléine, taephota airgid
is ceapairí cúcumair. Táimse ar thaobh na gcailíní,
is deirim léi cén dochar, go bhfuil siad fós óg,
is nach féidir ceann críonna a chur ar cholainn,
nach dtagann ciall roimh aois is gur mó craiceann . . .
is gur ag dul i minithe is i mbréagaí atá gach dream
dá dtagann: gach seanrá a thagann isteach i mo chloigeann.
aon rud ach an tseanbhean bhaoth seo a choimeád socair.

The Shan Van Vocht*

The faded cornflower blue of that old woman's eye
Stares through me – it's as if I wasn't there – back to where
The bright days of her youth shine through,
Lamenting all the halcyon monotony of that pluperfect time.
How come no common birds sang then,
Only nightingales?
How come her 'nice young men' would offer her,
Not just a bunch of flowers, but out-of-season orchids?
Or cold-weather, fragrant violets? And then, the eternal
Champagne on ice, the froth of lace at her wrists, diamonds
Dripping from her ears, pearls wound seven times
Around her neck, her fingers ponderous
With expensive rings, one with an emerald
As big as an Adam's apple.

That ice-blue pity stares through me, she
Whose eyes were radiant once with youth and blue fire –
How privileged they were, the poor unfortunates
Who caught a glimpse of her in all her majesty, gliding
On the promenade beneath a queenly parasol; the regiments
Of stricken youths who took to soldiering, who
Laboured in the White Man's Grave, anything
To flee the blue illicit lightning
She squandered from those eyes.

She's mumbling, babbling, murmuring
About that Long-Ago of a Year and a Day
When she held sway as Empress of the Zodiac;
And those who were born while she kicked and squealed
In a bath plonked down on the kitchen floor, well,
They were doomed to be drowned or smothered
And the ill-starred ones who came into the world
When the noose got tighter on her neck

* Trans. by Ciaran Carson.

Were doomed to be strung up
And those first smitten by the light of day
While she danced in the fire
Were doomed to be burned-out, dazzled and frazzled
With all-consuming love for her
So that it came to pass that they were mowed down
In their hundreds, left and right, not with love
That you or I know, no, not with ordinary love
But with a gnawing, migraine-bright black lust
And galloping consumption.

She's getting to be cranky, cantankerous
And cancered, slabbering of this and that, straight-
Jacketed to her wheelchair, locked
Into self-pity, whingeing on and on – damn
All to do all day, but stare at these four walls.
And servants, of course, aren't what they used to be.
Look how these two chits of girls
Have smeared their greasy paws on the antimacassar.
And that embroidered tablecloth – you know the ambassador?
Well, his wife gave that to her. And she wouldn't like
To see it ruined by those same two hussies.

And here they come now, tinkling in
With an overloaded tray – china tea-set, silver pot,
The dreaded cucumber sandwiches. Not a word from her,
I notice, about their *prospects. Well, I'm on their side*
And I mutter something, that they're young yet, that wisdom
Only comes with age, that you can't put an old head on young shoul- . . .
Folly, I'm saying, gets worse with every generation:
Anything, every old cliché in the book, anything at all
To get this old bitch to shut the fuck up.

Ceist na Teangan

Cuirim mo dhóchas ar snámh
i mbáidín teangan
faoi mar a leagfá naíonán
i gcliabhán
a bheadh fite fuaite
de dhuilleoga feileastraim
is bitiúman agus pic
bheith cuimilte lena thóin

ansan é a leagadh síos
i measc na ngiolcach
is coigeal na mban sí
le taobh na habhann,
féachaint n'fheadaraís
cá dtabharfaidh an sruth é,
féachaint, dála Mhaoise,
an bhfóirfidh iníon Fhorainn?

*The Language Issue**

*I place my hope on the water
in this little boat
of the language, the way a body might put
an infant*

*in a basket of intertwined
iris leaves,
its underside proofed
with bitumen and pitch,*

---

* Trans. by Paul Muldoon.

then set the whole thing down amidst
the sedge
and bulrushes by the edge
of a river

only to have it borne hither and thither,
not knowing where it might end up;
in the lap, perhaps,
of some Pharaoh's daughter.

LINTON KWESI JOHNSON (b.1952)

Linton Kwesi Johnson was born in Chapelton, Jamaica, in 1952, and came to London in 1963. As well as publishing poetry he has released a number of records and is well-known for his performances combining poetry and dub. Tings an Times was his most recent album, and also the title of his selected poems, published in 1991.

Inglan Is a Bitch

w'en mi jus' come to Landan toun
mi use to work pan di andahgroun
but workin' pan di andahgroun
y'u don't get fi know your way aroun'

Inglan is a bitch
dere's no escapin' it
Inglan is a bitch
dere's no runnin' whey fram it

mi get a lickle jab in a big 'otell
an' awftah a while, mi woz doin' quite well
dem staat mi aaf as a dish-washah
but w'en mi tek a stack, mi noh tun clack-watchah!

Inglan is a bitch
dere's no escapin' it
Inglan is a bitch
noh baddah try fi hide fram it

w'en dem gi' yu di lickle wage packit
fus dem rab it wid dem big tax racket
y'u haffi struggle fi mek en's meet
an' w'en y'u goh a y'u bed y'u jus' cant sleep

Inglan is a bitch
dere's no escapin' it
Inglan is a bitch fi true
a noh lie mi a tell, a true

mi use to work dig ditch w'en it cowl noh bitch
mi did strang like a mule, but, bwoy, mi did fool
den awftah a while mi jus' stap dhu ovahtime
den awftah a while mi jus' phu dung mi tool

Inglan is a bitch
dere's no escapin' it
Inglan is a bitch
y'u haffi know how fi suvvive in it

well mi dhu day wok an' mi dhu nite wok
mi dhu clean wok an' mi dhu dutty wok
dem seh dat black man is very lazy
but if y'u si how mi wok y'u woulda seh mi crazy

Inglan is a bitch
dere's no escapin' it
Inglan is a bitch
y'u bettah face up to it

dem have a lickle facktri up inna Brackly
inna disya facktri all dem dhu is pack crackry
fi di laas fifteen years dem get mi laybah
now awftah fifteen years mi fall out a fayvah

Inglan is a bitch
dere's no escapin' it
Inglan is a bitch
dere's no runnin' whey fram it

mi know dem have work, work in abundant
yet still, dem mek mi redundant
now, at fifty-five mi gettin' quite ol'
yet still, dem sen' mi fi goh draw dole

Inglan is a bitch
dere's no escapin' it
Inglan is a bitch fi true
is whey wi a goh dhu 'bout it?

ANDREW MOTION (b.1952)

Andrew Motion was born in 1952 in London, and his first volume of poetry, The
Pleasure Steamers, *was published in 1978. He is Professor of Creative Writing at
the University of East Anglia and has published prose fiction and also biography,
including* Philip Larkin: A Writer's Life *(1993) and* Keats *(1997). In 1982 he
co-edited* The Penguin Book of Contemporary British Poetry; *his recent
collections of poetry include* Salt Water, *published in 1997. He lives in London.*

The Letter

If I remember right, his first letter.
Found where? My side-plate perhaps,
or propped on our heavy brown tea-pot.
One thing is clear – my brother leaning
across asking *Who is he?* half angry
as always that summer before enlistment.

Then alone in the sunlit yard, mother
unlocking a door to call *Up so early?*
– waving her yellow duster goodbye
in a small sinking cloud. The gate creaks
shut and there in the lane I am running
uphill, vanishing where the woodland starts.

The Ashground. A solid contour swept
through ripening wheat, and fringe
of stippled green shading the furrow.
Now I am hardly breathing, gripping
the thin paper and reading *Write to me.*
Writer to me please. I miss you. My angel.

Almost shocked, but repeating him line
by line, and watching the words jitter
under the pale spidery shadows of leaves.
How else did I leave the plane unheard
so long? But suddenly there it was –
a Messerschmitt low at the wood's edge.

What I see today is the window open,
the pilot's unguarded face somehow
closer than possible. Goggles pushed up,
a stripe of ginger moustache, and his eyes
fixed on my own while I stand
with the letter held out, my frock blowing,

before I am lost in cover again,
heading for home. He must have banked
at once, climbing steeply until his jump
and watching our simple village below –
the Downs swelling and flattening, speckled
with farms and bushy chalk-pits. By lunch

they found where he lay, the parachute
tight in its pack, and both hands spread
as if they could break the fall. I still

imagine him there exactly. His face pressed
close to the sweet-smelling grass. His legs
splayed wide in a candid unshamable V.

Bathing at Glymenopoulo

Lotophagi. I can believe it:
first moment ashore the heat
stunned us – a lavish blast
and the stink of horses.
Then it was *Mister. Mister.*
Captain McKenzie – bathing girls
round from the beach, white
towels and parasols weaving
through gun-carriages, crates
and saddlery lined on the quay
to pelt us with flowers. *Want*
Captain McKenzie? I give you
good times. But we rode away,
eyes-front and smiling, pursued
until the Majestic gates.

Men to the grounds, officers
one to a cool high-ceilinged room –
mine with a balcony looking
down to the lake. There were pelicans
clambering carefully in and out
and in, never still, wrecking
the stagnant calm, fighting,
and shaking their throats
with a flabby rattle. Otherwise,
peace – the cedar layered
in enormous green-black slabs
and shading tents on the lawn;

the horses only a rumour –
stamping and snorting
out by the kitchen garden.

Each morning we rode early
to Christmas Hill – two hours
of dressage in dusty circuits
then home with the sun still low.
For the rest, time was our own –
no orders, no news from France,
but delicious boredom: polo
some evenings, and long afternoons
bathing at Glymenopoulo. Iras,
I have you by heart, giggling
and stumbling up from the breakers
into my photograph, one thin hand
pressed to your cheek, your knee-
length, navy-blue costume puckered
and clinging. I singled you out

day after day after day –
to swim with, to dawdle
arm in arm on the beach
as the furious sun sank, and later
to hear your pidgin whispers
dancing in waterfront cafés:
You not like anyone. Gentling
than other Captain McKenzies.
You not like others –
your lemon-smelling hair
loose and brushing my mouth,
your bracelets clinking,
and languorous slow waltzes
twirling us round and round
in the smoky half-light. *Luck.*

I kept telling myself. *Luck.*
It will end – but the lazy days
stretched into months,
and then we were riding out
on a clear pastel-blue morning
to Christmas Hill as ever.
And half-way, at Kalia,
stopped at our watering place –
a date grove fringing the pool,
and the whole troop fanned
in a crescent to drink.
I was dismounted, leading my horse
over packed sand, empty-headed
and waving flies from my face
when the firing began. Ten shots,

perhaps – flips and smacks
into date trunks or puffing the sand
and nobody hurt. But we charged –
all of us thinking *At last. Action
at last*, as our clumsy light brigade
wheeled under the trees and away
up a steady slope. I was far left,
drawing my sword with a stupid
high-pitched yelp as we laboured
through silvery mirage lakes.
They were waiting ahead –
Senussi, no more than a dozen,
their gypsy silhouettes crouching
and slinking back into stones
as we breasted the rise.

The end of the world. A sheer
wall falling hundreds of feet
to a haze of yellow scrub.

I wrenched myself round, sword
dropped, head low, to a dead
teetering halt as our line
staggered, and buckled, and broke
in a clattering slide. I can
hear it again – the panicking
whinneys, shouts, and the rush
of scree where they shambled off
into space. It has taken three days
to bury them – one for the trek
to the valley floor, one to scratch
their ranks of graves, one to return.

There is little the same. At six
we have curfew now: I am writing this
after dark, on my knee, in the School
of Instruction grounds, in a tent.
I cannot sleep – sirens disturb me,
groaning up from the harbour.
Those are the ships from Gallipoli,
unloading their trail of stretchers
to the Majestic, where you will be
waiting, Iras, I know, stopped
outside the gates, high-heeled
just as you were, with your hair
fluffed out after swimming, repeating
your tender sluttish call, *Want
Captain McKenzie? I give you good times.*

On the Table

I would like to make it clear that I have bought
this tablecloth with its simple repeating pattern
of dark purple blooms not named by any botanist
because it reminds me of that printed dress you had

the summer we met – a dress you have always said
I never told you I liked. Well I did, you know. I did.
I liked it a lot, whether you were inside it or not.

How did it slip so quietly out of our life?
I hate – I really hate – to think of some other bum
swinging those heavy flower-heads left to right.
I hate even more to think of it mouldering on a tip
or torn to shreds – a piece here wiping a dipstick,
a piece there tied round a crack in a lead pipe.

It's all a long time ago now, darling, a long time,
but tonight just like our first night here I am
with my head light in my hands and my glass full,
staring at the big drowsy petals until they start to swim,
loving them but wishing to lift them aside, unbutton them,
tear them, even, if that's what it takes to get through
to the beautiful, moon-white, warm, wanting skin of you.

HELEN DUNMORE (b.1952)

Helen Dunmore is a poet, novelist and children's writer. She was born in Yorkshire in 1952 and lives in Bristol. In 1996 her novel A Spell in Winter *won the Orange Prize, and her* New and Selected Poems: Short Days, Long Nights *(1991) contained work from four previous volumes. More recent collections are* Recovering a Body *(1994) and* Bestiary *(1997).*

The dream-life of priests

Do they wake careless and warm
with light on the unwashed windows
and a perpetual smell of bacon,

do their hearts sink at today's martyr
with his unpronounceable name
and strange manner of execution?

Do they wake out of the darkness
with hearts thudding like ours
and reach for the souvenir lamp-switch

then shove a chair against the door
and key facts into the desk-top computer
while cold rattles along the corridor?

Do they cry out in sleep
at some barely-crushed thought,
some failure to see the joke,

or do they rest in their dreams
along the surface of the water
like a bevy of dragonflies

slack and blue in the shallows
whirring among reed-mace and water-forget-me-not
while the ripples cluck?

Do they wake in ordinary time
to green curtains slapping the frame
of a day that'll cloud later on,

to cars nudging and growling for space,
to a baptismal mother, wan with her eagerness
and her sleepless, milk-sodden nights?

Do they reach and stroke the uneven plaster
and sniff the lime-blossom threading
like silk through the room,

or do they wait, stretched out like babies
in the gold of its being too early
with sun on their ceilings wobbling like jelly

while their housekeepers jingle the milk-bottles
and cry 'Father!' in sixty-year-old voices
and scorch toast with devotion –

do they sense the milk in the pan rising
then dive with their blue chins, blundering
through prayer under their honeycomb blankets?

Wild strawberries

What I get I bring home to you:
a dark handful, sweet-edged,
dissolving in one mouthful.

I bother to bring them for you
though they're so quickly over,
pulpless, sliding to juice,

a grainy rub on the tongue
and the taste's gone. If you remember
we were in the woods at wild strawberry time

and I was making a basket of dockleaves
to hold what you'd picked,
but the cold leaves unplaited themselves

and slid apart, and again unplaited themselves
until I gave up and ate wild strawberries
out of your hands for sweetness.

I lipped at your palm –
the little salt edge there,
the tang of money you'd handled.

As we stayed in the wood, hidden,
we heard the sound system below us
calling the winners at Chepstow,
faint as the breeze turned.

The sun came out on us, the shade blotches
went hazel: we heard names
bubble like stock-doves over the woods

as jockeys in stained silks gentled
those sweat-dark, shuddering horses
down to the walk.

SEAN O'BRIEN (b.1952)

*Sean O'Brien was born in London in 1952 and grew up in Hull. He read English
at Cambridge, was a schoolteacher in Sussex for several years and has held writing
fellowships and residences in England and Scotland. He won a Somerset Maugham
Award and a Cholmondeley Award for his books* The Indoor Park *(1983) and*
The Frighteners *(1987), and his most recent collection,* Ghost Train, *received the
1995 Forward Poetry Prize. He is a regular reviewer of poetry in the national press
and is the author of* The Deregulated Muse, *a series of essays on contemporary
verse. He lives in Newcastle-upon-Tyne.*

Cousin Coat

You are my secret coat. You're never dry.
You wear the weight and stink of black canals.
Malodorous companion, we know why
It's taken me so long to see we're pals,
To learn why my acquaintance never sniff
Or send me notes to say I stink of stiff.

But you don't talk, historical bespoke.
You must be worn, be intimate as skin,
And though I never lived what you invoke,
At birth I was already buttoned in.
Your clammy itch became my atmosphere,
An air made half of anger, half of fear.

And what you are is what I tried to shed
In libraries with Donne and Henry James.
You're here to bear a message from the dead
Whose history's dishonoured with their names.
You mean the North, the poor, and troopers sent
To shoot down those who showed their discontent.

No comfort there for comfy meliorists
Grown weepy over Jarrow photographs.
No comfort when the poor the state enlists
Parade before their fathers' cenotaphs.
No comfort when the strikers all go back
To see which twenty thousand get the sack.

Be with me when they cauterise the facts.
Be with me to the bottom of the page,
Insisting on what history exacts.
Be memory, be conscience, will and rage,
And keep me cold and honest, cousin coat,
So if I lie, I'll know you're at my throat.

A Rarity

It's under the X where the viaducts met.
It was round the back and further down
And it isn't that street but a vanished
Identical elsewhere that waits
In a different night with a different accent
Beneath a blue sign reading TIXE.
Kelly's *Apocrypha* offers no entry
But don't let that stop you from wasting
The middling years in pursuit of a number
Whose title escapes you, a band you can't
Even remember or swear to have heard.
Polish your shoes, climb into bed
And breathe in the sweetness of nylon and Bass.

The girls are done up to the nines,
Like racoons with affective disorders,
Rehearsing three steps round their handbags
And speaking in smoke-rings, a code
Meaning *Fuck off and die* or *Be older*,
Knowing it's to you the management reserves
The right to do pre-emptive violence.
You almost believe in the night you went
In on a whim and came out on a stretcher
With VOX back-to-front on your forehead.
Then rippling its skin of sweat
The bar retires to infinity, bulb
After bulb swinging back to the stillness
Your dreaming's disrupted, the night
Before music and after, the night of un-music –
No horn-chart, no thin, underamplified Fender,
No workaday-beautiful backline, no voice
Being torn from the soles of the feet:
No such matrix, no such number.
Everything is afterwards, a dripping jacket
Hung across a mirror, drinks becoming syrup,
A van spitting teeth on its way to the knacker's.
The culture of almost is married, divorced
And has always been forty. Yet now you step in –
The wrong hole, the wrong wall, but at least
It's not there in the hours of business –
To run down a shuddering spiral that ends
In a foyer intriguingly minus a door.
Knee-deep in water and flyers, it smells
Like your big sister's hairspray, supposing
She's used it or even existed.
Under the dandruff of whitewash and rust,
Behind traffic and ship-engines,
Wind in the stairwell, the pulse in your temple,
What you can hear will be nothing, the space
Made of wishing, the cousin of happiness,

Waiting to comfort the longing to know
There is something you still haven't got.
Why not pick up a leaflet? It mentions
The unnumbered white-label item
Unearthed by a rumour (one copy)
In Belgium. The price is an arm and a leg,
Your entire collection, your job and your marriage
And still you won't find it. It's perfect.

Reading Stevens in the Bath

It is Newcastle at evening. It is far
From the furnished banks of the coaly Tyne
But close beside the hidden and infernal banks

Of the unutterable Ouseburn. Howay. It cries
Its native cry, this poisoned soup of prawns.
Howay. The evil river sings. The mind,

In Forest Hall, the haunted disbelieving suburb
Like a field of snowmen, the mind in Forest Hall
Lays by its knitting and considers

Going to the Fusilier. Howay. But in the upper room,
The room upstairs, the upstairs room,
The blear of glass and heat wherein

Not much is visible, a large pink man
Is reading Stevens in the bath. Howay. It is bath-time,
The time of the bath, the green-watered, where the mind

Lies unencumbered by the body as by time.
It is the bath as absolute, admitting
No conditional of green, the bath in which the bather

Lies considering. And the mind takes out
Its lightness to inspect, and finding nothing there
Begins to sing, embodying, emboldening its note.

It is the singing body in the bath, the mind.
Bookless Fruiterers, tell me if you can
What he may find to sing about, that man

Half-audible, and howling, as it were, the moon
That rests its gravity on weary Forest Hall,
That sends its tidal song by Tyne,

By Ouseburn, by the purifying plant
And ultimately here, to this balneum absolute,
Steam-punkah'd bath at the end of the mind, whose singer

Sings beyond the scope of tongues and sanity
Of neighbours, howling like a wolf among the snowmen
To the moon which does not listen:

Say it's only a paper moon,
Sailing over a cardboard sea,
But it wouldn't be make-believe

If you believed in me.
Howay. Howay. Howay!

MATTHEW SWEENEY (b.1952)

Matthew Sweeney was born in Donegal in 1952 and lives in London. He co-edited
Emergency Kit (1996) with Jo Shapcott, and was recently the writer in residence at
London's South Bank Centre. He has published several books for children and his poetry
collections include Blue Shoes *(1989),* Cacti *(1992) and* The Bridal Suite *(1997).*

Blue Shoes

I see that day's non-headlines, as he did
        though they're smoky now –
a prince at playschool, a brat's betrothal.

Some days they rob the gossip entries
    in lieu of disasters.
    They missed his later.

The weather inch reads more like Sicily
    than England. I see him
hurrying towards the train, his hand
raised to his eyes, the sunglasses at home.
    I have his notes here,
    the last of any consequence.

All the women, it seems, wore blue shoes
    in keeping with the morning.
He played with patterns, with omens
he deciphered later. That particular day
    it was blue shoes
    for want of any better.

I see him with a letter and xeroxed map
    leaving the station.
He is sucking mints, perhaps hungover.
At the school gates he checks his flies.
    He goes in the office,
    is lost from sight.

Did they know the strain of these visits?
    Did the kids care?
It was a long day, but not outlandish.
In his honour they had lunch in a pub.
    On another day
    it would have relaxed him.

He was chauffeured to the train in the end,
    an overwound watch.
He queued at a phone, his heart chugging.
A woman was speaking, a man waiting –
    the woman, he wrote,
    wore blue shoes.

Hard for me in this library to imagine
    that home journey,
the mounting pain in his mind and chest,
the prison of that train in motion.
    All I know is
    he thought he was dead.

And got off at a suburban station
    to ride in an ambulance
through all the jams of South London
to nurses and a narrow bed with wheels
    and electric wires
    on feet, wrists and heart.

I am reading over his own description
    of that evening –
how later, at home, he imagined
he'd got away with it, and drank.
    He got away
    for the time being.

For years, even, but what does it matter –
    he never forgot
that day of the interrupted train,
the only time in his life, late sun
    and pretty women
    wearing blue shoes.

JO SHAPCOTT (b.1953)

Jo Shapcott was born in 1953 in London, and has worked for the Arts Council and as a lecturer and education officer. In 1991 she was the Judith E. Wilson Fellow at the University of Cambridge. Her publications include Electroplating the Baby *(1988) and* Phrase Book *(1992), the title poem of which was joint winner of the 1991 National Poetry Competition.*

Phrase Book

I'm standing here inside my skin,
which will do for a Human Remains Pouch
for the moment. Look down there (up here).
Quickly. Slowly. This is my own front room

where I'm lost in the action, live from a war,
on screen. I am an Englishwoman, I don't understand you.
What's the matter? You are right. You are wrong.
Things are going well (badly). Am I disturbing you?

TV is showing bliss as taught to pilots:
Blend, Low silhouette, Irregular shape, Small,
Secluded. (Please write it down. Please speak slowly.)
Bliss is how it was in this very room

when I raised my body to his mouth,
when he even balanced me in the air,
or at least I thought so and yes the pilots say
yes they have caught it through the Side-Looking

Airborne Radar, and through the J-Stars.
I am expecting a gentleman (a young gentleman,
two gentlemen, some gentlemen). Please send him
(them) up at once. This is really beautiful.

Yes they have seen us, the pilots, in the Kill Box
on their screens, and played the routine for
getting us Stealthed, that is, Cleansed, to you and me,
Taken Out. They know how to move into a single room

like that, to send in with Pinpoint Accuracy, a hundred Harms.
I have two cases and a cardboard box. There is another
bag there. I cannot open my case – look out,
the lock is broken. Have I done enough?

Bliss, the pilots say, is for evasion
and escape. What's love in all this debris?
Just one person pounding another into dust,
into dust. I do not know the word for it yet.

Where is the British Consulate? Please explain.
What does it mean? What must I do? Where
can I find? What have I done? I have done
nothing. Let me pass please. I am an Englishwoman.

ALISON BRACKENBURY (b.1953)

*Alison Brackenbury was born in Lincolnshire in 1953, read English at Oxford and
worked for some time as a librarian. She is now an electroplater and lives in Cheltenham.
Her books include* Dreams of Power *(1981),* Breaking Ground *(1984),* Christmas
Roses *(1988) and* Selected Poems *(1991).*

Grooming

Mud hangs its dry beads on your eyelid,
Not on red and glossy hair, but the dark skin
Too tender to be brushed. I hesitate
And then I lick the sponge and touch it to you.
You sigh with pleasure, slip your heavy head
Into my other hand: and let me rub.
Stepping round, stroking your ears, I think
We are too narrow, and our labels
Far too few.
All the loves and all the warmth shut out –
The yard is empty. Finished, like this horse
Who on the hill-top cries for his own kind –
How suddenly, intensely, I want you.

IAN DUHIG (b.1954)

Ian Duhig was born in 1954 in London and lives in Leeds. He was Fellow in Creative Writing at Leeds University in 1997. In 1987 he won first prize in the National Poetry Competition, and his collections include The Bradford Count *(1991) and* The Mersey Goldfish *(1996).*

From the Irish

According to Dineen, a Gael unsurpassed
in lexicographical enterprise, the Irish
for moon means 'the white circle in a slice
of half-boiled potato or turnip'. A star
is the mark on the forehead of a beast
and the sun is the bottom of a lake, or well.

Well, if I say to you your face
is like a slice of half-boiled turnip,
your hair is the colour of a lake's bottom
and at the centre of each of your eyes
is the mark of the beast, it is because
I want to love you properly, according to Dineen.

MONIZA ALVI (b.1954)

Moniza Alvi was born in Lahore in 1954 and moved to England at an early age. The Country at My Shoulder *(1993) was her first full-length collection, followed in 1996 by* A Bowl of Warm Air. *She works as a schoolteacher.*

Arrival 1946

The boat docked in at Liverpool.
From the train Tariq stared
at an unbroken line of washing
from the North West to Euston.

These are strange people, he thought –
an Empire, and all this washing,
the underwear, the Englishman's garden.
It was Monday, and very sharp.

MICHAEL DONAGHY (b.1954)

*Michael Donaghy was born in 1954 in America, and for several years was poetry editor of
the* Chicago Review, *before moving to England. He lives in London, and works as a
writer and musician. His collections include* Shibboleth *(1988) and* Errata *(1993), which
was selected as one of the New Generation Poets titles in 1994.*

Shibboleth

One didn't know the name of Tarzan's monkey.
Another couldn't strip the cellophane
From a GI's pack of cigarettes.
By such minutiae were the infiltrators detected.

By the second week of battle
We'd become obsessed with trivia.
At a sentry point, at midnight, in the rain,
An ignorance of baseball could be lethal.

The morning of the first snowfall, I was shaving,
Staring into a mirror nailed to a tree,
Intoning the Christian names of the Andrews Sisters.
'Maxine, Laverne, Patty.'

Liverpool

Ever been tattooed? It takes a whim of iron,
takes sweating in the antiseptic-stinking parlour,
nothing to read but motorcycle magazines
before the blood-sopped cotton and, of course, the needle,
all for – at best – some Chinese dragon.
But mostly they do hearts,

hearts skewered, blurry, spurting like the Sacred Heart
on the arms of bikers and sailors.
Even in prison they get by with biro ink and broken glass,
carving hearts into their arms and shoulders.
But women's are more intimate. They hide theirs,
under shirts and jeans, in order to bestow them.

Like Tracy, who confessed she'd had hers done
one legless weekend with her ex.
Heart. Arrow. Even the bastard's initials, R. J. L.,
somewhere where it hurt, she said,
and when I asked her where, snapped 'Liverpool'.

Wherever it was, she'd had it sliced away
leaving a scar, she said, pink and glassy,
but small, and better than having his mark on her,

(that self-same mark of Valentinus,
who was flayed for love, but who never
– so the cardinals now say – existed.

Desanctified, apocryphal, like Christopher,
like the scar you never showed me, Trace,
your (   ), your ex, your 'Liverpool').

Still, when I unwrap the odd anonymous note
I let myself believe that it's from you.

Reliquary

The robot camera enters the Titanic
And we see her fish-cold nurseries on the news;
The toys of Pompeii trampled in the panic;
The death camp barrel of babyshoes;

The snow that covered up the lost girl's tracks;
The scapular she wore about her neck;
The broken doll the photojournalist packs
to toss into the foreground of the wreck.

JOHN BURNSIDE (b.1955)

John Burnside was born in Fife in 1955, and has published several collections of poetry. In 1994 he was selected as one of the New Generation Poets for his collection The Myth of the Twin. The Dumb House *(1997) is his first novel, and further books of poetry are* Swimming in the Flood *(1995) and* A Normal Skin *(1997).*

Faith

You would have unravelled a soul
from fishbones and lice,
from the brightness that seeps through the floor

when you walk in the dark,
and the birdless, indelible shadows
amongst the laburnum.

You would have imagined the physics
of limbo,
and paradise suburbs, where only the chosen exist,
the self made systematic: lawns and woods
and quiet houses
peopled with like minds.

In the morning you would have stood
alone, at the edge of the world
with your face to the light,
and God would become the camphor in a bush,
the whisper of something local and banal,
a personal event, which you would grasp,
inferred from the wind like a shiver of ash or pollen.

Dundee

The streets are waiting for a snow
that never falls:
too close to the water,
too muffled in the afterwarmth of jute,
the houses on Roseangle
opt for miraculous frosts
and the feeling of space that comes
in the gleam of day
when you step outside for the milk
or the morning post
and it seems as if a closeness in the mind
had opened and flowered:
the corners sudden and tender, the light immense,
the one who stands here proven after all.

Science

Sound waves were never explained
to my satisfaction,

how they could travel through water, lacing the pool
with muffled voices,

or streaming away from the deep end, to fledge the walls
with faint harmonics, lapping semitones.

On Thursdays I went from school
to the public baths

and waited for the body I desired:
the swallow dive, the underwater glide,

the surface tension
of a second skin.

In physics I watched a light beam shatter and heal,
bleeding to crimson and blue in a prism of glass,

and wondered if a soul could change like that,
my father's shadow filtered through the lens

and disappearing, leaving something clean
and weighted, like the swimmer's earned fatigue,

rhythmic and steady,
a sine wave of grace and attunement.

JAMIE McKENDRICK (b.1955)

Jamie McKendrick was born in Liverpool in 1955 and lives in Oxford, where he is a part-time teacher. He was selected as one of the New Generation Poets in 1994. His publications include The Sirocco Room *(1991),* The Kiosk on the Brink *(1993) and* The Marble Fly, *which won the 1997 Forward Poetry Prize.*

On/Off

The switch stuck through the lampstand's neck
like an arrow shaft of walrus ivory
in a Welsh epic
has lost its feathers and its head.
Peacock feathers and a gold head.
Its Fiat Lux
with a length of flex,
its shift, its crick has made me
blink like a lemur at the lack
of the moon or a star
or a thing between. But it's good
how someone takes off their earrings
with the motion of shelling a pea.
A tiny snap. Like the hasp-click
of a calyx
at the press of a picker's thumb.
A sound like lifting an airtight lid
or a pin dropping in a pyramid.
Then the lobe's set free
and breathes with delight
to shed the slight weight
of the earrings.
Earrings that might be
twin filaments, a pair of ball-bearings
or a hammock-faced moon and a tarnished star.

PAULA MEEHAN (b.1955)

Paula Meehan was born in 1955 in Dublin, and has worked as a writer in settings such as schools, prisons and universities throughout Ireland. Her collections of poetry include Return and No Blame *(1984),* Reading the Sky *(1986) and* The Man who was Marked by Winter *(1991).*

The Man who was Marked by Winter

He was heading for Bridal Veil Falls,
an upward slog on a dusty path.
Mid May and hot as a mill–

stone grinding his shoulders, his back.
Each breath was a drowning.
And who's to say if it was a mirage

the other side of the creek's brown
water. He saw it, that's enough,
in the deep shade of a rocky overhang –

the spoor of winter, a tracery of ice. If
we'd reached him, we'd have warned him of the depth,
the secret current underneath.

He must have been half crazy with the heat.
He stripped off. Waded in.
His feet were cut from under him. He was swept

downriver in melt water from the mountain.
She clutched him to her breast, that beast of winter.
One look from her agate eyes and he abandoned

hope. He was pliant. She pulled him under.
If she had him once, she had him thrice.
She shook his heart and mind asunder.

And he would willingly have gone back to her palace
or her lair, whichever; whatever she was,
he would have lived forever in her realms of ice.

She must have grown tired of his human ways.
We found him tossed like a scrap on the bank,
hours or years or seconds later. His eyes

stared straight at the sun. His past is a blank
snowfield where no one will step. She made her mark
below his heart, a five-fingered gash – *Bondsman.*

CAROL ANN DUFFY (b.1955)

*Carol Ann Duffy was born in 1955 in Glasgow, grew up in Staffordshire, has lived in
Liverpool and London and currently lives in Manchester. She edited the anthology*
I Wouldn't Thank You for a Valentine *(1992), and has published five collections
of poetry, including* Mean Time *which won the 1993 Whitbread Award for Poetry
and the Forward Prize. Her* Selected Poems *was published in 1994.*

Warming Her Pearls

for Judith Radstone

Next to my own skin, her pearls. My mistress
bids me wear them, warm them, until evening
when I'll brush her hair. At six, I place them
round her cool, white throat. All day I think of her,

resting in the Yellow Room, contemplating silk
or taffeta, which gown tonight? She fans herself
whilst I work willingly, my slow heat entering
each pearl. Slack on my neck, her rope.

She's beautiful. I dream about her
in my attic bed; picture her dancing
with tall men, puzzled by my faint, persistent scent
beneath her French perfume, her milky stones.

I dust her shoulders with a rabbit's foot,
watch the soft blush seep through her skin
like an indolent sigh. In her looking-glass
my red lips part as though I want to speak.

Full moon. Her carriage brings her home. I see
her every movement in my head . . . Undressing,
taking off her jewels, her slim hand reaching
for the case, slipping naked into bed, the way

she always does . . . And I lie here awake,
knowing the pearls are cooling even now
in the room where my mistress sleeps. All night
I feel their absence and I burn.

Adultery

Wear dark glasses in the rain.
Regard what was unhurt
as though through a bruise.
Guilt. A sick, green tint.

New gloves, money tucked in the palms,
the handshake crackles. Hands
can do many things. Phone.
Open the wine. Wash themselves. Now

you are naked under your clothes all day,
slim with deceit. Only the once
brings you alone to your knees,
miming, more, more, older and sadder,

creative. Suck a lie with a hole in it
on the way home from a lethal, thrilling night
up against a wall, faster. Language
unpeels to a lost cry. You're a bastard.

Do it do it do it. Sweet darkness
in the afternoon; a voice in your ear
telling you how you are wanted,
which way, now. A telltale clock

wiping the hours from its face, your face
on a white sheet, gasping, radiant, yes.
Pay for it in cash, fiction, cab-fares back
to the life which crumbles like a wedding-cake.

Paranoia for lunch; too much
to drink, as a hand on your thigh
tilts the restaurant. You know all about love,
don't you. Turn on your beautiful eyes

for a stranger who's dynamite in bed, again
and again; a slow replay in the kitchen
where the slicing of innocent onions
scalds you to tears. Then, selfish autobiographical sleep

in a marital bed, the tarnished spoon of your body
stirring betrayal, your heart overripe at the core.
You're an expert, darling; your flowers
dumb and explicit on nobody's birthday.

So write the script – illness and debt,
a ring thrown away in a garden
no moon can heal, your own words
commuting to bile in your mouth, terror –

and all for the same thing twice. And all
for the same thing twice. You did it.
What. Didn't you. Fuck. Fuck. No. That was
the wrong verb. This is only an abstract noun.

Prayer

Some days, although we cannot pray, a prayer
utters itself. So, a woman will lift
her head from the sieve of her hands and stare
at the minims sung by a tree, a sudden gift.

Some nights, although we are faithless, the truth
enters our hearts, that small familiar pain;
then a man will stand stock-still, hearing his youth
in the distant Latin chanting of a train.

Pray for us now. Grade I piano scales
console the lodger looking out across
a Midlands town. Then dusk, and someone calls
a child's name as though they named their loss.

Darkness outside. Inside, the radio's prayer –
Rockall. Malin. Dogger. Finisterre.

Mrs Lazarus

I had grieved. I had wept for a night and a day
over my loss, ripped the cloth I was married in
from my breasts, howled, shrieked, clawed
at the burial stones till my hands bled, retched
his name over and over again, dead, dead.

Gone home. Gutted the place. Slept in a single cot,
widow, one empty glove, white femur
in the dust, half. Stuffed dark suits
into black bags, shuffled in a dead man's shoes,
noosed the double knot of a tie round my bare neck,

gaunt nun in the mirror, touching herself. I learnt
the Stations of Bereavement, the icon of my face
in each bleak frame; but all those months
he was going away from me, dwindling
to the shrunk size of a snapshot, going,

going. Till his name was no longer a certain spell
for his face. The last hair on his head
floated out from a book. His scent went from the house.
The will was read. See, he was vanishing
to the small zero held by the gold of my ring.

Then he was gone. Then he was legend, language;
my arm on the arm of the schoolteacher – the shock
of a man's strength under the sleeve of his coat –
along the hedgerows. But I was faithful
for as long as it took. Until he was memory.

So I could stand that evening in the field
in a shawl of fine air, healed, able
to watch the edge of the moon occur to the sky
and a hare thump from a hedge; then notice
the village men running towards me, shouting,

behind them the women and children, barking dogs,
and I knew. I knew by the shrill light
on the blacksmith's face, the sly eyes
of the barmaid, the sudden hands bearing me
into the hot tang of the crowd parting before me.

He lived. I saw the horror on his face.
I heard his mother's crazy song. I breathed
his stench; my bridegroom in his rotting shroud,
moist and dishevelled from the grave's slack chew,
croaking his cuckold name, disinherited, out of his time.

ROBIN ROBERTSON (b.1955)

Robin Robertson was born in 1955 and brought up in the north-east of Scotland. He is a fiction and poetry editor at Jonathan Cape, and his book A Painted Field *won the 1997 Forward Prize for the best first collection. He lives in London.*

Artichoke

The nubbed leaves
come away
in a tease of green, thinning
down to the membrane:
the quick, purpled,
beginnings of the male.

Then the slow hairs of the heart:
the choke that guards its trophy,
its vegetable goblet.
The meat of it lies, displayed,
up-ended, *al dente*,
the stub-root aching in its oil.

SUJATA BHATT (b.1956)

Sujata Bhatt was born in 1956 in Ahmedabad, India, and educated in the US. She works as a freelance writer and as a translator of Gujarati poetry into English, and lives in Germany. Her poetry collections include Brunizem *(1988),* Monkey Shadows *(1991) and* The Stinking Rose *(1994).*

શેરડી   (Shérdi)*

The way I learned
to eat sugar cane in Sanosra:
I use my teeth
to tear the outer hard *chaal*
then, bite off strips
of the white fibrous heart –
suck hard with my teeth, press down
and the juice spills out.

January mornings
the farmer cuts tender green sugar-cane
and brings it to our door.
Afternoons, when the elders are asleep
we sneak outside carrying the long smooth stalks.
The sun warms us, the dogs yawn,
our teeth grow strong
our jaws are numb;
for hours we suck out the *russ*, the juice
                    sticky all over our hand

So tonight
when you tell me to use my teeth,
to suck hard, harder,
then, I smell sugar cane grass in your hair
and imagine you'd like to be
shérdi   shérdi   out in the fields
            the stalks away
                    opening a path before us

---

* શેરડી   (*Shérdi*): sugar cane.

What Is Worth Knowing?

That Van Gogh's ear, set free
wanted to meet the powerful nose
of Nevsky Avenue.
That Spain has decided to help
NATO. That Spring is supposed to begin
on the 21st of March.
That if you put too much salt in the *keema*
just add a few bananas.
That although the Dutch were the first
to help the people of Nicaragua they don't say much
about their history with Indonesia.
That Van Gogh collected Japanese prints.
That the Japanese considered
the Dutch to be red-haired barbarians.
That Van Gogh's ear remains full of questions
it wants to ask the nose of Nevsky Avenue.
That the vaccinations for cholera, typhoid and yellow fever
are no good – they must be improved.
That red, green and yellow are the most
auspicious colours.
That turmeric and chilli powder are good
disinfectants. Yellow and red.
That often Spring doesn't come
until May. But in some places
it's there in January.
That Van Gogh's ear left him because
it wanted to become a snail.
That east and west
meet only in the north and south – but never
in the east or west.
That in March 1986 Darwinism is being
reintroduced in American schools.
That there's a difference
between pigeons and doves, although

a ring-dove is a wood-pigeon.
That the most pleasant thing is to have a fever
of at least 101 – because then the dreams aren't
merely dreams but facts.
That during a fever the soul comes out
for fresh air, that during a fever the soul bothers to
speak to you.
That tigers are courageous and generous-hearted
and never attack unless provoked –
but leopards,
leopards are malicious and bad-tempered.
That buffaloes too,
water-buffaloes that is, have a short temper.
That a red sky at night is a good sign for sailors,
for sailors . . . what is worth knowing?
What is worth knowing?

MICK IMLAH (b.1956)

Mick Imlah was born in Aberdeen in 1956. He was editor of Poetry Review *and poetry editor at Chatto & Windus, and now works part-time at the* Times Literary Supplement. *His collection* Birthmarks *was published in 1988.*

Tusking

In Africa once
A herd of Harrow
Elephants strayed
Far from their bunks;
Leather, they laid
Their costly trunks
And ears of felt
Down on the Veldt.

All forgot
The creep of dusk;
A moonbeam stole
Along each tusk:
Snores and sighs.
Oh, foolish boys!
The English elephant
Never lies!

★

In the night-time, lithe
Shadows with little
Glinting teeth
Whisked tusks away;
Drew through the dark
Branches of ivory,
Made a great hue
On their rapid run.

Hunters, at home
They curl up the bare
Soles of their feet
With piano-pleasure;
Sammy plays
A massacre song
With the notes wrong
On Massa's baby.

★

Out in the bush
Is silence now:
Savannah seas
Have islands now,
Smelly land-masses,
Bloody, cold,
Disfigured places
With fly-blown faces;

And each of us rests
After his fashion:
Elephant, English,
Butcher, Bushman;
Now only the herding
Boy in a singlet
Worries his goat
With a peaceful prod.

★

But if, one night
As you stroll the verandah
Observing with wonder
The place of the white
Stars in the universe,
Brilliant, and clear,
Sipping your whisky
And pissed with fear

You happen to hear
Over the tinkle
Of ice and Schubert
A sawing – a drilling –
The bellow and trump
Of a vast pain –
Pity the hulks!
Play it again!

SARAH MAGUIRE (b.1957)

Sarah Maguire was born in London in 1957 and trained as a gardener before reading English at the University of East Anglia. She has taught creative writing in many different settings and is a regular contributor to BBC arts programmes. Her collections include Spilt Milk *(1991) and* The Invisible Mender *(1997).*

Uisge Beatha

Such a glutton for pleasure. Absorbed on your sofa
I watch this fire, its heat, its mutations.
Your keen knife slips into the flesh of an orange
and a cacophony of Os ravels into your lap, unbroken.

Not for years – but I'm too late: already
you're spanning my wrist, have taken my arm
right up to the elbow. Then the stem of my glass.
What do I remember? – a litany of whiskies:

Lagavulin, Laphroaig, Talisker, Aberlour,
The Macallan – the hot sweet smoked malt
that I burned of and for you. Or your exact,
fluent fingers. The perfume near your throat.

And how I dreamt of that house with red doors,
a huge garden, and two weeping willows.
A cool brook I'd fall into and not wish to leave.

OLIVER REYNOLDS (b.1957)

Oliver Reynolds was born in Cardiff in 1957 and educated at Hull University. His collections of poetry include Skevington's Daughter *(1985),* The Player Queen's Wife *(1987) and* The Oslo Tram *(1991). He has also written for the stage and for children.*

Anna Colutha in Suffolk

I first saw her in a teashop in Eye.
We had both been stood up
And it showed.
She kept looking at her watch

As if it was to blame.
I marshalled a smile
Then crossed to her table.
We had a pot for two
And drank to absent shits.
The hatchback is easier to load.

She was an astronomer
Working on black holes.
If sucked into one head first
The greater pull on the upper body
Results in stretching of the trunk.
This is known as spaghettification.
She spoke quickly,
Holding up a glass as the black hole
And circling it with one very white hand.
Boycott had just made his hundredth hundred.

I was working my way up to Diss.
At each stop
I puzzled over
Araucaria's latest
Until all but 10 Down were done.
Anna had it straight away,
Filling it in with her propelling pencil.
(It was 'jerboa' which I later learned
Is also known as *Jaculus jaculus*.)
In Walberswick I went to the dentist's.

Random passion is rather confusing;
After I had dropped her off
I missed the turning for the A140.
Anna was very taken with my stomach
And used it as a pillow.
Moles ran in the Colutha family
And she had a beauty on her back,

Stuck there like a squashed sultana
Against the skin's eidetic white.
Bulk orders are on the up.

MICHAEL HOFMANN (b.1957)

Michael Hofmann was born in 1957 in Germany, the son of the novelist Gert Hofmann.
His publications include Nights in the Iron Hotel *(1983),* Acrimony *(1986) and*
Corona, Corona *(1993). He works as a writer, reviewer and translator, teaches in the*
US and lives in London.

Between Bed and Wastepaper Basket

There hasn't been much to cheer about in three years
in this boxroom shaped like a loaf of bread,
the flimsy partitions of the servants' quarters,
high up in the drafty cranium of the house.

All things tend towards the yellow of unlove,
the tawny, moulting carpet where I am commemorated
by tea- and coffee-stains, by the round holes of furniture –
too much of it, and too long in the same place.

Here, we have been prepared for whatever comes next.
The dishonest, middle-aged anorexic has been moved on.
The radio-buff is now responsible for contact
in the cardboard huts of the British Antarctic Survey.

(His great antenna was demolished here one stormy night.)
The tiny American professor is looking for tenure.
On occasional passionate weekends, the vinegary
smell of cruel spermicide carried all before it.

Familiarity breeds mostly the fear of its loss.
In winter, the ice-flowers on the inside of the window
and the singing of the loose tap; in summer,
the thunderflies that came in and died on my books

like bits of misplaced newsprint . . . I seize the day
when you visited me here – the child's world in person:
gold shoes, grass skirt, sky blouse and tinted, cirrus hair.
We went outside. Everything in the garden was rosy.

Prefabs ran down the back of the Applied Psychology Unit.
Pigeons dilated. The flies were drowsy from eating
the water-lilies on the pond. A snake had taken care of
the frogs. Fuchsias pointed their toes like ballerinas.

My hand tried to cup your breast. You were jail-bait,
proposing a miraculous career as county wife
and parole officer. We failed to betray
whatever trust was placed in us.

BENJAMIN ZEPHANIAH (b.1958)

Benjamin Zephaniah was born in Birmingham in 1958 and grew up in Jamaica and Handsworth. A musician as well as a poet, he has released several records and performed as a reggae DJ. He has also written for the stage and worked with other media such as film, television and radio. His books include City Psalms *(1992) and* Propa Propaganda *(1996), and he lives in the East End of London.*

Dis Poetry

Dis poetry is like a riddim dat drops
De tongue fires a riddim dat shoots like shots
Dis poetry is designed fe rantin
Dance hall style, Big mouth chanting,

Dis poetry nar put yu to sleep
Preaching follow me
Like yu is blind sheep,
Dis poetry is not Party Political
Not designed fe dose who are critical.

Dis poetry is wid me when I gu to me bed
It gets into me Dreadlocks
It lingers around me head
Dis poetry goes wid me as I pedal me bike
I've tried Shakespeare, Respect due dere
But dis is de stuff I like.

Dis poetry is not afraid of going ina book
Still dis poetry need ears fe hear an eyes fe hav a look
Dis poetry is Verbal Riddim, no big words involved
An if I hav a problem de riddim gets it solved,
I've tried to be more Romantic, it does nu good for me
So I tek a Reggae Riddim an build me poetry,
I could try be more personal
But you've heard it all before,
Pages of written words not needed
Brain has many words in store,
Yu could call dis poetry Dub Ranting
De tongue plays a beat
De body starts skanking,
Dis poetry is quick an childish
Dis poetry is fe de wise an foolish,
Anybody can do it fe free,
Dis poetry is fe yu an me,
Don't stretch yu imagination
Dis poetry is fe de good of de Nation,
Chant,
In de morning
I chant
In de night
I chant

In de darkness
An under de spotlight,
I pass thru University
I pass thru Sociology
An den I got a Dread degree
In Dreadfull Ghettology.

Dis poetry stays wid me when I run or walk
An when I am talking to meself in poetry I talk,
Dis poetry is wid me,
Below me an above,
Dis poetry's from inside me
It goes to yu
WID LUV.

MEG BATEMAN (b.1959)

Meg Bateman was born in Edinburgh in 1959. She learnt Gaelic at Aberdeen University and on South Uist where she worked as an auxiliary nurse. Her first full-length collection of Gaelic poetry with her own facing English translations was Aotromachd agus dàin eile / Lightness and Other Poems *(1997). She teaches in the Celtic Studies department at Aberdeen University.*

Aotromachd

B' e d' aotromachd a rinn mo thàladh,
aotromachd do chainnte 's do ghàire,
aotromachd do lethchinn nam làmhan,
d' aotromachd lurach ùr mhàlda;
agus 's e aotromachd do phòige
a tha a' cur trasg air mo bheòil-sa,
is 's e aotromachd do ghlaic mum chuairt-sa
a leigeas seachad leis an t-sruth mi.

Lightness

It was your lightness that drew me,
the lightness of your talk and your laughter,
the lightness of your cheek in my hands,
your sweet gentle modest lightness;
and it is the lightness of your kiss
that is starving my mouth,
and the lightness of your embrace
that will let me go adrift.

GWYNETH LEWIS (b.1959)

Gwyneth Lewis was born in 1959 in Cardiff, where she works as a television producer.
She writes both in Welsh, her first language, and in English. Her first Welsh language
collection was Sonedau Redsa, *and her first volume of poetry in English,* Parables &
Faxes, *was published in 1995.*

Pentecost

The Lord wants me to go to Florida.
I shall cross the border with the mercury thieves,
as foretold in the faxes and prophecies,
and the checkpoint angel of Estonia
will have alerted the uniformed birds
to act unnatural and distract the guards

so I pass unhindered. My glossolalia
shall be my passport – I shall taste the tang
of travel on the atlas of my tongue –
salt Poland, sour Denmark and sweet Vienna,
and all men in the Spirit shall understand
that, in His wisdom, the Lord has sent

a slip of a girl to save great Florida.
I'll tear through Europe like a standing flame,
not pausing for long, except to rename
the occasional city; in Sofia
thousands converted and hundreds slain
in the Holy Spirit along the Seine.

My life is your chronicle; O Florida
revived, look forward to your past
and prepare your perpetual Pentecost
of golf course and freeway, shopping mall and car
so the fires that are burning in the orange groves
turn light into sweetness and the huddled graves

are hives of the future – an America
spelt plainly, translated in the Everglades
where palm fruit hang like hand grenades
ready to rip whole treatises of air.
Then the S in the tail of the crocodile
will make perfect sense to the bibliophile

who will study this land, his second Torah.
All this was revealed. Now I wait for the Lord
to move heaven and earth to send me abroad
and fulfil His bold promise to Florida.
As I stay put, He shifts His continent:
Atlantic closes, the sheet of time is rent.

FRED D'AGUIAR (b.1960)

Fred D'Aguiar was born in London in 1960, grew up in Guyana and lives in America,
where he teaches creative writing at the University of Miami, in Florida. Playwright and
novelist, he edited the Black British section of The New British Poetry *(1988), and his*
collections include Mama Dot *(1985),* Airy Hall *(1989) and* British Subjects *(1993).*

Mama Dot

I

Born on a sunday
in the kingdom of Ashante

Sold on monday
into slavery

Ran away on tuesday
cause she born free

Lost a foot on wednesday
when they catch she

Worked all thursday
till her head grey

Dropped on friday
where they burned she

Freed on saturday
in a new century

II

Old Mama Dot
old Mama Dot
boss a de stew-pot
she nah deal in vat
she nah bap
no style
so stop
look at Mama Dot
windin on de spot

Old Mama Dot
old Mama Dot
watch her squat

full o de nat–
-tral goodness dat
grow in de lann
she use to farm
bare hann
up evry dawn

Old Mama Dot
old Mama Dot
she nah deal wid vat–
-igan nah mek no fuss
she a deal wid duss
she swing cutlass
play big boss
lick chile rass
go to mass

The Day Mama Dot Takes Ill

The day Mama Dot takes ill,
The continent has its first natural disaster:
Chickens fall dead on their backs,
But keep on laying rotten eggs; ducks upturn
In ponds, their webbed feet buoyed forever;
Lactating cows drown in their sour milk;
Mountain goats lose their footing on ledges
They used to skip along; crickets croak,
Frogs click, in broad daylight; fruits
Drop green from trees; coconuts kill travellers
Who rest against their longing trunks;
Bees abandon their queens to red ants,
And bury their stings in every moving thing;
And the sun sticks like the hands of a clock
At noon, drying the very milk in breasts.

Mama Dot asks for a drink to quench her feverish thirst:
It rains until the land is waist-deep in water.
She dreams of crops being lost: the water drains
In a day leaving them intact. She throws open her window
To a chorus and rumpus of animals and birds,
And the people carnival for a week. Still unsteady
On her feet, she hoes the grateful ashes
From the grate and piles the smiling logs on it.

PETER SIRR (b.1960)

Peter Sirr was born in Ireland in 1960 and has spent time in Italy. His several collections of poetry include Marginal Zones *(1984),* Talk, Talk *(1987) and* The Ledger of Fruitful Exchange *(1996).*

Recognition

I had spread them out between us
so often our bed was like a map:
the heraldic crunch of the gravel path,
the pines going through their old routines
of boredom and sudden laughter

Now your car door slams in the drive
and I am
only a little surprised

My mother looks through the kitchen window,
years falling like the suds
she rinses from her hands

and I can believe the familiar room
in which we turn and turn
as my body thins, as I grow
more awkward in your arms

I am retreating before your eyes

and this is the photograph you must take away,
the girl not quite fitting the clothes she wears
or your need to possess her,
whose wary eye you must return
like unlooked for treasure to the bed we share:

in the morning we will struggle with the year, the day
the sky outside the window exactly
as I said it would be

and the bodies lying so close together
someone must surely break the silence
with a name, a gesture; someone must rise, easily,
into the known room, the recognition.

STEPHEN KNIGHT (b.1960)

*Stephen Knight was born in 1960 in Swansea, where he grew up. He read English
at Oxford and now lives in London where he works as a theatre director. His poetry
collections are* Flowering Limbs *(1993) and* Dream City Cinema *(1996). He won
the 1992 National Poetry Competition.*

The Mermaid Tank

Beneath my weight, the duckboards bow.
    Two buckets, slopping water, weigh me down.
A cold wind howls around the cages now,
    While rain sweeps in – across the town –

Again; and while our rheumy-eyed,
   Arthritic monsters fall asleep
      Or vegetate
         I kneel beside
The Songstress Of The Deep
   And wait.

All afternoon, the punters pass
   Her tank in single file; because it's dark
Inside, they press their faces to the glass.
   I breathe, at night, on every mark.
Behind my cloth, the water churns
   And curls around our fat dugong
      And when it clears
        (Like smoke) she turns
Away, and any song
   I hear

Is 'just the wind' or 'my mistake' . . .
   Outside, discarded handbills catch their wings
On tents or in the mud while, in their wake,
   Paper cups, ticket stubs and things
The rain dismantles every night
   Turn cartwheels in the foreign air
      Before they throng
        The sky, too light
To settle anywhere
   For long.

W. N. HERBERT (b.1961)

W. N. Herbert was born in Dundee in 1961. He has worked as a magazine editor, and held a number of teaching positions and residencies in England and Scotland. He has published work in English and Scots, and his collections include Sharawaggi *(1990, with Robert Crawford),* Forked Tongue *(1990, selected as a New Generation Poets title in 1994) and* Cabaret McGonagall *(1996).*

Coco-de-Mer

Dinna bathir wi thi braiggil o wir lends
that maks a cothaman o gravy
i thi cot, but famine in wir crullit herts –
let gae oan thi dumbswaul, be
brankie i thi breakirs, an flocht,
flocht lyk thi crospunk intae Lewis –
thi lucky-bean tae thi haunds o thi misk.

braiggil: a dangerously unstable article; *lends*: loins; *cothaman*: surfeit; *crullit*: cowering; *dumbswaul*: a long, noiseless sea-swell in calm, windless weather; *brankie*: pranked-up, ready for fun; *crospunk, coco-de-mer*: the Molucca bean, drifted to the shores of some of the Western Islands; *misk*: land covered in coarse, moorish grasses.

Morn-Come-Never

Sall ilka morn's licht hae this motherie
waurmth o yir *nganga* haunds that clap
aa glawnicies fae
ma body's een? That far countrie
o bairnhood that
we aa replace wi fear
becomes a bed.

This is thi glamir-gift, tae shift
time frae thi shouthirs o thi lift,
this brichtness o thi branchis shufflin cloods,
yir herr. Thi semm
renn skuds in us
as you muve, slamp ti conjerr
wi smoorikins an
yir fingirs' hurlochs
sic misgruggilment o miserie.

Eh feel yir sma haunds catch
up coonties in me, coup and
creel crans o aa thir datchie toons,
meh industrial hert,
Eh feel'um thring
this dunchit wean's crune
oot o me, lyk
ficklin wi a clarinet.

motherie: shell-like; *nganga*: (Zimbabwean) traditional midwife with mediumistic and herbal skills; *glawnicies*: optical illusions caused by witchcraft; *glamir-gift*: the talent to enchant; *lift*: sky; *skud*: to rain slightly; *slamp*: supple; *smoorikins*: stolen kisses; *hurloch*: a falling or rolling mass; *misgruggilment*: rough handling; *coup and creel crans*: entirely overturn; *datchie*: cunning, secret; *thring*: squeeze; *dunchit*: tightly bundled; *crune*: a murmuring or menacing sound, like that made by an angry bull; *ficklin*: doing something intricate that others cannot.

JACKIE KAY (b.1961)

Jackie Kay was born in 1961 in Edinburgh, and has lived in Glasgow, London and Manchester. A playwright and librettist as well as a poet, her adult collections include The Adoption Papers *(1991) and* Other Lovers *(1993). A collection of poetry for children,* Two's Company, *was published in 1992.*

Brendon Gallacher (For my brother Maxie)

He was seven and I was six, my Brendon Gallacher.
He was Irish and I was Scottish, my Brendon Gallacher.
His father was in prison; he was a cat burglar.
My father was a communist party full-time worker.
He had six brothers and I had one, my Brendon Gallacher.

He would hold my hand and take me by the river
Where we'd talk all about his family being poor.
He'd get his mum out of Glasgow when he got older.
A wee holiday someplace nice. Some place far.
I'd tell my mum about my Brendon Gallacher

How his mum drank and his daddy was a cat burglar.
And she'd say, 'why not have him round to dinner?'
No, no, I'd say he's got big holes in his trousers.
I like meeting him by the burn in the open air.
Then one day after we'd been friends two years,

One day when it was pouring and I was indoors,
My mum says to me, 'I was talking to Mrs Moir
Who lives next door to your Brendon Gallacher
Didn't you say his address was 24 Novar?
She says there are no Gallachers at 24 Novar

There never have been any Gallachers next door.'
And he died then, my Brendon Gallacher,
Flat out on my bedroom floor, his spiky hair,
His impish grin, his funny flapping ear.
Oh Brendon. Oh my Brendon Gallacher.

LAVINIA GREENLAW (b.1962)

Lavinia Greenlaw was born in 1962 in London, where she lives. She has worked in publishing, arts administration and as a writer in residence. Her collections include Night Photograph *(1993) and* A World Where News Travelled Slowly *(1997), the title poem of which won the 1997 Forward Prize for the best single poem.*

A World Where News Travelled Slowly

It could take from Monday to Thursday
and three horses. The ink was unstable,
the characters cramped, the paper tore where it creased.
Stained with the leather and sweat of its journey,
the envelope absorbed each climatic shift,
as well as the salt and grease of the rider
who handed it over with a four-day chance
that by now things were different and while the head
had to listen, the heart could wait.

Semaphore was invented at a time of revolution;
the judgement of swing in a vertical arm.
News travelled letter by letter, along a chain of towers,
each built within telescopic distance of the next.
The clattering mechanics of the six-shutter telegraph
still took three men with all their variables
added to those of light and weather,
to read, record and pass the message on.

Now words are faster, smaller, harder
     . . . *we're almost talking in one another's arms.*
Coded and squeezed, what chance has my voice
to reach your voice unaltered and then to leave no trace?

Nets tighten across the sky and the sea bed.
When London made contact with New York,
there were such fireworks, City Hall caught light.
It could have burned to the ground.

GLYN MAXWELL (b.1962)

Glyn Maxwell was born in Welwyn Garden City, and after a poetry scholarship at
Boston University in the United States, worked as a freelance writer and a publisher's
editor. As well as poetry, he has written a novel, Blue Burneau *(1994); three of his verse*
plays are collected in Gnyss the Magnificent *(1993), and he continues to write for the*
theatre. His poetry books include Tale of the Mayor's Son *(1990),* Out of the Rain
(1992) and Rest for the Wicked *(1995). He lives in Amherst, Massachusetts, where he*
teaches, and in London.

Helene and Heloise

So swim in the embassy pool in a tinkling breeze
The sisters, *mes cousines*, they are blonde-haired
    Helene and Heloise,
One for the fifth time up to the diving board,
The other, in her quiet shut-eye sidestroke
Slowly away from me though I sip and look.

From in the palace of shades, inscrutable, cool,
I watch exactly what I want to watch
    From by this swimming pool,
Helene's shimmer and moss of a costume, each
Soaking pony-tailing of the dark
And light mane of the littler one as they walk;

And the splash that bottles my whole life to today,
The spray fanning to dry on the porous sides,
    What these breathtakers say
In their, which is my, language but their words:
These are the shots the sun could fire and fires,
Is paid and drapes across the stretching years.

Now Heloise will dive, the delicate slimmer,
Calling Helene to turn who turns to see
    One disappearing swimmer
Only and nods, leans languorously away
To prop on the sides before me and cup her wet
Face before me near where I'd pictured it.

I was about to say I barely know them. –
I turn away because and hear of course
    Her push away. I see them
In my rose grotto of thought, and it's not a guess,
How they are, out of the water, out
In the International School they lie about,

What they can buy in the town, or the only quarters
Blondes can be seen alighting in, and only
    As guided shaded daughters
Into an acre of golden shop. 'Lonely?'
Who told me this had told me: 'They have no lives.
They will be children. Then they will be wives.'

Helene shrieks and is sorry – I don't think – my
Ankles cool with the splash of her sister's dive:
    I wave and smile and sigh.
Thus the happiest falling man alive,
And twenty-five, and the wetness and the brown
Hairs of my shin can agree, and I settle down.

'Already the eldest – suddenly – the problems.
The other draws, writes things.' I had heard
    Staccato horrid tantrums

Between earshot and the doorbell, held and read
Heloise's letters in chancery
  Script to her dead grandmother, to me,
To nobody. They have a mother and father,
And love the largest pandas in the whole
  World of Toys. The other
Sister rang from Italy and was well,
But wouldn't come this time. 'She'll never come.
She has a home. They do not have a home.'

Stretching out in her shiny gold from the pool,
Heloise swivels, and sits and kicks
  Then reaches back to towel
Her skinny shoulders tanned in a U of lux-
Uriant material. Helene
Goes slowly to the board, and hops again

Into the dazzle and splosh and the quiet. Say,
Two, three miles from here there are heaps of what,
  Living things, decay,
The blind and inoculated dead, and a squad
Of infuriated coldly eyeing sons
Kicking the screaming oath out of anyone's.

Cauchemar. – We will be clear if of course apart,
To London again me, they to their next
  Exotic important spot,
Their chink and pace of Gloucestershire, Surrey, fixed
Into the jungles, ports or the petrol deserts.
I try but don't see another of these visits;

As I see Helene drying, Heloise dry,
The dark unavoidable servant seeming to have
  Some urgency today
And my book blank in my hands. What I can love
I love encircled, trapped and I love free.
That happens to, and happens to be, me,

But this is something else. Outside the fence,
It could – it's the opposite – be a paradise
    Peopled with innocents,
Each endowed with a light inimitable voice,
Fruit abundant, guns like dragons and giants
Disbelieved, sheer tolerance a science –

Still, I'd think of Helene, of Heloise
Moving harmless, shieldless into a dull
    And dangerous hot breeze,
With nothing but hopes to please, delight, fulfil
Some male as desperate and as foul as this is,
Who'd not hurt them for all their limited kisses.

We Billion Cheered

We billion cheered.
    Some threat sank in the news and disappeared.
It did because
    Currencies danced and we forgot what it was.

It rose again.
    It rose and slid towards our shore and when
It got to it,
    It laced it like a telegram. We lit

Regular fires,
    But missed it oozing along irregular wires
Towards the Smoke.
    We missed it elbowing into the harmless joke

Or dreams of our
    Loves asleep in the cots where the dolls are.
We missed it how
    You miss an o'clock passing and miss now.

We missed it where
   You miss my writing of this and I miss you there.
We missed it through
   Our eyes, lenses, screen and angle of view.

We missed it though
   It specified where it was going to go,
And when it does,
   The missing ones are ten to one to be us.

We line the shore,
   Speak of the waving dead of a waving war.
And clap a man
   For an unveiled familiar new plan.

Don't forget.
   Nothing will start that hasn't started yet.
Don't forget
   It, its friend, its foe and its opposite.

Either

A northern hill aghast with weather
Scolds and lets me hurry over.
Someone phoned to tell my father
Someone died this morning of a
Stroke. The news has tapped me with a
Stick. I vaguely knew his brother.
No one knows where I am either.

Now I'm lost. I don't know whether
This road runs along the river
Far enough. I miss my lover,
Town and all the south. I'd rather
Die than be away forever,
What's the difference. Here's another
Field I don't remember either.

KATHLEEN JAMIE (b.1962)

Kathleen Jamie was born in 1962 in Renfrewshire, and lives in Fife. Her poetry has won a Somerset Maugham Award and the Geoffrey Faber Memorial Award. She has published a travel book, The Golden Peak *(1992), as well as her collections of poetry, which include* The Way We Live *(1987) and* The Queen of Sheba *(1994).*

Wee Wifey

I have a demon and her name is
WEE WIFEY
I caught her in a demon trap – the household of my skull
I pinched her by her heel throughout her wily transformations
until
     she confessed
her name indeed to be WEE WIFEY
and she was out to do me ill.

So I made great gestures like Jehovah: dividing
land from sea, sea from sky,
My own self from WEE WIFEY
(*There*, she says, *that's tidy!*)

Now I watch her like a dolly
keep an eye,
     and mourn her:
For she and I are angry/cry
because we love each other dearly.
It's sad to note
     that without
WEE WIFEY
I shall live long and lonely as a tossing cork.

Arraheids

See thon raws o flint arraheids
in oor gret museums o antiquities
awful grand in Embro –
Dae'ye near'n daur wunner at wur histrie?
Weel then, Bewaur!
The museums of Scotland are wrang.
They urnae arraheids
but a show o grannies' tongues,
the hard tongues o grannies
aa deid an gaun
back to thur peat and burns,
but for thur sherp
chert tongues, that lee
fur generations in the land
like wicked cherms, that lee
aa douce in the glessy cases in the gloom
o oor museums, an
they arenae lettin oan. But if you daur
sorn aboot an fancy
the vanished hunter, the wise deer runnin on;
wheesht . . . an you'll hear them,
fur they cannae keep fae muttering
ye arenae here tae wonder,
whae dae ye think ye ur?

Mr and Mrs Scotland are dead

On the civic amenity landfill site,
the coup, the dump beyond the cemetery
and the 30-mile-an-hour sign, her stiff
old ladies' bags, open mouthed, spew
postcards sent from small Scots towns
in 1960: Peebles, Largs, the rock-gardens

of Carnoustie, tinted in the dirt.
Mr and Mrs Scotland, here is the hand you were dealt:
fair but cool, showery but nevertheless,
Jean asks kindly; the lovely scenery;
in careful school–room script –
The Beltane Queen was crowned today.
But Mr and Mrs Scotland are dead.

Couldn't he have burned them? Released
in a grey curl of smoke
this pattern for a cable knit? Or this:
tossed between a toppled fridge
and sweet-stinking anorak: *Dictionary for Mothers*
M: – Milk, *the woman who worries . . . ;*
And here, Mr Scotland's John Bull Puncture Repair Kit;
those days when he knew intimately
the thin roads of his country, hedgerows
hanged with small black brambles' hearts;
and here, for God's sake, his last few joiners' tools,
SCOTLAND, SCOTLAND, stamped on their tired handles.

Do we take them? Before the bulldozer comes
to make more room, to shove aside
his shaving brush, her button tin.
Do we save this toolbox, these old-fashioned views
addressed, after all, to Mr and Mrs Scotland?
Should we reach and take them? And then?
Forget them, till that person enters
our silent house, begins to open
to the light our kitchen drawers,
and performs for us this perfunctory rite:
the sweeping up, the turning out.

The Tay Moses

What can I fashion
for you but a woven
creel of river-
rashes, a golden
oriole's nest, my gift
wrought from the Firth –

and choose my tide; either
the flow, when water-tight
you'll drift to the uplands –
my favourite hills; held
safe in eddies, where salmon,
wisdom and guts
withered in spawn,
rest between moves: that
slither of body as you were born;

or the ebb, when the water
will birl you to snag
on reeds, the river-
pilot leaning over the side:
'*Name o God!*' and you'll change hands
tractor-man, grieve,
to the farm-wife, who
takes you into her
competent arms

even as I drive, slamming
the car's gears;
spitting gravel on tracks
down between berry-fields,
engine still racing, the door wide,
as I run toward her, crying
LEAVE HIM! Please,
it's okay, he's mine.

DON PATERSON (b.1963)

Don Paterson was born in Dundee in 1963. He left school at sixteen, and has worked as a writer in residence and as a musician, co-leading the jazz-folk ensemble Lammas. He won an Eric Gregory Award in 1990, and his volume, Nil Nil, *won the 1993 Forward Poetry Prize for the best first collection. His second book,* God's Gift to Women, *was published in 1997, and he divides his time between London and Scotland.*

Exeunt

I

DROP SERENE

He poured the warm, clear guck into the mould
in which he'd already composed, with tweezers,
dead wasps on an everlasting flower
or ants filing over a leaf. When it was cold
he slaved at the surface, softening the camber
till it sat with the row of blebs on his mantelpiece,
each with its sequestered populace
like a hiccup in history, scooped out of amber.

As if it might stall the invisible cursor
drawing a blind down each page of his almanac
or the blank wall of water that always kept pace,
glittering an inch, half an inch from his back.
He was out in the garden, digging the borders
when it caught him, in a naturalistic pose.

II

CURTAINS

You stop at the tourist office in Aubeterre,
a columbarium of files and dockets.
She explains, while you flip through the little leaflets
about the chapel and the puppet-theatre,

that everything is boarded up till spring,
including – before you can ask – the only hotel.
A moped purrs through the unbroken drizzle.
You catch yourself checking her hands for rings.

She prepares a light supper; you chat,
her fussy diction placing words in air
like ice in water. She leads you to her room
but gets the shivers while you strip her bare;
lifting her head, you watch her pupils bloom
into the whole blue iris, then the white.

III
BIRD

The wind baffled lightly as they filled the grave
and a queasy flutter left us, the last faint
ripple of the peristaltic wave
that ushered her out. In eight months, her complaint
had whittled her down to the palsied sylph
who filched the car-keys from her snoring spouse
and went out to prove a point; then found herself,
like Alice, on the wrong side of the glass.

Later, back at the house, I overheard
the disembodied voices in the hall
where George, who'd only last another year,
was trying to be philosophical:
Ach, there was nothin' o' her. She was nae mair
than a sparra, nae mair than a wee bird.

IV
THE ELECTRIC BRAE

For three days and three nights, he has listened
to the pounding of a terrible jug band
now reduced to a wheezy concertina

and the disinterested thump of a tea-chest bass.
It seems safe to look: wires trail on the pillowcase,
a drip swings overhead; then the clear tent

becomes his father's clapped-out Morris Minor,
rattling towards home. The windscreen presents
the unshattered myth of a Scottish spring;
with discreet complicity, the road
swerves to avoid the solitary cloud.
On an easy slope, his father lets the engine
cough into silence. Everything is still.
He frees the brake: the car surges uphill.

A Private Bottling

So I will go, then. I would rather grieve over your absence
than over you.
Antonio Porchia

Back in the same room that an hour ago
we had led, lamp by lamp, into the darkness
I sit down and turn the radio on low
as the last girl on the planet still awake
reads a dedication to the ships
and puts on a recording of the ocean.

I carefully arrange a chain of nips
in a big fairy-ring; in each square glass
the tincture of a failed geography,
its dwindled burns and woodlands, whin-fires, heather,
the sklent of its wind and its salty rain,
the love-worn habits of its working-folk,
the waveform of their speech, and by extension
how they sing, make love, or take a joke.

So I have a good nose for this sort of thing.

Then I will suffer kiss after fierce kiss
letting their gold tongues slide along my tongue
as each gives up, in turn, its little song
of the patient years in glass and sherry-oak,
the shy negotiations with the sea,
air and earth, the trick of how the peat-smoke
was shut inside it, like a black thought.

Tonight I toast her with the extinct malts
of Ardlussa, Ladyburn and Dalintober
and an ancient pledge of passionate indifference:
Ochon o do dhóigh mé mo chlairsach ar a shon,
wishing her health, as I might wish her weather.

When the circle is closed and I have drunk myself sober
I will tilt the blinds a few degrees, and watch
the dawn grow in a glass of liver-salts,
wait for the birds, the milk-float's sweet nothings,
then slip back to the bed where she lies curled,
replace the live egg of her burning ass
gently, in the cold nest of my lap,
as dead to her as she is to the world.

★

Here we are again; it is precisely
twelve, fifteen, thirty years down the road
and one turn higher up the spiral chamber
that separates the burnt ale and dark grains
of what I know, from what I can remember.
Now each glass holds its micro-episode
in permanent suspension, like a movie-frame
on acetate, until it plays again,
revivified by a suave connoisseurship
that deepens in the silence and the dark
to something like an infinite sensitivity.
This is no romantic fantasy: my father
used to know a man who'd taste the sea,

then leave his nets strung out along the bay
because there were no fish in it that day.
Everything is in everything else. It is a matter
of attunement, as once, through the hiss and backwash,
I steered the dial into the voice of God
slightly to the left of Hilversum,
half-drowned by some big, blurry waltz
the way some stars obscure their dwarf companions
for centuries, till someone thinks to look.

In the same way, I can isolate the feints
of feminine effluvia, carrion, shite,
those rogues and toxins only introduced
to give the composition a little weight
as rough harmonics do the violin-note
or Pluto, Cheiron and the lesser saints
might do to our lives, for all you know.
(By Christ, you would recognise their absence
as anyone would testify, having sunk
a glass of *North British*, run off a patent still
in some sleet-hammered satellite of Edinburgh:
a bleak spirit, no amount of caramel
could sweeten or disguise, its after-effect
somewhere between a blanket-bath and a sad wank.
There is, no doubt, a bar in Lothian
where it is sworn upon and swallowed neat
by furloughed riggers and the Special Police,
men who hate the company of women.)

O whiskies of Long Island and Provence!
This little number catches at the throat
but is all sweetness in the finish: my tongue trips
first through burning brake-fluid, then nicotine,
pastis, *Diorissimo* and wet grass;
another is silk sleeves and lip-service
with a kick like a smacked puss in a train-station;

another, the light charge and the trace of zinc
tap-water picks up at the moon's eclipse.
You will know the time I mean by this.

Because your singular absence, in your absence,
has bred hard, tonight I take the waters
with the whole clan: our faceless ushers, bridesmaids,
our four Shelties, three now ghosts of ghosts;
our douce sons and our lovely loudmouthed daughters
who will, by this late hour, be fully grown,
perhaps with unborn children of their own.
So finally, let me propose a toast:
not to love, or life, or real feeling,
but to their sentimental residue;
to your sweet memory, but not to you.

The sun will close its circle in the sky
before I close my own, and drain the purely
offertory glass that tastes of nothing
but silence, burnt dust on the valves, and whisky.

KATE CLANCHY (b.1965)

Kate Clanchy was born in Glasgow in 1965 and educated in Edinburgh. Until recently she worked as a schoolteacher, and her first collection, Slattern, *was published in 1995. She lives in London.*

Poem for a Man with No Sense of Smell

This is simply to inform you:

that the thickest line in the kink of my hand
smells like the feel of an old school desk,
the deep carved names worn sleek with sweat;

that beneath the spray of my expensive scent
my armpits sound a bass note strong
as the boom of a palm on a kettle drum;

that the wet flush of my fear is sharp
as the taste of an iron pipe, midwinter,
on a child's hot tongue; and that sometimes,

in a breeze, the delicate hairs on the nape
of my neck, just where you might bend
your head, might hesitate and brush your lips,

hold a scent frail and precise as a fleet
of tiny origami ships, just setting out to sea.

ACKNOWLEDGEMENTS

The editors and publisher gratefully acknowledge permission to reprint the following copyright poems in this book:

DANNIE ABSE: 'White Balloon' from *Selected Poems* (Penguin Books, 1994), to The Peters Fraser and Dunlop Group Limited on behalf of the author; FLEUR ADCOCK: 'A Surprise In The Peninsula', 'Country Station', 'Against Coupling', and 'The Ex-Queen among the Astronomers' from *Selected Poems* (1983), to Oxford University Press; JOHN AGARD: 'Listen Mr Oxford don' from *Mangoes and Bullets*, © 1990 by John Agard, to Serpent's Tail, London; GILLIAN ALLNUTT: 'Convent' from *Beginning the Avocado* (Virago, 1987), to the author; MONIZA ALVI: 'Arrival 1946' from *The Country at My Shoulder* (1993), to the author and Oxford University Press; JOHN ASH: 'Unwilling Suspension', and 'Party Damage' from *Disbelief* (Carcanet Press, 1987), to the publisher. 'Early Views of Manchester and Paris: First View' from *Branching Stairs* (Carcanet Press, 1984), to the publisher; W. H. AUDEN: 'The Fall of Rome (for Cyril Connolly)', 'The Shield of Achilles', 'First Things First', and 'In Praise of Limestone' from *Collected Shorter Poems 1927–1957* (Faber & Faber, 1966), to the publisher; GEORGE BARKER: 'On a Friend's Escape from Drowning off the Norfolk Coast', and lines from 'Villa Stellar' from *Collected Poems* (Faber & Faber, 1987), to the publisher; ELIZABETH BARTLETT: 'Charlotte, Her Book' from *Two Women Dancing: New and Selected Poems* (Bloodaxe Books, 1995), to the publisher; MEG BATEMAN: 'Aotromachd/Lightness' from *Lightness and Other Poems* (Polygon, 1997), to the publisher; PATRICIA BEER: 'The Fifth Sense', and 'Head of a Snowdrop' from *Collected Poems* (Carcanet Press, 1990), to the publisher; JAMES BERRY: 'Folk Proverbs Found Poems' from *Hot Earth Cold Earth* (Bloodaxe Books, 1995), to the publisher; JOHN BETJEMAN: 'A Subaltern's Love-Song', 'I. M. Walter Ramsden ob. March 26, 1947, Pembroke College, Oxford', and 'Executive' from *Collected Poems* (John Murray, 1958), to the publisher; SUJATA BHATT: 'શેરડી (Shérdi)', and 'What Is Worth Knowing?' from *Brunizem* (Carcanet Press, 1988), to the publisher; EAVAN BOLAND: 'Mountain Time', 'The Black Lace Fan my Mother Gave Me', and 'The Dolls Museum in Dublin' from *Collected Poems* (Carcanet Press, 1995), to the publisher. 'That the Science of Cartography is Limited' from 'Writing in a Time of Violence: A Sequence' from *In a Time of Violence* (Carcanet Press, 1994), to the publisher; ALISON BRACKENBURY: 'Grooming' from *Selected Poems* (Carcanet Press, 1991), to the publisher; GEORGE MACKAY BROWN: 'The Old

Women', 'Kirkyard', 'Taxman', and 'The Stone Cross' from 'Stations of the Cross' from *Selected Poems 1954–1983* (John Murray, 1991), to the publisher; BASIL BUNTING: lines from 'Briggflatts' from *Complete Poems* (1994), to Oxford University Press; JOHN BURNSIDE: 'Science' from *Swimming in the Flood* (Jonathan Cape, 1995), to Random House UK Ltd. 'Faith', and 'Dundee' from *The Myth of the Twin* (Jonathan Cape, 1994), to Random House UK Ltd; CIARAN CARSON: 'Bloody Hand' from *Belfast Confetti* (1989), to the author and The Gallery Press. 'Dresden', and 'Belfast Confetti' from *The Irish for No* (1987), to the author and The Gallery Press. 'The Brain of Edward Carson' from *First Language* (1993), to the author and The Gallery Press; CHARLES CAUSLEY: 'My Friend Maloney', and 'Loss of an Oil Tanker' from *Collected Poems* (Macmillan, 1992), to David Higham Associates Ltd; KATE CLANCHY: 'Poem for a Man with No Sense of Smell' from *Slattern* (Chatto & Windus, 1995), to Random House UK Ltd; AUSTIN CLARKE: 'Mabel Kelly' from *Collected Poems*, edited by Liam Miller (The Dolmen Press, in association with Oxford University Press, 1974), to R. Dardis Clarke, 21 Pleasants Street, Dublin 8; GILLIAN CLARKE: 'Chalk Pebble', and 'Overheard in County Sligo' from *Selected Poems* (Carcanet Press, 1985), to the publisher; JOHN COOPER CLARKE: 'beezley street' from *Ten Years in an Open Necked Shirt* (Arrow Books, 1983), © April Music 1977, 1978, 1979, 1980, 1981, 1982, 1983; DAVID CONSTANTINE: 'The Door', and 'Watching for Dolphins' from *Selected Poems* (Bloodaxe Books, 1991), to the publisher; WENDY COPE: 'Two Cures for Love' from *Serious Concerns* (Faber & Faber, 1992), to the publisher. 'Waste Land Limericks' from *Making Cocoa for Kingsley Amis* (Faber & Faber, 1986), to the publisher; FRED D'AGUIAR: 'Mama Dot', and 'The Day Mama Dot Takes Ill' from *Mama Dot* (Chatto & Windus, 1985), to Random House UK Ltd; DONALD DAVIE: 'The Priory of St Saviour, Glendalough', and 'Revulsion' from *Collected Poems* (Carcanet Press, 1990), to the publisher; PETER DIDSBURY: 'The Guitar' from *The Classical Farm* (Bloodaxe Books, 1987), to the publisher. 'The Shore', and 'An Expedition' from *That Old Time Religion* (Bloodaxe Books, 1994), to the publisher; MICHAEL DONAGHY: 'Shibboleth' from *Shibboleth* (Oxford University Press, 1988), to the author. 'Liverpool', and 'Reliquary' from *Errata* (Oxford University Press, 1993), to the author; CAROL ANN DUFFY: 'Mrs Lazarus' from *Selected Poems* (Penguin Books, 1994), to the author. 'Warming Her Pearls' from *Selling Manhatten* (Anvil Press Poetry, 1987), to the publisher. 'Adultery', and 'Prayer' from *Mean Time* (Anvil Press Poetry, 1993), to the publisher; IAN DUHIG: 'From the Irish' from *The Bradford Count* (Bloodaxe Books, 1991), to the publisher; HELEN DUNMORE: 'The dream-life of priests', and 'Wild strawberries' from *Short Days, Long Nights: New and Selected Poems* (Bloodaxe Books, 1991), to the publisher; DOUGLAS DUNN: 'On Roofs of Terry Street', 'The Come-on', 'St Kilda's Parliament: 1879–1979', 'Reading Pascal in the Lowlands', and 'Land Love' from *Selected Poems 1964–1983* (Faber & Faber, 1986), to the publisher; PAUL DURCAN: 'The Hay-Carrier', 'In Memory of Those Murdered in the Dublin Massacre, May 1974', and 'Ulysses' from *A Snail in My Prime*. First published in Great Britain in 1993 by Harvill. © Paul Durcan, to The Harvill Press; MENNA ELFYN: 'Dyn Eira', translated by Gillian Clarke, from *Cell Angel* (Bloodaxe Books, 1996), to the publisher; D. J. ENRIGHT: 'Oyster Lament', and 'Entertaining Women' from *Selected Poems* (Oxford University Press, 1990), to Watson, Little Ltd; GAVIN EWART: 'The Dildo' from *Selected Poems 1933–1993* (Hutchinson, 1995), to Margo Ewart. 'Crimewatch' from the *Independent on Sunday* (February 7, 1993), to Margo Ewart; U. A. FANTHORPE: 'The Poet's Companion' from *Neck Verse* (1992), to Peterloo Poets; VICKI FEAVER: 'Rope' from *The Handless Maiden* (Jonathan Cape, 1994), to Random House UK Ltd; ELAINE FEINSTEIN: 'Father', and 'Mother Love' from *Selected Poems* (Carcanet Press, 1994), to the publisher; JAMES FENTON: 'A German Requiem', and 'A Staffordshire Murderer' from *The Memory of War and Children in Exile: Poems 1968–1983* (Penguin Books, 1983), to The Peters Fraser and Dunlop Group Ltd. 'The Ballad of the Imam and the Shah' from *Out of Danger* (Penguin Books, 1993), to The Peters Fraser and Dunlop Group, Ltd; IAN HAMILTON FINLAY: 'Star/Steer', 'The Cloud's Anchor', 'Acrobats', and 'Evening Will Come' from *Ian Hamilton Finlay: A Visual Primer* by Yves Abrioux and Stephen Bann (Reaktion Books 1985, 2nd edition 1992), © Yves Abrioux and Stephen Bann 1985, 1992, to Ian Hamilton Finlay and Reaktion Books. 'sf' sequence from *SF* (1978), to Ian Hamilton Finlay; ROY FISHER: 'The Entertainment of War', and 'Report on August' from *Poems 1955–1980* (Oxford University Press, 1980), to the author and Bloodaxe Books; JOHN FULLER: 'The Cook's Lesson', and 'Concerto for Double Bass' from *Selected Poems 1954–1982* (Secker & Warburg, 1985), to the author; ROY FULLER: '1948' from *Collected Poems 1936–1961* (André Deutsch, 1962), to John Fuller; ROBERT GARIOCH: 'The Wire' from *Complete Poetical Works*, edited by Robin Fulton (Macdonald Publishers, 1983), to The Saltire Society; KAREN GERSHON: 'I Was Not There' from *Collected Poems* (Papermac, 1990), to C. V. M. Tripp; W. S. GRAHAM: 'Listen. Put On Morning', 'Malcolm Mooney's Land', 'I Leave This At Your Ear', and 'Greenock at Night I Find You' from *Collected Poems 1942–1977* (Faber & Faber, 1979), © The Estate of W. S. Graham, to Michael and Margaret Snow, Literary Administrators for Nessie Graham; ROBERT GRAVES: 'Apple Island', and 'Surgical Ward: Men' from *Selected Poems* (Carcanet Press, 1995), to the publisher. 'The White Goddess' from *Collected Poems* (Cassell, 1965), to Bloodaxe Books; LAVINIA GREENLAW: 'A World Where News Travelled Slowly' from *A World Where News Travelled Slowly* (Faber & Faber, 1997), to the publisher; THOM GUNN: 'The Unsettled Motorcyclist's Vision of his Death', 'Touch', 'The Discovery of the Pacific', and 'The Man with Night Sweats' from *Collected Poems* (Faber & Faber, 1993), to the publisher; TONY HARRISON: 'Them & [uz]', 'Book Ends', 'Continuous', 'Marked with D.', and 'Timer' from *Selected Poems* (Penguin

Books, 1987), to the author; SEAMUS HEANEY: 'Seeing Things' from *Seeing Things* (Faber & Faber, 1991), to the publisher. 'Digging', 'Punishment', 'The Harvest Bow', and 'The Railway Children' from *New Selected Poems 1966–1987* (Faber & Faber, 1990), to the publisher; W. N. HERBERT: 'Morn-Come-Never' from *Forked Tongue* (Bloodaxe Books, 1994), to the publisher. 'Coco-de-Mer' from *Sharawaggi* by Robert Crawford and W. N. Herbert (Polygon, 1990), to the publisher; JOHN HEWITT: 'I Write For . . .', and 'The Scar' from *The Collected Poems of John Hewitt*, edited by Frank Ormsby (The Blackstaff Press, 1991), to the publisher; GEOFFREY HILL: 'Genesis', 'Two Formal Elegies', 'Ovid In The Third Reich', 'September Song', and lines from 'Mercian Hymns' from *Collected Poems* (Penguin Books, 1985), to the publisher; SELIMA HILL: 'The Significance of Significance', and 'The Unsuccessful Wedding-Night' from *Trembling Hearts in The Bodies of Dogs: New and Selected Poems* (Bloodaxe Books, 1994), to the author and publisher. 'Cow', and 'Don't Let's Talk About Being in Love' from *A Little Book of Meat* (Bloodaxe Books, 1993), to the author and publisher; MICHAEL HOFMANN: 'Between Bed and Wastepaper Basket' from *Acrimony* (Faber & Faber, 1986), to the publisher; TED HUGHES: 'The Thought-Fox', 'Wind', 'Full Moon and Little Frieda', 'February 17th', and 'The Last of the 1st/5th Lancashire Fusiliers' from *New Selected Poems 1957–1994* (Faber & Faber, 1995), to the publisher; MICK IMLAH: 'Tusking' from *Birthmarks* (Chatto & Windus, 1988), to Random House UK Ltd; KATHLEEN JAMIE: 'Wee Wifey', 'Arraheids', and 'Mr and Mrs Scotland are dead' from *The Queen of Sheba* (Bloodaxe Books, 1994), to the publisher. 'The Tay Moses' from *Penguin Modern Poets 9* (1996), to Bloodaxe Books; ELIZABETH JENNINGS: 'Lazarus', 'The Diamond Cutter', and 'My Grandmother' from *Collected Poems* (Carcanet Press, 1986), to David Higham Associates Ltd; LINTON KWESI JOHNSON: 'Inglan Is a Bitch' from *Tings an Times* (Bloodaxe Books, 1991), to the publisher; BOBI JONES: 'Mynwent Bilbo', 'Aber-porth', and 'Merch Siop' from *Casgliad O Gerddi* (Cyhoeddiadau Barddas, 1989), to the publisher. The translation of 'Mynwent Bilbo/Bilbao Cemetery' by Joseph P. Clancy is from *Modern Poetry in Translation*, New Series/No. 7 (1995), edited by Daniel Weissbort, published by King's College, London; and the translations of 'Aber-porth' and 'Merch Siop/Shop Girl' by Joseph P. Clancy are from *Selected Poems* by Bobi Jones (Swansea: Christopher Davies Publishers, 1987), to the translator and publisher; DAVID JONES: lines from 'The Sleeping Lord' from *The Sleeping Lord and Other Fragments* (Faber & Faber, 1974), to the publisher; JENNY JOSEPH: 'The lost sea' from *Selected Poems* (Bloodaxe Books, 1992), to John Johnson (Authors' Agent); PATRICK KAVANAGH: 'A Christmas Childhood', and 'The Long Garden' from *Patrick Kavanagh: The Complete Poems* (Goldsmith Press, 1984), to the Trustees of the Estate of Patrick Kavanagh, c/o Peter Fallon, Literary Agent, Loughcrew, Oldcastle, Co. Meath, Ireland; JACKIE KAY: 'Brendon Gallacher (For my brother Maxie)' from *Two's Company* (Blackie, 1992), copyright © Jackie Kay,

1992, to Penguin Books Ltd; BRENDAN KENNELLY: 'A Holy War', and 'The Visit' from *Cromwell* (Bloodaxe Books, 1983), to the publisher; THOMAS KINSELLA: 'Ancestor' from *Poems 1956–1973* (Dolmen Press), to the author; STEPHEN KNIGHT: 'The Mermaid Tank' from *Dream City Cinema* (Bloodaxe Books, 1996), to the publisher, FRANK KUPPNER: lines from 'A Bad Day for the Sung Dynasty' from *A Bad Day for the Sung Dynasty* (Carcanet Press, 1984), to the publisher; PHILIP LARKIN: 'The Whitsun Weddings', 'Here', 'This Be The Verse', 'Sad Steps', and 'Water' from *Collected Poems* (Faber & Faber, 1988), to the publisher; TOM LEONARD: 'The Voyeur', 'Unrelated Incidents – 3', and 'hangup' from *Intimate Voices: Selected Works 1965–1983* (Vintage, 1985), © Tom Leonard, to the author; DENISE LEVERTOV: 'Casselden Road, NW:10 (For Marya)' from *Collected Earlier Poems 1940–1960* (New Directions Publishing Corporation, 1979), copyright © 1949, 1979 by Denise Levertov, to Laurence Pollinger Limited. 'Psalm Concerning the Castle', 'The Rainwalkers', and 'A Map of the Western Part of the County of Essex in England' from *Selected Poems* (Bloodaxe Books, 1986), to Laurence Pollinger Limited; GWYNETH LEWIS: 'Pentecost' from *Parables and Faxes* (Bloodaxe Books, 1995), to the publisher; LIZ LOCHHEAD: 'My Mother's Suitors', and 'What The Pool Said, On Midsummer's Day' from *Dreaming Frankenstein and Collected Poems* (Polygon, 1984), to the publisher; CHRISTOPHER LOGUE: 'The Song of the Dead Soldier' from *Selected Poems* (Faber & Faber, 1996), to the publisher; MICHAEL LONGLEY: 'Detour', and 'An Amish Rug' from *Gorse Fires* (Secker & Warburg, 1991), to Random House UK Ltd. 'Ceasefire' from *The Ghost Orchid* (Jonathan Cape), to Random House UK Ltd. 'Wounds', and 'The Linen Industry' from *Poems 1963–1983* (Penguin Books, 1986), to The Peters Fraser and Dunlop Group Ltd on behalf of the author; NORMAN MACCAIG: 'Summer Farm', 'July Evening', 'Aunt Julia', 'Toad', and 'Small boy' from *Collected Poems* (Chatto & Windus, 1990), to Random House UK Ltd on behalf of the estate of Norman MacCaig; HUGH MACDIARMID: 'Crystals Like Blood', and 'To a Friend and Fellow-Poet' from *Complete Poems*, edited by M. Grieve and W. R. Aitken (Martin Brian & O'Keeffe, 1978), to Carcanet Press Ltd; ROGER MCGOUGH: 'Goodbat Nightman' from *The Mersey Sound*, edited by Roger McGough et. al. (Penguin Books, 1967), to The Peters Fraser and Dunlop Group Ltd on behalf of the author; MEDBH MCGUCKIAN: 'Yeastlight' from *On Ballycastle Beach* (1995), to the author and publisher. 'Venus and the Rain' from *Venus and the Rain* (1994), to the author and The Gallery Press. 'Slips' from *The Flower Master and Other Poems* (1993), to the author and The Gallery Press; JAMIE MCKENDRICK: 'On/Off' from *The Marble Fly* (1997), to Oxford University Press; SORLEY MACLEAN: 'Soluis/Lights', 'Hallaig', and 'A'Bheinn air Chall/The Lost Mountain' from *From Wood to Ridge: Collected Poems in Gaelic and English* (Carcanet Press, 1989), to the publisher; LOUIS MACNEICE: 'All Over Again', 'Soap Suds', 'The Suicide', and 'The Taxis' from *Collected Poems* (Faber & Faber,

1966), to David Higham Associates Ltd; SARAH MAGUIRE: 'Uisge Beatha' from *Spilt Milk* (Secker & Warburg, 1991), to the author; DEREK MAHON: 'As It Should Be', 'The Last of the Fire Kings', 'Matthew V. 29–30', and 'A Disused Shed in Co. Wexford' from *Poems 1962–1978* (1979), to Oxford University Press; GLYN MAXWELL: 'Helene and Heloise', and 'We Billion Cheered' from *Out of the Rain* (Bloodaxe Books, 1992), to the publisher. 'Either' from *Rest for the Wicked* (Bloodaxe Books, 1995), to the publisher; PAULA MEEHAN: 'The Man who was Marked by Winter' from *The Man who was Marked by Winter* (1991), to the author and The Gallery Press; CHRISTOPHER MIDDLETON: 'A Forge in Darkness' from *Selected Writings* (Carcanet Press, 1989), to the publisher; ADRIAN MITCHELL: 'Celia Celia' from *Heart on the Left: Poems 1953–1984* (Bloodaxe Books, 1997), © Adrian Mitchell, to The Peters Fraser and Dunlop Group Ltd on behalf of the author. Educational Health Warning! Adrian Mitchell asks that none of his poems are used in connection with any examinations whatsoever; EDWIN MORGAN: 'Message Clear', 'Canedolia', 'The First Men On Mercury', and 'Cinquevalli' from *Collected Poems* (Carcanet Press, 1990), to the publisher; BLAKE MORRISON: lines from 'The Ballad of the Yorkshire Ripper' from *The Ballad of the Yorkshire Ripper and Other Poems* (Chatto & Windus, 1987), to The Peters Fraser and Dunlop Group Ltd; ANDREW MOTION: 'On the Table' from *Salt Water* (Faber & Faber, 1997), to the Peters Fraser and Dunlop Group Ltd. 'The Letter', and 'Bathing at Glymenopoulo' from *Dangerous Play: Poems 1974–1984* (Penguin Books, 1985), to The Peters Fraser and Dunlop Group Ltd; EDWIN MUIR: 'The Interrogation', 'The Annunciation', and 'The Horses' from *Complete Poems*, edited by P. H. Butter (Association for Scottish Literary Studies, 1991); PAUL MULDOON: lines from 'Incantata' from *The Annals of Chile* (Faber & Faber, 1994, to the publisher; RICHARD MURPHY: 'Slate' from *The Battle of Aughrim* (Faber & Faber, 1968), to the author; GRACE NICHOLS: 'Thoughts drifting through the fat black woman's head while having a full bubble bath' from *The Fat Black Woman's Poems* (Virago, 1984), copyright Grace Nichols 1984, to Curtis Brown Ltd, London, on behalf of the author. 'Mystery', from *Lazy Thoughts of a Lazy Woman* (Virago, 1989), copyright Grace Nichols 1989, to Curtis Brown Ltd, London, on behalf of the author; NORMAN NICHOLSON: 'The Tame Hare', and 'The Shape of Clouds' from *Collected Poems* (Faber & Faber, 1994), to the publisher; EILÉAN NÍ CHUILLEANÁIN: 'Deaths and Engines' from *The Magdalene Sermon* (1989), to the author and The Gallery Press; NUALA NÍ DHOMHNAILL: 'Geasa (The Bond'/English version by Medbh McGuckian), 'An tSeanbhean Bhoct (The Shan Van Vocht'/English version by Ciaran Carson), and 'Ceist na Teangan (The Language Issue'/English version by Paul Muldoon) from *Pharaoh's Daughter* (1990), to the author and The Gallery Press; SEAN O'BRIEN: 'A Rarity', and 'Reading Stevens In The Bath' from *Ghost Train* (1995), to Oxford University Press. 'Cousin Coat' from *The Frighteners* (Bloodaxe Books, 1987), to the publisher; BERNARD

O'DONOGHUE: 'O'Regan the Amateur Anatomist' from *The Weakness* (Chatto & Windus, 1991), to Random House UK Ltd; JOHN ORMOND: 'Design for a Quilt' from *Selected Poems* (Seren, 1987), to the publisher; DON PATERSON: 'Exeunt' from *Nil Nil* (Faber & Faber, 1993), to the publisher. 'A Private Bottling' from *God's Gift to Women* (Faber & Faber, 1997), to the publisher; TOM PAULIN: 'Settlers', 'Peacetime', and 'A Lyric Afterwards' from *Selected Poems 1972–1990* (Faber & Faber, 1993), to the publisher; RUTH PITTER: 'Old Nelly's Birthday' from *Collected Poems* (Enitharmon Press, 1996), to the publisher; SYLVIA PLATH: 'You're', 'The Arrival of the Bee Box', 'Daddy', and 'Edge' from *Collected Poems*, edited by Ted Hughes (Faber & Faber, 1981), to the publisher; PETER PORTER: 'Annotations of Auschwitz', 'Eat Early Earthapples', 'Soliloquy at Potsdam', and 'An Exequy' from *Collected Poems* (1984), to Oxford University Press; CRAIG RAINE: 'The Man Who Invented Pain' from *Rich* (Faber & Faber, 1984), to the publisher. 'The Onion, Memory' from *The Onion, Memory* (1978), to Oxford University Press. 'A Martian Sends a Postcard Home' from *A Martian Sends a Postcard Home* (1979), to Oxford University Press; KATHLEEN RAINE: 'Air', and 'The Pythoness' from *The Collected Poems of Kathleen Raine* (Hamish Hamilton, 1956); PETER READING: 'Midnight', and lines from 'Ukulele Music', to the author; PETER REDGROVE: 'A Twelvemonth', and 'Six Odes (IV. Wardrobe-Lady)' from *The Moon Disposes: Poems 1954–1987* (Secker & Warburg, 1987), to David Higham Associates Ltd. 'The First Earthquake' from *The First Earthquake* (Secker & Warburg, 1989), to David Higham Associates Ltd; CHRISTOPHER REID: 'Stones and Bones' from *Expanded Universes* (Faber & Faber, 1996), to the publisher; OLIVER REYNOLDS: 'Anna Colutha in Suffolk' from *Skevington's Daughter* (Faber & Faber, 1985), to the publisher; DENISE RILEY: 'Shantung' from *Penguin Modern Poets 10* (Penguin Books, 1996), © Denise Riley 1993, 1996, to the author and publisher; ROBIN ROBERTSON: 'Artichoke' from *A Painted Field* (Picador, 1997), to Macmillan Ltd; CAROL RUMENS: 'Stealing the Genre' from *Thinking of Skins: New and Selected Poems* (Bloodaxe Books, 1993), to the publisher; PETER SCUPHAM: 'Going Out: Lancasters, 1944' from *Selected Poems, 1972–1990*, to Oxford University Press; JO SHAPCOTT: 'Phrase Book' from *Phrase Book* (1992), to Oxford University Press; PENELOPE SHUTTLE: 'Taxing the Rain' from *Taxing the Rain* (Oxford University Press, 1992), to David Higham Associates Ltd; PETER SIRR: 'Recognition' from *The Ledger of Fruitful Exchange* (1995), to the author and The Gallery Press; IAIN CRICHTON SMITH: 'The Exiles', 'Old Woman', and 'Owl and Mouse' from *Collected Poems* (Carcanet Press, 1992), to the author and publisher. 'Gaelic Stories' from *The Faber Book of Twentieth Century Scottish Poetry*, edited by Douglas Dunn (1993), to Carcanet Press Ltd; KEN SMITH: 'The road to Henrietta's house' from *Tender to the Queen of Spain* (Bloodaxe Books, 1993), to the author; STEVIE SMITH: 'Do Take Muriel Out', 'Not Waving but Drowning', 'The Jungle Husband', and 'Piggy to Joey' from *The Collected Poems of Stevie Smith* (Penguin

Twentieth Century Classics, 1985), to James MacGibbon; SYDNEY GOODSIR SMITH: 'The Grace of God and the Meth-Drinker' from *Collected Poems 1941–1975* (John Calder, 1975), to Calder Publications Ltd; PAULINE STAINER: 'Sighting the Slave Ship' from *Sighting the Slave Ship* (Bloodaxe Books, 1992), to the publisher; ANNE STEVENSON: 'The Marriage', 'The Fish are all Sick', 'Where the Animals Go', and 'The Fiction-Makers' from *The Collected Poems 1955–1995* (1996), to Oxford University Press; MATTHEW SWEENEY: 'Blue Shoes' from *Blue Shoes* (Secker & Warburg, 1989), to the author; DYLAN THOMAS: 'In my craft or sullen art', 'Lie still, sleep becalmed', 'Do not go gentle into that good night', 'Fern Hill', and 'A Refusal to Mourn the Death, by Fire, of a Child in London' from *Poems* (Dent, 1971), to David Higham Associates Ltd; R. S. THOMAS: 'A Peasant', 'Because', 'Concession', 'The Coming', 'The Way of It', and 'Gift' from *Collected Poems 1945–1990* (Dent, 1993), to The Orion Publishing Group Ltd; DERICK THOMSON: 'Clann-Nighean an Sgadain/The Herring Girls', and 'Cisteachan-Laighe/Coffins' from *Plundering the Harp: Collected Poems 1940–1980* (Macdonald Publishers, 1982, distributed by Gairm Publications, Glasgow), © Derick Thomson, to the author; ANTHONY THWAITE: 'Mr Cooper' from *Selected Poems 1956–1996* (Enitharmon Press, 1997), © Anthony Thwaite, 1961, to the author; CHARLES TOMLINSON: 'A Given Grace' from *Collected Poems* (1985), to Oxford University Press. 'The Blade' from *Annunciations* (1989), to Oxford University Press; JEFFREY WAINWRIGHT: 'As He Found Her' from *Selected Poems* (Carcanet Press, 1985), to the publisher; HUGO WILLIAMS: 'Old Boy', and 'Standstill' from *Dock Leaves* (Faber & Faber, 1994), to the publisher. 'A Picture of a Girl in a Bikini' from *Writing Home* (1985), to Oxford University Press; KIT WRIGHT: 'I Found South African Breweries Most Hospitable' from *Penguin Modern Poets* (Penguin Books, 1962), to the author; BENJAMIN ZEPHANIAH: 'Dis Poetry' from *City Psalms* (Bloodaxe Books, 1992), to the publisher.

Every effort has been made to obtain permission from all copyright holders whose material is included in this book, but in some cases this has not proved possible. We therefore wish to thank all copyright holders who are included without acknowledgement. Penguin UK apologizes for any errors or omissions in the above list and would be grateful to be notified of any corrections that should be incorporated in the next edition of this volume.

INDEX OF POETS

INDEX OF FIRST LINES